THE POLITICS OF POLICY
IN LOCAL GOVERNMENT

THE POLITICS OF POLICY IN LOCAL GOVERNMENT

The making and maintenance of public policy in the Royal Borough of Kensington and Chelsea

JOHN DEARLOVE

Lecturer in Politics, University of Sussex

Cambridge University Press

Published by the Syndics of the Cambridge University Press
Bentley House, 200 Euston Road, London NW1 2DB
American Branch: 32 East 57th Street, New York, N.Y.10022

© Cambridge University Press 1973

Library of Congress Catalog Card Number: 73–77179

ISBN: 0 521 20244 2

First published 1973

Printed in Great Britain
by Cox & Wyman Ltd, London, Fakenham and Reading

Contents

Acknowledgements

People in Kensington and Chelsea helped me in this study. The University of Sussex made available a limited amount of finance. Professor Peter Self, Professor Bernard Schaffer, and Professor Bruce Graham, all read through an earlier draft. I had useful meetings with Jim Danziger, and politics teachers and students at Sussex have been an important source of criticism. A number of people typed the manuscript, but Joan Robson and Rei Stark did the bulk of the work. To all the above, my thanks.

The figure on p. 64 appears by permission of Rand McNally & Co.

Should his systematic inquiry only confirm what had been widely assumed . . . he will of course be charged with 'laboring the obvious', He becomes tagged as a bore, telling only what everybody knows. Should investigation find that widely held social beliefs are untrue . . . he is a heretic, questioning value-laden verities. If he ventures to examine socially implausible ideas that turn out to be untrue, he is a fool, wasting effort on a line of enquiry not worth pursuing in the first place. And finally, if he should turn up some implausible truths, he must be prepared to find himself regarded as a charlatan claiming as knowledge what is patently false.

R. K. Merton, 'Notes on problem-finding in sociology', in R. K. Merton, L. Broom, and L. S. Cottrell, *Sociology Today: Problems and Prospects* (New York Basic Books, 1959), pp. x–xxxiv, xv–xvi

Introduction: political science and public policy

It is a characteristic of our time that everyone wants to be connected with policy.

> C. J. Friedrich, 'Policy: A Science?', *Public Policy*, 4, 1953, pp. 269–81, p. 269.

An increasing number of political scientists would agree that 'in one way or another, directly or indirectly, political research has to deal with the determinants of public policy' (Social Science Research Council, Committee on Historiography, 1954). However, although we hear much about the 'policy approach' (C. O. Jones, 1969), and the 'policy sciences' (*Policy Sciences*, 1970; Lerner & Lasswell, 1951), and although such terms as 'policy', 'process' and 'decision' are part of the everyday vocabulary of those in the discipline of political science, the terms themselves are rarely defined by those who use them, and such definitions as are available reveal little or no consistency one with another.[1] Frequently, many of the terms are used almost interchangeably, and an impression is created that anything to do with 'policies' or 'decisions' is automatically political and should, therefore, absorb the energies of those who claim to be political scientists.

In this introductory chapter I do not intend to offer particularly tight and exclusive definitions of the concepts which have been used by political scientists in their studies of public policy, and neither do I wish to suggest that only public or governmental policy is the appropriate subject matter of political enquiry. However, it is important to make certain distinctions between concepts which need to be used in discussions about public policy, as the absence of this conceptual clarity can lead to confusion and partial research.

---

1. Barnard (1940) lists twelve distinct meanings which have been used to describe the term 'policy'.

I. CONCEPT CLARIFICATION

I shall use the term 'public policy' to refer to the substance of what government does; to the pattern of resources which they actually commit as a response to what they see as public problems or challenges warranting public action for their solution or attainment. Public policy is the product or output of governmental activity and has consequences primarily outside of government itself.[2] Indeed it is precisely these commitments which have consequences outside the immediate circle of government which can be regarded as particularly important and worthy of study.[3] Even though this definition is very general, I do not pretend that all students of public policy would agree with the meaning which I attach to this term, but then I do not consider that goals, intentions, principles, decisions, wishes, objectives, or anything else that has been seen as constituting a public policy represents an appropriate usage of the term. I view a public policy as a pattern of resources committed by government which has an effect on those outside of government.

Now, there are a large number of questions that could legitimately absorb the energy of the student of public policy. He could identify the citizens' views of public policy, and see how far the policy decisions of government are being obeyed without the necessity of force; he could see how far the articulated intentions of political decision-makers are actually being translated into hard patterns of resource commitments; he could establish what were the effects or consequences of a particular pattern of public policies;[4] or he could suggest ways in which public policy might be improved. Recently, some political scientists have been making a renewed and rather uncertain effort to make the content of public policy a subject of research attention, and scholars have developed a number of taxonomies to categorise public policies (Lowi, 1964; and, Froman, 1967) arguing that the preoccupation with explanation (dependent variables) has meant that the description of public policies has gone largely unexplored. I have a considerable sympathy with this research orientation, but this study was conceived before it was developed,[5] and almost unthinkingly I elected to search for the determinants of public policy, seeing it as something to be

2. Van Dyke (1968) makes a distinction between what he calls 'substantive policy', and 'procedural policy'. The former has consequences primarily outside the system, whereas the latter 'is designed to have consequences primarily within the system'.
3. Sharkansky (1970*c*, p. 3) makes the point that policy refers to the 'important activities of government', and he considers an activity as important 'if it involves large amounts of resources or if it is relevant to the interests of many people'.
4. A number of writers have made a distinction between 'outputs' and 'outcomes'. See, Easton, 1965*a*, pp. 351–2; Robinson & Majak, 1967; and, Ranney, 1968.
5. In the past, the 'activist' strain in the discipline has been a strong one, but in recent years it has been but little developed.

explained. There is no doubt that this concern with explanation constitutes the major thrust of political science writing on public policy, but more specifically, in modern political science, explaining public policy has been seen as demanding a consideration of the process of policy-*making*, and 'at least since 1945 most American political scientists [when studying public policy] have focused their professional attention mainly on the *processes* by which public policies are made' (Ranney, 1968, p. 3, original emphasis). Explaining public policy ideally demanded lengthy historical studies, but explaining instead the process of public policy-making involved the more limited consideration of the forces which resulted in certain governmental decisions being taken.

Now it has to be admitted that explaining public policy – explaining, that is, why any government has its own particular pattern of resource commitments – is difficult, since the critical decisions which established any pattern will invariably be lost in history. Nevertheless, it is not adequate to shift from this to *only* considering the process of policy-making, explaining the forces which result in governments taking particular policy decisions. It is also vitally important to consider the factors which inhibit and resist this sort of decisional activity and result in governments confining their energy to routine matters which involve maintaining established policies. The political science literature on public policy in concentrating on explaining the process[6] of policy-making has dealt with only half the question that needs to be answered if we wish to adequately explain public policy. In other words, although we can perhaps take the existing pattern of public policies for granted, we must look not only at the forces which encourage and lead to policy decisions, but also at those factors which inhibit this and result in policy-*maintaining* activity so that certain policy decisions are not taken even though there may be those who urge these options upon government. The problem with the emphasis on the process of public policy-making, is that it has tended to confuse distinctions which need to be carefully borne in mind between public policy, public policy-making and different types of decisions. If those distinctions are not maintained then there is the danger, not only of equating public policy with any *decision* which is made by government, but also of ignoring altogether the extent to which the bulk of governmental activity may well involve the maintenance and implementation of established policies where there is little or no policy 'making' as such. Indeed the whole emphasis on case-studies of decision-making, and on process, with the inevitable concentration of dramatic decisions and 'important' activity, is a research strategy which is particularly ill-adapted to dealing with policy-maintenance; with steady-state politics; the scope of non-decisions and non-decision-making (Bachrach & Baratz, 1962, 1963, 1970), the day-to-day, humdrum routine of political decision-makers; and the extent to which

6. Although some writers have pointed out that there is not one process but a number, Lowi, 1964.

policy-making is itself avoided and resisted by those in government.[7] Questions of this kind are really only given prominence if *structure*, and not process or decisional activity, is given prominence and made the centre of research enquiry.

The distinction between public policy and public policy-making is, conceptually at least, clear enough. A public policy as I defined it is a pattern of resources which is committed by government. In this sense all governments must have policies. However, not all governments need necessarily be involved in actually making all their policies, and no government is forever making policies. Any government when it comes to power, or any newly elected decision-makers, will invariably face a whole range of commitments which are left by their predecessors. Now in many cases these commitments are neither changed nor challenged. The particular public policy continues in the same form and is in no sense 'made' by the present governmental decision-makers. Councillors from Kensington and Chelsea were aware of this distinction. A senior councillor pointed out that when a new councillor joins the council, 'it is rather like coming in to Act III of a play, where much has already been established and must be taken for granted' so that certain actions must follow on irrespective of what new councillors might think should be council policy. Similarly, a new councillor thought he would be involved in 'making policy' but found that he was attending meetings where well-developed plans were laid before him where he had little choice but to say 'yes': he found, in other words, that he was really servicing a well-established range of commitments by participating in the making of decisions which he himself saw as of a 'non-policy' kind.

A public policy is, then, distinct from the particular process of critical decision-making which may have established any particular pattern of resource commitments. However, the actual maintenance or continuance of a public policy does itself require particular decisions. The distinction between public policy-maintenance, and public policy-making comes almost to be a distinction between different types of decisions. The decisions which maintain a public policy and implement a policy decision are of a different order to those decisions which involve innovation and the establishment of a new range of commitments, or else the complete reversal of an existing pattern of commitments.[8] There is an important distinction to be made between policy decisions and routine decisions (Loewenstein, 1965; Bauer, 1968; Gore & Dyson, 1964; Selznick, 1957; Simon, 1958; and, Gore, 1964).

Most decision-making activity that occurs within governments – or anywhere else for that matter – does not in any sense involve the

7. Salisbury (1968, p. 153) makes the point that 'the concept of policy . . . is anti-case study in its implications for research'. Note too, the 'elitist' criticism of 'pluralist' writing in the American community-power debate of the 1950s and 1960s.
8. There is also the idea of a policy *without* any decision. See, Eulau & March, 1969, p. 19; Schilling, 1961; and, Robinson, 1962, p. 3, who refers to this as the 'decision paradox'.

taking of policy decisions, or policy-making. Decisions of this kind are important in 'establishing rules for future contingencies' (Snyder & Paige, 1959, p. 336) and have 'long run implications for the organisation' (Selznick, 1957, p. 56), but they are, nevertheless, 'relatively rare' (Loewenstein, 1965, p. 44. See also, Gore & Dyson, 1964, p. 3) precisely because, in raising questions about organisational purpose, they open up scope for organisational conflict which leaders within any organisation would usually rather avoid. A considerable amount of activity within organisations is, in fact, devoted to avoiding and resisting the necessity for taking trauma-producing decisions of this kind in favour of confining activity to the taking of decisions which are only routine and work within the framework of established policies, maintaining the pattern of commitments and implementing the implications of earlier policy decisions. The distinction between these two types of decision may be made clearer if I give an example from Kensington and Chelsea.

A spokesman from the Kensington Housing Trust pointed out that the Housing Act of 1957 made it very much easier for local authorities to make loans and grants to housing trusts, and as a result of this representatives of the Trust went to the Kensington Borough Council to point out this possibility to councillors and officials: 'We didn't borrow from the council till very recently . . . Our first loan was in fact to buy a house for a homeless family, and this was the first time that we had ever bought on a mortgage. Our relationship with the Council really began when we found section 119 of the Housing Act 1957. We saw the Town Clerk, the Borough Treasurer and the leading lights on the council and we pointed this out to them. Anyway, they said they didn't believe in it. But we asked them to consider it, and they know that what we say does bear examination because we're an established group of integrity and don't just go to the Council with anything – and they know it. At first we were received with sardonic amusement, but later with more attention, and after a lot of humming and haaing we got our loan and from then on it's been fairly automatic'.

The initial decision by the council to give a loan to the Kensington Housing Trust represents a clear example of a policy decision which set a precedent and established a commitment to a particular course of action so that when there were later applications by the Trust they were treated as purely routine matters which could be quickly acceded to in such a way that a decision was scarcely involved. Now, if other housing trusts apply to the council for assistance in this way, once it is established by the council that they are what they call 'bona fide', then they too can be assured of a loan. Nowadays, any request from a housing trust for a loan to purchase property meets with the following standardised council response: '(*a*) that subject to (i) the approval of the Ministry of Housing and Local Government, (ii) the concurrence of the Finance Committee, and (iii) the completion between the Council and —— in the matter, a loan of £—— be made to the —— on such terms and conditions as the Finance Committee may deem to be appropriate for the purchase by the —— of the —— properties in ——. (*b*) that the Common Seal of the Council be affixed to the agreement and to any other necessary document'.

I have perhaps created the impression that the distinction between policy-making and policy-maintaining, between that is, policy decisions and routine decisions, is a clear-cut one, but in fact this is not always the case. In many organisations, policy change is often 'incremental' and gradual (Dahl & Lindblom, 1953; and, Lindblom, 1959) so that a lot of the time decisions are being taken which, although not strictly policy decisions are not simply routine, since even though they do not really establish a new commitment, they do nevertheless imperceptibly shift the existing pattern so that over time with a number of these sorts of decisions the particular pattern of resource commitments is quite drastically changed without there ever having been a consciousness of this or one or two decisions which clearly established the break. In practice then, it is rather difficult to distinguish and categorise the different decisions, but nevertheless it is important for the student of public policy to be aware of these distinctions, for this awareness can draw attention away from considering policy-making alone to the important and more prevalent activity of policy-maintenance.

II. THE DESIGN OF THIS STUDY

The empirical base of this study is a limited one since I am concerned to look for the determinants of public policy in just one local authority in Britain, the Royal Borough of Kensington and Chelsea. This London Borough first gained authority in 1965 as a result of the merging of the two separate Metropolitan Boroughs of Kensington, and Chelsea occasioned by the London Government Act of 1963, which also transferred powers from the county authority to the rejuvenated borough units. The Royal Borough comprises a roughly 'L' shaped area of 2,951 acres, bounded eastwards by the City of Westminster, to the north and west by the boroughs of Brent and Hammersmith respectively, and having a southern boundary midstream in the Thames. The population of the borough is something under a quarter of a million, and it has a rateable value of £25 million. It would be foolish to claim that the borough is somehow typical of other local authorities, but at the same time unless the supposed criteria of typicality are clearly spelled out and comparison made with a specified sample of local authorities, then it is not really possible to point to the typical and untypical features. Indeed, this is not my intention, and at any event I suggest that careful enquiry would show the uniqueness of every local authority. However, it is worth noting, first, that the council of the Royal Borough is safely controlled by the Conservative Party, but second, that their strength derives from support from the wards in the constituencies of South Kensington and Chelsea, for North Kensington returns a Labour

Member of Parliament and most of the wards there are usually safe for the Labour Party. This electoral geography reflects the fact that 'one of the most distinctive features about the Royal Borough is the sharp contrast between North Kensington and the rest of the Borough' (Notting Hill Housing Service, *Housing Survey*, 1968, p. 10). In North Kensington there is a lower percentage of non-manual workers, more overcrowding, a greater deficiency of open-space, and children are proportionately over-represented in that part of the borough. The very distinctiveness of North Kensington when compared to the rest of the borough, and its comparative political weakness, have meant not only that the problems of that area have received inadequate council attention, but also that it is from there that has come the loudest cry for change and innovation in the pattern of council policies.

Now although I am concerned with public policy in Kensington and Chelsea, I will not be dealing centrally with processes and structures in that area until the second part of this study, precisely because I am mindful of a critique directed against case and community studies which, quite rightly, suggests that they have frequently been engaged in 'producing a steady stream of hypotheses and questions while making no effort to inquire into the scores, perhaps the hundreds, [other] . . . cases already contain' (Kaufman, 1958, p. 56). In other words, it is important to be self-conscious in reviewing and assessing established work which confronts the central intellectual problem of any particular enquiry, and also once this task has been accomplished, to be articulate in stressing the ideas which will guide the interpretation and selection of facts from a particular case. Only if this exercise is undertaken, and when there is a continual readjust-ment between theory and fact-finding research can we expect to move beyond hunches and the tacit acceptance of inherited theories to newer and more realistic theories, 'more realistic in the sense that they are in a higher degree adequate to the facts' (Myrdal, 1957, p. 163).

Since this is a study of a local authority in Britain, I must obviously look to the literature on British local government, and I do this in Chapters 1 and 2. At the same time, however, I am concerned to explain public policy within this authority and so it is important that I also look to the work of political scientists who have concerned themselves with this question (regardless of whether or not they have focused their attention on local government) in order to see how far they have developed ideas and hypo-theses which are logically coherent and so may have a potential relevance for my case. I do this in Chapters 2, 3, 4 and 5, which comprise Part One of this study.

In one sense the study of public policy is a comparatively new area of enquiry within political science, but at the same time, students of politics have had a long-standing interest in making sense of the behaviour of government and these enquiries mean that there is a rich backlog of material which indirectly offers a partial explanation of public policy by dealing with the processes and forces which lead up to government decision. The difficulty is that 'because the policy-making process is not a well-defined, established field in political science, it is not possible to refer to books that stand squarely and explicitly in the middle of it' (Lindblom, 1968, p. 119), and so the student who wishes to identify established theories and hypotheses has to cull a vast literature. In Part One, I offer a partial review of particular theories which have been developed by political scientists to explain the policy-making activity of government. These theories, which I see as in the mainstream of the discipline, all assign causal importance to the environmental forces which surround government and which are said to critically affect governmental activity and the form of public policy. In *Chapter 2* I assess the utility of the differing theories which have pointed to the importance of elections and the electorate in the policy-making process. In *Chapter 3*, I outline work on pressure groups – work which represents the major body of empirical political theory explaining public policy-making. In *Chapter 4* I look at the more recent 'demographic approach', which argues that the characteristics of the socio-economic environment of government explains the form of public policy. *Chapter 5* is an overview chapter to this part of the study, and I look at the similarities and deficiencies of these theories as explanations for public policy. I suggest that they all pay insufficient regard to the structures of government; they ignore the importance of factors internal to government; and they fail to recognise that in order to adequately assess the impact of environmental forces on public policy-making it is necessary to see how political decision-makers relate to inputs and demands. I suggest that the cumulative effect of these deficiencies has meant that political scientists have failed to study the structure of policy-maintenance, and I further suggest that the organisational situation which the council of the Royal Borough enjoys in relation to its environment means that within that authority the forces for policy-maintenance are particularly firmly established. In other words, when I move on to Part Two and deal more centrally with Kensington and Chelsea I will be doing so against the backdrop of my critique of established theories which I consider just do not fit the facts of my case since they ignore or underplay factors which I see as of more crucial importance in accounting for the development of public policies within that authority. The result will be that I will be emphasising the forces which encourage the maintenance of public policy. I will be stressing the extent to which decisional activity is limited to the taking of routine decisions and the working out of the implications of established policies, so that there is not just limited policy-making activity, but also an active resistance to, and avoidance of, this activity.

There are three sections in Part Two, each of which takes up a theme which, although outside the mainstream of political-science writing explaining public policy, I see as of critical importance in enabling me to make sense of the behaviour of the Council of the Royal Borough as it develops and defends its pattern of policies. In Section A, I deal with what I call 'The internal regulation of council activity'. In *Chapter 6*, after I have outlined work on the 'conventions' of British government and the 'rules of the game' of American legislatures, I will argue that this work represents an attempt to apply role theory to the explanation of governmental behaviour. Towards the end of this chapter I will suggest an application of role theory which I consider can be fruitfully used to make sense of the behaviour of councillors as it is likely to affect the future development of public policy. These ideas guide the selection of material in *Chapter 7*, where I identify two sorts of rules which can be expected to have implications for, or an impact upon, the likely behaviour of councillors in policy situations. I catalogue the 'recruitment rules' which are used to select people for the council and for positions within the council, and I also outline the 'behaviour rules' which have a guiding and restraining effect on the behaviour of those positions. I will argue that the predominant effect of these rules will be to confine decisional activity to the maintenance of established policies.

In Chapter 5 I do not only argue that the established literature explaining public policy ignores the importance of factors internal to government, but I also suggest that if we wish to assess the impact of environmental forces upon the decisional activity of government adequately then it is particularly important not just to study inputs and pressures, but also to see how those in government relate to external influence attempts and perhaps reach out to surrounding structures. In Section B, I develop these themes in two chapters. In *Chapter 8*, I look at the framework which councillors use to assess and allow differential access to interest groups and their demands, and in *Chapter 9*, I look at the important, but neglected, question of the councillors' use of information. The conclusion of this section is that the way councillors relate to interest groups and use information selectively is such that they are likely to defend established policies and avoid and resist opportunities for change and innovation.

Behavioural political scientists have tended to pay scant attention to political ideology, particularly in the context of Western democracies, and where parties of the moderate right are concerned. Public policies do, however, embody certain values and political decision-makers are not, and cannot be, neutral and devoid of preferences as to what government should and should not be doing since their job is to manage the scope of government. In the single chapter of Section C, *Chapter 10*, I outline the political ideology of the Conservative councillors in Kensington and Chelsea. I suggest that their views as to the proper role of government, together with the justifications which they use to sustain these views are such as to confine government to a relatively narrow scope so that it tends not to interfere with established private interests and the natural working of market forces.

Finally, in the *Conclusions*, I will summarise some of the themes which

I will have developed in the preceding chapters, and suggest ideas which I feel need to be developed if we are to progress in our understanding of governmental behaviour and the development of public policy.

In fact all this is to rather jump the gun, for I have tended to already assume that the Council of the Royal Borough of Kensington and Chelsea can be regarded as having sufficient authority to make and maintain public policies. One group of writers deny that it is possible to study the making and maintenance of public policy in the context of British local government, claiming that the extent of 'central control' is such as to reduce local authorities to agents of the central government responsible only for the administration of policies. In *Chapter 1*, I criticise this view and suggest that it is a mistaken characterisation of the position of local authorities in this country, which have substantial autonomy to make and maintain their own policies.

1 Local government as administration

One school of thought insists that local authorities are not policy-making bodies since all their powers and duties are defined by a higher body.

A. J. Burkett, 'Conventions and Practices in the Committee System in Selected Local Authorities in the East Midlands' (M.A. Thesis, University of Nottingham, 1960), p. 308.

A dominant tradition of writing about British local government states that local authorities are the 'agents' of the central government (L. P. Green, 1959, p. 156. See also, Robson, 1966, p. 67; Jackson, 1965, p. 275; and, A. Jones, 1968), and serve only as administrative structures to implement the policies decided by the higher authority.[1] It is argued that during this century, and particularly since the Second World War (A West Midland Study Group, 1956, p. 32; Jackson, 1965, p. 275; and, Robson, 1948, p. 7), local authorities have gradually been transformed 'into mere receptacles for Government policy' (Robson, 1933, p. 89), where 'Ministers and their departments [have] become the policy-making body in local affairs' (A West Midland Study Group, 1956, p. 2). A situation is described in which the 'central government is the determination of policy and principle. Local government is the application of those principles to the peculiarities of local fact' (J. J. Clarke, 1969, p. 1. See also, Rose, 1965, p. 193; and, G. D. H. Cole, 1947, pp. 28–9). This result has been attributed to the central government's reliance, not only on its formal powers of intervention, but also on its ability to impose its will upon local authorities by means of informal persuasion, for the existence of extensive legal powers of control has had a 'cumulative' and 'psychological effect' where local authorities submit questions to the minister 'over which he has no legal

1. Sharpe (1967a, p. 2) makes the point that 'academic interest in it, [local government] where it has not been predominantly legal in character, has usually treated it as a branch of public administration rather than as a representative institution.' MacKenzie (1951, pp. 348–9) rather more pointedly says that 'the notion of "government" seems to have dropped out of our discussion of local "government"'.

control' (Jennings, 1947, p. 258). These informal consultations between central and local government ensure that 'the policy of a department works its way into the practice of local authorities, perhaps imperceptibly.' We have a situation which has been termed by one commentator, 'government by circular' (Cross, 1966, p. 167).

Writers who advance this thesis provide two theories which purport to account for the increase and the extent of central control. It is important to explore the cogency of their evidence and argument in order to see how far they provide adequate support for their conclusions as to the current position of local authority autonomy.

The most popular explanation accounting for the extent of central control is based upon a consideration of the dependence of local authorities upon central finance. There is the idea that 'he who pays the piper calls the tune' (A West Midland Study Group, 1956, p. 2; Marshall, 1960, p. 15, and, 1970; G. D. H. Cole, 1921, pp. 4–5; Robson, 1966, p. 149; Sullivan, 1939; and, H. Finer, 1945). Writers refer to the increasing dependence of local authorities on central grants, note increasing central control, and weld these two separate (and often unsubstantiated) observations together to form a causal explanation which suggests that central control has been increasing because of the increased dependence of local authorities upon central government finance: 'The more finance is supplied by the central government from nationally raised taxes the less tends to be the discretion allowed to local government. Conversely, the greater the ability of local government to raise finance from its own sources then the less able the central government is to control local government' (Hepworth, 1970, pp. 14–15). Chester suggests that 'it could be argued with strong support from the history of central–local relations that the giving of a grant enabled the central Government to "purchase" many of the administrative powers it now possesses' (Chester, 1951, p. 84), and Jackson makes the causal connection even more forcefully when he states that 'a rule . . . developed in England, which is now regarded as an axiom, namely that the provision of money from the exchequer entitles the central government to ensure that the money is properly spent and that the conception of proper spending goes beyond a mere matter of audit and includes the duty to see that money has been spent economically and in accordance with central government conception of what is desirable' (Jackson, 1965, p. 267). Not surprisingly, this belief has led to the argument that 'if local authorities are to function as anything more than advisory committees, helping to administer national services on standards laid down by Whitehall, they must have at least one large independent source of revenue at their disposal' (Fogarty, 1946, p. 3). There have been large numbers of suggestions for reform which would enable local authorities to gain more financial independence and with this a supposed increase in decisional autonomy (Chester, 1951, p. 333; G. D. H. Cole, 1921, p. 96; Banwell, 1959, p. 204; Committee on the Management of Local Government, 1967, vol. 1, p. xi; and, Royal Institute of Public Administration, 1956).

In examining the cogency of this argument it is important to note that the balance sheet as between local and central sources of income is not always accurately drawn up, for writers choose to ignore the locally generated income which derives from rents, charges, fees, and trading services in order to strengthen their argument quite bogusly (See the table in Robson, 1966, p. 54). In fact in Kensington and Chelsea only about 20 per cent of income is derived from central government grant, but even then it must be borne in mind that the specific grants which provide a greater potential for control are a still smaller (and reducing) percentage of total income. In order to sustain the argument effectively that increasing central control is caused by, and based upon, local authority dependence on central finance, it would be necessary to point to a situation where there was more control in services and authorities which were particularly dependent on an exchequer contribution. In fact, writers who advance this thesis have not undertaken this crucial test and there 'has been no full examination of the implications of that form of control for local action' (Boaden, 1970, p. 177). However, Davey (1971, p. 50) has stated that 'the degree of dependence upon Government for revenue does not . . . determine the extent to which local autonomy is impaired by central regulation.'[2]

The other argument which has been developed to account for the supposed increase in central control points to 'the prevailing desire for uniformity of public services' (Marshall, 1960, p. 15), and suggests that the 'public demand for equality, . . . drove the central government into detailed control' (Smellie, 1968, p. 108). Although Redlich could refer to the necessity of administrative supervision in order to 'secure uniformity and prevent the general interests of the nation suffering from local eccentricity' (Redlich, 1903, vol. 2, p. 372), this thesis has really only been developed since the advent of the Labour Government of 1945, for their interest in the social services 'brought with it an increasing desire to lay down standards at the centre' (Banwell, 1959, p. 206). A quite distinct impression is created that although at one time there was 'a wide divergence of practice from district to district' (Hasluck, 1936, p. 94. But see, Dolman, 1895), this is now no longer the case, for a grey uniformity based on the minimum standards of the central government everywhere prevails.

Although the writers we are considering fail to put their thesis to the test by examining the actual extent of uniformity of service provision in different local authorities, when this exercise is undertaken we find (quite contrary to the impression these writers create), that there are 'vast

2. Davies (1968, pp. 303–4) notes that authorities are generally . . . unresponsive to price incentives', and consequently he considers that the 'influential theories about how grant systems affect local authorities' are invalid', for they are based on the false 'assumption that local authorities respond to price incentives as do firms in a market.'

differences . . . between the same services in different areas' (Holman, 1970, p. 164), and 'examples of the variation of service can be found over the whole range of local government activity' (Boaden & Alford, 1969, p. 204). There is evidence of erratic provision of day nurseries (Packman, 1968; Ryan, 1964; and, Central Advisory Council for Education, 1967), services for old people (Slack, 1960; and, Townsend, 1962), and welfare services generally (Ruck, 1963; Davies, 1968; and, J. Parker, 1965), as is further reflected in the numbers of social workers and other workers employed by local authority social service departments. Townsend has commented that even taking population proportions into account, some 'councils possess from four to ten times as many home helps as others . . . there are three and four times as may health visitors and social workers' (Townsend, 1963). More specifically, White depicted a range between authorities of one child care officer to 101, 210 population, to one for every 3,467 (T. White, 1968). There is evidence that local authorities make different use of their permissive powers to support the arts (Political and Economic Planning, 1965; and, Higgins, 1965), and more important, in the crucial field of housing a number of studies are suggestive of different provision by local authorities (Burnett & Scott, 1962; Layton, 1961; Committee on Housing in Greater London, 1965; and, Meacher, 1971), with Spencer pointing to great differences concerning the numbers of dwellings built, methods of council house allocation, rent levels, interpretation of statutory standards of dwellings, and the use of powers to designate improvement areas (Spencer, 1970), In education too, even though the responsible Ministry has conceived of its role in 'promotional'[3] terms, the influential Robbins Report pointed to 'variations in the provision of primary and secondary schooling from area to area' (Committee on Higher Education, 1963, p. 64), and careful work by Douglas has suggested that 'many differences in educational opportunities and in the methods of secondary school selection . . . exist between one local education authority and another' (Douglas, 1964, pp. 1–2. See also, Douglas, Ross & Simpson, 1968; and, Brand, 1965). Although political scientists have not generally concerned themselves with the question of the local variation in public policies because of their tacit acceptance of the dominant orthodoxy of uniformity and central control, a recent study by Boaden points to wide variation in service provision in the county boroughs of England and Wales. (Boaden, 1971. See also, Peterson, 1969). It would be comforting to suppose that all these variations in service provision reflect differences in local need, but the evidence suggests that this is not the case (Davies, 1968; Committee on Local Authority and Allied Personal Social Services, 1968; and, Holman, 1970).

These findings must surely challenge the view which suggests that the

3. Griffith (1966) argues that the various central government departments concerned with local authorities conceive of their role in different ways. I will return to this theme later.

demand for minimum standards has brought with it more control and greater uniformity in the provision of various services throughout the country. There is a pressing need to account for variations, and this is likely to demand a consideration of the politics within local authorities.[4]

The truth of the matter is that the literature I am considering consists, in large part, of unsupported hunches based on partial research. It has failed to explore adequately central–local relations and this inadequacy has almost certainly resulted in the exaggeration of the extent of central control and the lack of local autonomy.

A major deficiency of the research base of these studies derives from the assumption that legal prescriptions as to how things should operate can be used as descriptions of how things actually do operate, and consequently writers have centred almost exclusive attention on the study of law, failing to deal with the implementation and enforcement of that law as it comes to affect local authorities in their day-to-day workings. Now of course it is true that in theory 'local authorities have no powers except such as are defined by statute' so that 'if a local authority wants to do something, the Clerk of the Council . . . must be able to put his finger on the section of the Act of Parliament or other legislative instrument which says that a local authority may do that thing' (J. J. Clarke, 1969, p. 5; and, Jackson, 1965, p. 39), but in practice the doctrine of *ultra vires* does not have the effect of holding a local authority within a legal straitjacket. Few cases of a breach of the *ultra vires* rule have come before the courts and similarly orders of *mandamus* and default powers are rarely put into effect. A chairman from the Royal Borough of Kensington and Chelsea assessed the effect of local government law on the work of the authority in the following way: 'Some [law] is cut and dried and there is nothing you can do about it, but there is a lot you can do, and one can invariably find a law to enable you to do something if you want to. I can't think of an instance when someone said "Let's do something" and they were told, "No, it's not possible, the law won't let us".' An officer of the Royal Borough made much the same point: 'You can always find some law to enable you to do something, and the officers are to blame if they can't advise the members as to how to do something they are keen to do. It's not so much a question of why something can't be done, but how a thing can be done.'

The inadequacy of much of this work is further reflected in the fact that although the various instruments of central control are listed at length, there is invariably a failure to identify their use by the central government, still less an examination of the way in which local authorities respond to them. These omissions mean that the central government's potential for control is equated with the actual extent and effect of control, and the

4. Boaden and Alford, 1969; and, G. W. Jones, 1969, p. 346; both suggest that policies will differ as between local authorities, depending on which party is in control.

result of this is to exaggerate the lack of local autonomy and to ignore the ways in which local authorities may be able to resist even quite explicit directives from the central government. I will return to this point later.

The dice are further loaded against noting local autonomy because central–local relations are usually just seen in terms of central control, and little work has been undertaken to show the influence which local authorities and their associations have upon the development of local government law; and yet as Griffith reminds us it is 'difficult to exaggerate' their importance in this area of politics (Griffith, 1966, p. 33).[5] Instead of choosing to characterise central–local relations in terms of a 'partnership, in which each partner has his recognised rights and privileges' (G. M. Harris, 1939, p. 296), and where influence runs both ways so that the standards which are said to affect local government are often 'fixed after consultation' (Cross, 1966, p. 183. See also, Brand, 1965), many writers instead see central–local relations in terms of warfare with one-way domination from the centre (Robson, 1948, p. 9).

A final factor which has the effect of giving a possible exaggerated picture of the extent of central control derives from the setting of the attack on central control within the context of a wider discussion about 'the march of centralisation'. However, if we wish to accurately assess the impact of the central government upon the on-going activity of local authorities then we need to strip away other arguments from our attention and we must not confuse central control with the loss of services[6] which some local authorities have suffered, as central control can hardly affect the services that are no longer handled by local authorities.

These research deficiencies mean that we must be cautious in accepting conclusions about the crushing weight of central control, and this caution should be heightened by the knowledge that most British writers are not detached observers of central–local relations, but are extremely committed to local self-government.[7] This commitment finds its expression in the

5. The Post-War Labour Government pointed out that one of the reasons why it did not feel that the time was right for a general recasting of the structure of local government was that there was 'no general desire in local government circles for a disruption of the present system' (*Local Government in England and Wales During the Period of Reconstruction*, 1945, p. 14). For a case-study which points to the role of local authorities in affecting legislation, see Smallwood, 1965.

6. At any event arguments about the loss of local authority services are frequently overdrawn because of the failure to recognise the intensification of local responsibility within the fields of welfare and planning, the huge amount of permissive legislation, and the fact that in recent times Parliament has 'given several widely-drawn powers to local authorities, powers which enable them to act . . . in ways not specified by statute' (Cross, 1966, p. 16).

7. The reasons why writers are attached to local self-government differ. One group stresses its value as a check on the central government (G. D. H. Cole, 1921, p. 26; and Sharpe, 1965, p. 5.). Another group sees the value of local self-government as lying in the way in which it can contribute to an educated citizenry and a democratic climate of opinion (Robson, 1948, 1966; Warren, 1950; Panter-Brick, 1953, 1954; MacKenzie, 1961; and H. Finer, 1945).

applause which writers have showered on those nineteenth-century reforms which democratised local authorities and extended their powers and responsibilities. However, frequently the perception of nineteenth-century developments is partial, for although writers such as Toulmin-Smith, Gneist, and Redlich pointed to the extension of central control during this period, this development was largely ignored by twentieth-century writers.[8] This selective attention to nineteenth-century reform coupled with the attachment to local self-government has meant that the increase in central control after the Second World War was seen as both a novelty and as something to be attacked for causing the problems which are said to beset local government today, such as the lack of interest by both the local electorate and the potential councillors of calibre. The result of this has been a build-up of writing which has stressed the extent of central control as the major fact of local government. In the period well before the Second World War there was probably a tendency to underplay the extent of central control, whereas now there is probably a strong tendency to underplay the extent of local authority autonomy.

An adequate assessment of the impact of the central government on the decisional activity of local authorities demands that full information be assembled on two points. First, we have to appreciate the willingness, or disposition of the central government to use the control techniques which it has at its disposal, and second, we need to assess the responsiveness of different local authorities to control attempts, for they cannot be seen simply as passive responders to central direction. An important study has looked at the first question, but there is no published work which has dealt with the second question and for this reason I will give a number of examples from Kensington and Chelsea which suggest how one local authority has resisted control attempts.

The notion of 'disposition' is hard to conceptualise, but Davies has argued that the Local Government Manpower Committee (1950, 1951), played a part 'in settling the ideology of central–local relations prevalent in the following decade' (Davies, 1968, p. 93), and that ideology was one which was prepared to allow local authorities a considerable amount of autonomy, in part reversing the policy of the 1945–8 period (although he points out that the extent of control in that early period can easily be exaggerated) (Davies, 1968, p. 104). It is not suffiicient to deal only in general terms with the central government's preparedness to intervene in the work of local authorities, since many different departments are involved and they may not share a common view as to what should be their role in relation to local authorities. It is only recently that this question has been systematically explored and Griffith has outlined the different 'philosophies

8. Though both Smellie (1968) and Richards (1968) show a fine appreciation of the contrasting developments which have affected local government since the nineteenth century.

about local government' held by the various departments with an involvement in local authority activity, noting that 'three separate attitudes are broadly distinguishable: one is basically *laissez faire*; one is basically regulatory; and one is basically promotional' (Griffith, 1966, p. 515). Both the Ministry of Health in relation to health and welfare services, and the Ministry of Housing and Local Government in relation to local housing authorities adopt the *'laissez faire'* attitude, and their activity 'stops short at exhortation and advice' (Griffith, 1966, pp. 289, 488). Although the powers of the Ministry of Health are 'limited,' its interpretation is 'narrower than need be' (Griffith, 1966, p. 491), and in the Ministry of Housing and Local Government 'no one, . . . looks to see whether local housing authorities are fulfilling their statutory obligations' (Griffith, 1966, p. 518). The Home Office in relation to children's services and the Ministry of Housing and Local Government in relation to town and country planning have assumed an essentially 'regulatory' role, with the Home Office relying on the inspectorate to serve as their link with the local authorities. Griffith is aware that there are differences in attitude *within* departments (Griffith, 1966, p. 515), and he is mindful of the fact that there are changes in how the departments see their role, with the Ministry of Housing and Local Government, for example, tending to move from a regulatory role in relation to its planning functions and shifting from 'the more negative control of development to the more positive improvement of the environment' (Griffith, 1966, p. 521). The greatest change in function has been assumed by the Ministry of Transport in relation to highway functions, where there has been a tendency for it to assume an increasingly promotional role. It is, however, the Department of Education and Science that constitutes the 'clearest example of a Department with a positive, promotional attitude to local authorities' (Griffith, 1966, p. 522),[9] and yet even in this most controlled service there is, as I suggested earlier, considerable local service variation.

It is important to note that the Royal Borough of Kensington and Chelsea is not an education authority and has only a limited responsibility for traffic matters, and so in consequence has little involvement with those central departments which have adopted a promotional role. Notwithstanding the fact that the Royal Borough has most contact with non-interventionist ministries, how has the council responded to central control and direction?

Section 74 of the London Government Act 1963 stated: 'Without prejudice to section 106 of the Local Government Act 1933, the officers of each London Council and the Common Council shall as soon as reasonably practicable, and in any event not later than the 1st April 1968, include an architect for the Borough or, as the case may be, the City.' Subsequent statements by the Minister, Sir Keith Joseph, and a later circular, made it clear that the architect should be of chief officer status. The Royal Borough

9. Davies (1968, p. 295) notes a similar pattern of central involvement.

of Kensington and Chelsea appointed an architect, as the Act required, but did not appoint him at the chief officer level. As a senior councillor of the Royal Borough said: 'People said that Sir Keith's statement in the House made it clear that the London Boroughs should appoint an architect as a chief officer. The Council considered, however, that they were entitled to act on the basis of what the Act said and not on the basis of what Sir Keith Joseph may, or may not, have meant.'

Ernest Marples, as Minister of Transport, was extremely keen to encourage the Inner London Boroughs to implement schemes of parking control which would involve the use of parking meters. Both Kensington, and Chelsea Councils were opposed to this, and successfully resisted the Ministry, only introducing a scheme once the law had been changed which made it possible for them to make special provision for residents. A senior councillor: 'I fought this parking meter idea with Marples. He said "Look here, you've got to have meters," and I said, "No, we're not that sort of Borough." We really stood out against a scheme which we thought would penalise our residents.'

A more notable case of the Royal Borough standing out against the advice of the central government came in the period 1966–7, over the question of rent increases for council tenants. In July 1966, the government issued a White Paper (*Prices and Incomes Standstill*, 1966), which requested local authorities 'to prevent or postpone rent increases, including those already announced'. Eventually, and not without opposition inside the party, the council decided to postpone the increases scheduled to begin in October 1966, but stated that it intended, at a later date, to collect the increases that would have been due from the initially planned date. The Ministry sent a letter requesting the Royal Borough to leave open the question of collecting the 'technical arrears'. In January the council decided to collect rent arrears for the three months October 1966–January 1967, caused by their postponing the collection of intended increases. In July the Ministry wrote to the Royal Borough and asked them to 'consider again the effect that this decision may have on their relations with the tenants', but at their August meeting the council reaffirmed its decision to collect the arrears. The implementation of this decision raised some £14,000, an amount equal to the product of one-seventh of an old penny rate.

In the summer of 1967 local people urged the Council of the Royal Borough to buy an unused garden square as a public amenity. The council were not sympathetic to this demand, and in January 1968 deferred decision on the matter, justifying their line of action by referring to a 'personal message from the Minister of Housing and Local Government referring to the gravity of the economic situation facing the country'. After the elections of 1968, there was a new leader of the council and a new group of North Kensington councillors who were more impressed by the need for additional play facilities. In the summer of 1968 the council bought the square for under £10,000. There was no hint of any problem regarding loan sanction.

It might be thought that this example at last provides proof of the reality of 'government by circular'. I would suggest that this is not so, but rather shows how a local authority can use a central government circular to justify and defend a particular position which it is keen to adopt, and so enable it to insulate itself from local criticism by deflecting criticism to the central government which the authority quite erroneously claims to be the cause of its action. It should not be forgotten that the council which accepted the minister's advice as it affected the possibility of their buying the garden square, refused to accept the far more forceful advice and direction when it came to the question of council house rents.

These cases show that the Royal Borough is prepared to stand out against the advice and direction contained in government White Papers, circulars, private meetings with ministers, and personal letters directed solely to them, if their own view as to what should be the proper scope of government is challenged. At the same time such cases also show how a local authority may use the supposed obstacle of central control for the purposes of internal political defence. Examples like this (which could be multiplied many times over if attention were directed to other local authorities) must question the validity of statements which refer to 'control through suggestion' and the 'cumulative and psychological effect' of control. These cases suggest that the impact of the central government upon the day-to-day decisions of local authorities often depends on local responsiveness, and the preparedness of local authorities to accept advice or guidance which in law the central government has no strict authority to give and no legal power to enforce.

In this chapter I have set out to counter the arguments of those who conclude that the weight of central control has effectively destroyed the independence and initiative of local authorities. I have suggested, not only that they have not proved their case, but also that there are firm grounds for claiming that local authorities are by no means the passive agents of the central government but have scope to develop their own policies. If local authorities are not prepared to accept central guidance and advice, then the central government can really only impose its will if it can apply sanctions, and this means that they are 'likely to be more fruitful in curtailing an above-average level of local activity than in stimulating individual Authorities to achieve such a level' (Chester, 1951, p. 121). A local authority which conceives of its role in small terms may find its pattern of public policies but little affected by central control.

It must be admitted that this study will be one-sided. It presumes that the reader has read the other side. Most books on local government in Britain have dwelt on the extent of central control and have consequently failed to see local authorities as structures which can make and maintain public policies. I will do the opposite, but in ignoring the effect of central control I will be able to devote more time to making sense of the way in which the Council of the Royal Borough makes and maintains the public policies for its area. In the first part of this study I will be looking at the established literature of political science which has shown a concern to explain public policy and at the start of the next chapter I will be assessing the value of another, but smaller, tradition, of writing about British local government.

Part One
PUBLIC POLICY-MAKING: THE IMPACT OF ENVIRONMENT

Although public policy is not a well-defined and established field in political science, there is nevertheless a literature which does attempt to make sense of public policy-making. Some students point to the importance of the class or personality of the political decision-makers, but the major explanatory ideas in the discipline of political science point to the impact which environmental forces have upon government. Some students point to the importance of elections, others to the impact of pressure groups, and still others have argued that the socio-economic environment of government has the major effect on the form of public policy. In the four chapters of this Part, I will look at each of these differing approaches one by one, and then in the final overview chapter, I will offer a more general critique of these explanations and suggest a way forward which should enable us to make better sense of public policy in the Royal Borough of Kensington and Chelsea.

2 Elections: the citizen as policy-maker

How is the country governed? *By the Government*, is the first answer that you will be likely to give, and in a way the answer is right. *But who governs the Government?* The answer is that Parliament does. But last of all, *who governs Parliament?* And the answer to that is that the *People of this Country* govern Parliament. And so you will see that the real answer to the question 'Who governs the country' is that '*The country governs itself*'.

> H. O. Arnold-Forster, *The Citizen Reader* (London, Cassell, 1900), p. 35, original emphasis.

There are two distinct traditions of writing about local government in Britain. There is the dominant one I discussed in the last chapter which sees local authorities as administrative structures, but there is another which asserts that local authorities are policy-makers. Within this latter body of writing there is a consistent range of ideas about local political relationships, with the argument that the process of local policy-making can best be explained by a theory which regards the structures of government as institutions of representative democracy at the end of a chain of command reaching back to the local electorate.

The fact that I have already rejected the first tradition as an adequate characterisation of the position of local government in Britain, and have accepted the view that local authorities are policy-making bodies, means that I need to explore the cogency of the arguments of those in this second tradition in order to see whether their theory is adequate to the facts of local government in general and to my case in particular.

I. THE ELECTORAL CHAIN OF COMMAND THEORY

In the last chapter I pointed out that British writers attach considerable importance to the value of local self-government and show enthusiasm for those nineteenth-century reforms which they saw as creating representative and responsible government at the local level. If writers have not explained the working of local government by referring to the dominating force of central control, then they have generally been content to refer to the motivating force of the local electorate, assuming and asserting that local governors fulfil the role provided for them in the normative theory of representative government. This theory is rarely subjected to empirical test.

In these discussions of the local political process causal connections are posited between electors, councillors and officers, and the vote is regarded as the starting point of a chain of command. Consider the following statement: 'Under this historic system of "local self-government" local authorities have even now a substantial amount of discretion. They consist of persons responsible to the local electorate, or of persons appointed by other persons who are responsible to the local electorate. Within the limits laid down by Parliament and of central control, they adopt a policy which accords, as they think, with the views of the local electorate' (Jennings, 1947, p. 17. See also, Howe, 1907).

Writers who use these arguments stress the degree of responsibility and responsiveness of local councils to their electorate, and claim that local councillors are 'in touch with the circumstances, feelings and needs of their areas' (Chester, 1951, p. 342. See also, Brooke, 1953, p. 183; A West Midland Study Group, 1956, p. 289; and, Hart, 1968, p. 90). They point out that if the policies being pursued by any council are unpopular with the ordinary citizens – if the chain of command breaks down so that the council can no longer be regarded as behaving responsibly – then this will only be a temporary occurrence, for 'the electoral process should remove them, just as the parliamentary election removes an unpopular government' (Chester, 1951, p. 342). In order to understand the local political process, it is simply necessary to realise that, 'the public in any area, or those members of the public who are local government electors, choose their representatives who collectively undertake the statutory responsibility of making development plans as well as a host of other local government functions. If the electors do not like what their representatives do, they have the right to change them periodically' (Town Planning Institute, 1968, pp. 343–4. See also, Redlich, 1903, vol. 1, pp. 215–16; and, Chapman, 1965).

In the relationship between the councillors and the electorate, it is the electors who are in the commanding position because 'not the Town Councillors but *all* the citizens are the municipality. . . . The councillors are merely the representatives of the citizens, elected by them to carry out their desires' (Suthers, 1905, p. 10).[1] When we move on to consider the

1. In the Electoral Chain of Command Model, the ideal representative would serve as an agent (as is suggested in this reference). However, even if a representative assumes more of a 'Burkean' role, this does not really conflict with the requirements of the model, as he will still be acting in accordance with the wishes of a disinterested and informed electorate which is ever-mindful of the general interest. At any event, whatever role the representative assumes, there is still the possibility of public recall through the vehicle of free elections.

relationship between the councillors and the officers, then the councillors are in command because they are seen as closer to the electorate, the ultimate source of political power: 'The Municipal Civil Service occupies a position in relation to the Local Authorities of Great Britain not unlike that occupied by the National Civil Service in relation to the Central Government. It is the elected members of the Authority, be they Cabinet Ministers of Town Councillors, who determine the policy and issue the orders of the Authority. But in the local Council, as in Whitehall, it is the Civil Service that carries on the day-to-day administration, advises the Council and its Committee, and is, in the last resort, obedient to any decision the Council may choose to make' (Atlee & Robson, 1925, p. 34. See also, Warren, 1950; Jennings, 1947, p. 119; and, M. Cole, 1956, pp. 115–16).

This statement not only describes the relationship between councillors and officers, but also highlights the fact that similar ideas have been used in discussions of national politics. Certainly the particular 'language'[2] I am considering at one time dominated the academic consensus and still today 'appears to command most general acceptance and to underlie most of the comments on political affairs that are to be found in the popular press' (Birch, 1967, p. 31).

Perhaps the classic discussion of British politics which relies on this liberal language of electoral control and command is that offered by Dicey who considers that the 'conventions' of government have 'one ultimate objective. Their end is to secure that Parliament, or the Cabinet which is indirectly appointed by Parliament, shall in the long run give effect to the will of that power which in modern England is the true political sovereign of the State – the majority of electors' (Dicey, 1959, p. 429). Writers argue that the convention of Ministerial Responsibility ensures that the civil service are checked by Parliament; that the convention of Collective Responsibility holds both Cabinet and Government accountable to Parliament (S. E. Finer, 1956*a*; Brown, 1955; and, Mackintosh, 1962.); and finally that the dominant House in Parliament – the House of Commons – is in its turn held accountable to the electorate by the device of regular, free, general elections. In this view of politics there is the 'transmission of orders from the many to the controlling few', a transmission which is 'ideally something of an automatic mechanism – almost indeed a sort of slot-machine by which votes inserted at one end turn out laws at the other' (Tivey, 1958, pp. 111–12).

Although the working of government at the central and the local level have both been explained by using this liberal theory of electoral control and command, there are two points which must be borne in mind when we consider this theory in the context of local politics.

2. Birch, 1964. Tivey, 1958, refers to the 'People's Will' theory, and Wahlke, 1971, to the 'Policy–Demand Input' conception of government.

First, the Electoral Chain of Command Theory is especially strongly entrenched as an explanation for local policy-making because writers have taken the view that there is more scope for extensive and informed public participation at the local level (Mill, 1861), and at the same time they have argued that there is no necessity for political parties. Both these two ideas are central to the theory I am considering. The stress on informed public participation is not surprising given the crucial initiating and controlling role which the electorate is seen as filling (Bryce, 1923, vol. 1, pp. 53–4; Hasluck, 1936; and, Lindsay, 1935). The attack on political parties reflects the fact that proponents of this theory see a social order characterised by only limited conflict and hence see no necessity for organised political competition. Society is regarded as an organic whole for which there exists a general interest, which publicity, discussion and common-sense can divine as a guide to the correct pattern of public policies. In many ways this theory is almost one which eliminates politics from policy-making and makes government merely a matter of administering what is largely agreed by all who have regard for the national interest over and above narrow sectional advantage.

Second, however, we must be cautious in accepting this theory as an adequate characterisation of the local policy process because writing on the functioning of the central government, which has been increasingly mindful of the lack of fit between this theory and current political reality,[3] should alert us to look for similar problems when we attempt to rely on the theory to make sense of local politics. In particular, writers dealing with national politics have been increasingly prepared to admit that political parties play a crucial role in the policy process in spite of the fact that these organisations are omitted from consideration in the Electoral Chain of Command Theory. Developments in the study of national politics have not really filtered down to the study of politics at the local level where 'there has been little formal study of the workings of party in local government, and much of the discussion that does take place is still largely concerned with whether or not party in local government is desirable' (Brennan, Cooney, & Pollins, 1954, p. 76. See also, MacColl, 1949; Block, 1962; Gowan, 1963; and, Warren, 1952). In the 'discussion of local democracy too great an emphasis is placed on the role of the individual elected representative and the individual elector, as if the two interacted one upon the other within the framework of an ideal representative system' (Sharpe, 1960, pp. 170–1), and although it would be reassuring to know that parties in local politics have not been studied because they have not existed until recently, Bulpitt reminds us that 'the search for a golden age (in the nineteenth and early twentieth centuries) when politics and parties played no part whatsoever in local government is quite futile; conflict has always existed, and

3. Birch (1964, p. 80) has noted that 'since the nineteen-thirties, adherents to the Liberal theory of the state have been regretfully aware that political practice has departed from Liberal principles.'

parties were always present' (Bulpitt, 1967, p. 5. See also, Keith-Lucas, 1961). The existence of local parties should not have been ignored, for Hadfield and MacColl make the point that 'an account of British local government that left out a description of the working of political parties would be formally correct. . . . Yet such an account would be hopelessly unrealistic. Everyone associated with a council recognises that the influence of political parties has increased and is increasing' (Hadfield & MacColl, 1948, p. 90). The fact is that parties have not been systematically integrated into a theory of politics at the local level because they have lacked normative acceptability. The Electoral Chain of Command Theory has been especially strongly developed in discussions of local politics and has served as much as a prescription of how things should be as a description of how things are. From this perspective parties should be non-existent, and at any event they are regarded as undesirable: ostrich-like, they have been ignored. The failure to study the role of parties in the local political process is an omission from this theory which means that it provides only a misleading picture of the electoral and representative process, and as such it has no real relevance in enabling us to make sense of the policy process in those local authorities – such as Kensington and Chelsea – where parties are firmly established.

This failure to study the role of political parties is not the only factor which must lead us to question the utility of the Electoral Chain of Command Theory as an accurate characterisation of the local political process, for, in addition to this omission, the theory is grounded on an assumption of high levels of public participation and involvement which when checked against available information is shown to be false. Election statistics and sample surveys show, not only restricted turnout, but also a low state of knowledge about even quite gross political phenomena at the local level. Many writers have refused to recognise evidence of this kind, or else they choose to interpret its relevance in a way which does not challenge the appropriateness of the liberal language. High voting is taken as an indication of protest or an over-efficient party machine, whereas a low poll is interpreted as indicating general satisfaction with the way local government is administered or as reflecting the electorate's awareness that either party will serve the people well (*Planning*, 1947, 1948, 1955; Bealey, Blondel & McCann 1965). The extent to which turnout at the polls is a good measure of interest in local government has been questioned (Bonnor, 1954), and more recently more favourable light has been cast on the extent of non-voting by suggesting that some is 'involuntary' and may be based on 'good reasons' (Sharpe, 1962*b*, p. 74; and, Grundy, 1950). In as far as it is admitted that voter turnout and general interest are low, then these effects are attributed to the excessive weight of central control. One writer has claimed that 'if the relationship between central and local government is adjusted so that the sense of responsibility returns to the latter, local government may recover from its sickness' (A West Midland Study Group, 1955, p. 5. See also,

Howe, 1907, pp. 174–5, and p. 190; Jennings, 1947, p. 187; and, Chester, 1951, p. 342).

A theory which takes little account of parties and public disinterest in local politics is obviously inadequate as a means of studying the making of public policy at this level, but in spite of this many writers still cling to assumptions and orientations which are rooted in an acceptance of liberal theories.[4] Recent empirical work on local government has been carried out within the framework of these ideas, for elections, electors, and the elected are still put right in the centre of the research stage,[5] and the line of continuity between these and older studies lies in the similarity of the roles and processes that are discussed as being relevant to an understanding of the functioning of local authorities. Of course the reasons why elections are studied today are rather different. Sharpe argues that 'building up from below . . . we can really begin to understand the electoral geography of this country in . . . depth' (Sharpe, 1967*a*, p. 8), and Stanyer considers that 'local elections ought to play a crucial role in the comparative study of electoral systems because only local elections yield enough cases for the use of modern techniques and concepts' (Stanyer, 1968, p. 1). Students of local elections may now lack an overt attachment to a liberal theory of the effects of elections on representatives and policies but the fact that 'elections take on an importance in the methodology of studying politics . . . tends to translate itself into a corresponding – and possibly exaggerated – importance in the analysis of political process. In addition it makes the voter or elector an excessively important actor in politics; usually exaggerating his role where any assessment of its importance is undertaken' (Nettl, 1967, p. 158). For the most part recent case-studies of local authorities simply describe selected facets of local politics, but the repeated isolation of the electorate for special attention reveals an implicit acceptance of the old liberal theory with the assumption that the electorate has a particularly decisive influence on public policy (Birch, 1959; Bealey *et al*, 1965; and, G. W. Jones, 1969).

I have outlined two themes in this section. First, I have suggested that there is a particular theory implicit in much of the work on local government which purports to describe the nature of the local political process, and to explain the making of public policy. I have called this the Electoral Chain of Command Theory. Second, I have suggested that certain of the assumptions on which this theory are based are so much at variance with

4. Similar comments about the survival of old modes of discussion are made by Plamenatz, 1958. Note too the comment that 'in many ways the traditional terms in which local democracy is still frequently discussed have little relevance to existing conditions' (Royal Commission on Local Government in England, Research Studies, 1, 1968, p. 31).
5. Sharpe, 1967*b*. In Bealey *et al*, 1965, over 100 pages are devoted to a discussion of the information derived from a sample survey of 1,576 electors. See also, Birch, 1959.

the reality of local politics that it is not even necessary to examine the theory within the specific context of the Royal Borough of Kensington and Chelsea in order to conclude that it is quite incapable of helping us to make sense of the policy process within that authority. Not only are political parties involved in the organisation of elections and the arrangement of council business, but also the levels of public participation and knowledge are very different from those which one would expect to be the case if the theory were taken as an accurate description. However, the realisation that this particular theory is inadequate does not mean that we must abandon the study of elections, but it does mean that if we wish to rely on theories of the policy process in which they play an important part, then we must look to theories which have been developed outside the body of writing on local government which are less at variance with the reality of electoral politics in local government and which may therefore be of utility in making sense of my case.

For the moment I will leave aside a consideration of the implications of the information which we have on the knowledge and orientations of the electorate, and will concentrate instead on studying how we can assess the role of elections once it is recognised that political parties are critically involved in the politics of virtually all urban local authorities in England, and that parties have been evident in the politics of Kensington and Chelsea at least back until 1900. The Doctrine of Responsible Party Government, born of American admiration of British practice, is a model of the political process which does recognise that parties assume a role of key importance, and as such it is likely to provide a more realistic model of the political process in British local authorities. In the next section I will outline this theory and then see how far the reality of politics in Kensington and Chelsea conforms to the requirements of the model.

II. THE DOCTRINE OF RESPONSIBLE PARTY GOVERNMENT

Although work on representative government has been slow to recognise the part which political parties play (for similar comments see, Birch, 1964, p. 114; and, Ranney, 1962a, p. 3), there has been increasing recognition of their existence and of the indispensability of a special type of party system (Bassett, 1935, pp. 33–7; Butler & Stokes, 1969, p. 23; and, Barker, 1945, p. 66), if public policy is to be in harmony with the wishes of the majority of the electorate. In order to appreciate whether any particular party system approximates to the ideal of the Responsible Party Model, it is necessary to see if the following five requirements of the model are met in that system.

1. 'the parties are able to bring forth *programs* to which they commit themselves' (American Political Science Association, Committee on Political Parties, 1950, p. 1).

2. 'the parties possess sufficient *internal cohesion* to carry out these programs' (American Political Science Association, Committee on Political Parties, 1950, p. 1).

3. Two parties are needed with an *opposition*, 'which all along has been "keeping its ear to the ground" to learn and anticipate the people's wants, pointing out the errors and deficiencies of the rulers in power, and which . . . stands ready to assume power' (Ranney, 1962*a*, p. 11).

4. *Neither party should be in a permanent majority*, because unless the opposition party has some hope of forming a government then the electoral situation holds little 'threat' for the ruling party.

5. If government is going to be responsible to, and controlled by, the electorate, then it has to be the case that *party programmes are drawn up in order to appeal to, and secure support from, the electorate*. There has, in other words, to be something of an 'exchange' between parties and voters – in return for favourable policies, parties can expect to gain the votes of electors. Parties, it is argued, should be geared to winning elections and gaining control of government, and this leads to their forming policies and programmes with the electors' wishes specifically in mind. The incentive to do this is, of course, dependent on the electoral situation being competitive (Dahl, 1961*b*, pp. 97–103, and 218–20; Downs, 1957, p. 28).

The Electoral Chain of Command Theory implied that the act of voting led directly to popular policies, whereas this model sees parties assuming a critically important linking role. If there are two parties each putting forward clear programmes which they are pledged to carry out if elected, and which they are able to carry out because they possess sufficient internal cohesion and discipline, then the electorate in choosing a particular programme (and a programme at that which has been drawn up with a view to recruiting electorate support) 'mandates' a party to carry out its programme and holds the party accountable for its adequate fulfilment at the next election (Epstein, 1964; and, Emden, 1956). If electors then consider that the successful party has broken its pledges, or that the opposition has since worked out more popular policies, it will vote the present government out and give the opposition a chance. If this situation obtains, it is argued that government will be controlled, and public policy will be congruent with the wishes of the majority of the electorate.

Although the Responsible Party Model is seen as a characterisation of the reality of British national politics (McKenzie, 1955), and although it represents 'the popular belief' about how the British constitution is 'supposed to work' (S. E. Finer, 1956*b*, pp. 751–2), it has rarely been used to make sense of the local policy process because of the general failure to recognise the existence of parties at that level. However, when the existence of parties has been noted and their role approved, then writers have had the Responsible Party Model in mind. Cole argues that with Parties, 'the policy upon which the party fought the elections is known, and every successful candidate has given adhesion to it; if therefore it is afterwards not carried out, and promises broken, it is no use for the individual Councillor, meeting his constituents, to say, "You voted for this, and I promised to do it; but I can't. My fellow-Councillors won't let me." His business is, if the policy is not being carried out and the promises not being fulfilled, to go to his party group or his party leader, and explain that confidence is being betrayed, and if the promises are not being carried out, without good reason given, the result will not simply be that he will fail to be re-elected; the party as a whole will be discredited and may easily lose power at the next election' (M. Cole, 1956, p. 174).[6]

Local government is the poor relation in the political science research-house, and like the poor relation wears the cast-off clothes of its elders: there are signs that the Responsible Party Model is filtering down to provide us with a description and explanation of how the local political process really works. A recent study of Wolverhampton illustrates the point, for the author concludes by suggesting that, 'the most important conclusion of this book is that on balance the growing involvement of parties in local government has had good results. Parties have made the Council more democratic and less oligarchic. More people vote, stand for and are elected to the Council now than before the days of party, and they come from a wider range of occupations. Parties have enabled individuals to devise a programme of policies and to implement it, and they have presented these programmes to the public in a dramatic and comprehensible way, enabling the public to judge a team of men and measures; thus the accountability of government to the electorate has been strengthened. Further, the organisation of parties, both inside and outside of the Council has enabled the humblest member of the rank and file to exercise influence on the party leaders, and to reject them and their policies if necessary. Although public participation in local government is small, it is more than it was in the days before political parties became actively involved, and for that increase parties deserve the credit' (G. W. Jones, 1969, pp. 348–9).

The study of party in local government introduces a greater realism into research, but it is to be hoped that the recognition of the existence of parties does not lead to the immediate assertion that local politics functions in accord with the Responsible Party Government Model. The specifications of the model only supply a useful list of research questions, and how far practice conforms to the model depends on the facts of the situation in a particular case. How far does the doctrine hold in the Royal Borough of Kensington and Chelsea?

There are fifteen wards in the Royal Borough. In Chelsea all wards with the exception of Stanley have returned only Conservative councillors since

6. See also, Shelley, 1939, pp. 182–3: 'If those who supported him [the councillor] at the last election are seriously offended by his course of action they may then abstain from voting, or even vote against other candidates representing the same party'.

1922;[7] in South Kensington, all five wards have only ever returned Conservative councillors since the election of 1900;[8] and in North Kensington the situation is rather more fluid – one ward is 'safe' Conservative, two wards are 'safe' Labour,[9] and the remaining ward has been won by Labour in six elections since the Second World War and by the Conservatives in the remaining three elections. Of the fifteen wards in the borough, ten have returned Conservative councillors since 1922, and at the present time these wards account for 39 of the 60 councillors. After the 1964 election the party balance (including aldermen) was Conservative 53, Labour 17; after the 1968 elections the balance was Conservatives 66, Labour 4; and following the 1971 elections the balance was Conservatives 46, Labour 24. The Conservative majority is large, the party has always been in control of the council, and there is no prospect of the opposition party either winning control, or posing an election threat to the ruling Party so that it is forced to keep a close ear to the ground in order to secure future victory. In terms of the requirements of the Responsible Party Model, although there is an opposition (Requirement Three), that opposition has no prospect of graduating to government (Requirement Four).

Two critical requirements of the Responsible Party Model relate to party programmes: parties should not only bring forth a programme of policies at an election (Requirement One), but they should also devise their programmes so as to appeal to the electorate (Requirement Five). Although part of the ritual of each council election involves the publication and circulation of biographies of the candidates together with brief details of their policy proposals, it is hardly possible to regard these election addresses as constituting a party programme which will guide the policy activity of the winning party till the next election. Not only are the policy proposals very general (usually advocating more and better services together with lower rates), but they also cover only a limited area of local government activity.

7. Prior to 1949 North and South Stanley were just the one ward – Stanley – which was not consistently held by any one party, although it was more often Conservative. North Stanley has only returned Conservatives; South Stanley has always been more marginal and has returned both Labour and Conservative councillors. In more recent times it has been regarded as a safe Labour ward, but in 1968 all seats there were won by the Conservatives for the first time.

8. Brompton ward has been in a rather strange position. Prior to the creation of the Royal Borough of Kensington and Chelsea, Brompton ward returned councillors to the Kensington council, but in parliamentary elections Brompton was part of the Chelsea constituency. With the creation of the new borough, Brompton is a ward which is in Chelsea, and candidates were selected by the Chelsea Conservatives, but in fact of the four Conservative councillors from that ward on the first and second councils, two had sat on the old Kensington council.

9. Pembridge was regarded as the safe Conservative ward, but it was lost to Labour in the 1971 elections. The two safe wards are regarded as Colborne and Saint Charles, though the latter ward was lost to the Conservatives in 1968, but won back in 1971.

TABLE 1 *Kensington and Chelsea: Party representations by wards, 1900–71*

	1900	1903	1906	1909	1912	1919	1922	1925	1928	1931	1934	1937	1945	1949	1953	1956	1959	1962	1964	1968	1971
North Kensington																					
Saint Charles	5c/1p	6p	1c/5p	2c/4p/2L	4c/2p	6c	6c	6c	6c	6c	5L/1c	6L	6L	6L	6L	6L	6L	6L	6L	6c	6L
Golborne	6p	6p	6L	6L	6L	6L	6L	6L	5L/1c	6L	6L	6L	6L	6L	6L	6L	6L	6L	3L	3L	3L
Norland	3p/3c	3p/3c	6E*	4p	6c	6c	6c	6c	6c	6c	3L/3c	6c	6c	6c	6c	6c	6c	6L	4L	4c	4L
Pembridge	6c	6c	6c	6c	6c	6c	6c	6c	6c	6c	6c	6c	6c	6c	6c	6c	6c	6c	6c	6c	6L
South Kensington:																					
Holland	8c/1i	8c/1i	9c	9c	9c	9c	9c	9c	9c	9c	9c	9c	9c	9c	9c	9c	9c	9c	6c	6c	6c
Earls Court	5c/1i	6c	5c/1mc†	6c	6c	6c	6c	6c	6c	6c	9c	6c	6c	6c	6c	6c	6c	6c	6c	6c	6c
Queens Gate	6c	6c	6c	6c	6c	6c	6c	6c	6c	6c	6c	6c	6c	6c	6c	6c	6c	6c	4c	4c	4c
Redcliffe	6c	6c	6c	6c	6c	6c	6c	6c	6c	6c	6c	6c	6c	6c	6c	6c	6c	6c	7c	7c	7c
Brompton**	8c/1i	9c	9c	9c	9c	9c	9c	9c	9c	9c	9c	9c	9c	9c	9c	9c	9c	9c	4c	4c	4c
Chelsea:																					
Cheyne	5c/1p	6c	6c	6c	6c	6c	6c	6c	6c	6c	6c	6c	6c	6c	6c	6c	6c	6c	2c	2c	2c
Church	6p	6p	2p/4c	6c	6c	1L/5c	6c	6c	6c	6c	6c	6c	6c	6c	6c	6c	6c	6c	3c	3c	3c
Hans Town	9c	9c	9c	9c	9c	9c	9c	9c	9c	9c	9c	9c	6c	6c	6c	6c	6c	6c	3c	3c	3c
Royal Hospital	6c	6c	6c	6c	6c	6c	6c	6c	6c	6c	6c	6c	6c	6c	6c	6c	6c	6c	2c	2c	2c
Stanley	6p/3c	9p	9c	9c	9c	7L/2c	9c	9c	9c	9c	9c	9c	9L								
North Stanley														6c	6c	6c	6c	6c	2c	2c	2c
South Stanley														4L/2c	6L	6L	6L	6L	1L/1c	2c	2L

c = Conservative; i = Independent; L = Labour; p = Progressive.   mc† = Middle Classes Defence Organisation.
E* = Economic Party.   ** = See footnote 8.

Election addresses of Conservative candidates in Kensington and Chelsea, May, 1968

1 SOUTH KENSINGTON

CONSERVATIVE CONTROL ENSURES FULL VALUE FOR ALL RATEPAYERS' MONEY

FINANCE

Wise management has enabled the demands made on our ratepayers to be kept to a minimum and this year has seen a substantial reduction in the domestic rate. We shall continue our policy of avoiding waste, providing first class services and giving our ratepayers full value for their money.

TOWN PLANNING

The importance of planning and of the Borough Development Plan cannot be overstressed. Our aims are to ensure that the Borough is predominantly a residential area; to conserve our unique heritage; to lay the foundations for slum clearance and improvement of twilight areas, and to keep residents informed so that they can actively participate in planning the type of environment in which they wish to live.

HOUSING

Your Council resources are devoted to slum clearance and redevelopment—this emphasis has been proved absolutely correct. Since April 1965, 333 families have been rehoused as a result of slum clearance work and your Council is at present engaged on one of the largest programmes ever undertaken by a comparable Borough Council. This, covering areas totalling approximately 46 acres, will provide some 2400 units of accommodation and envisages the rehousing of about 7800 persons. It is truly a great programme, due to Conservative initiative and drive.

Published by C. V. Brook, 23 Stratford Rd., London, W.8. and Printed by Errington & Martin, 25 Elsdale Street, London, E.9.

RENTS

For many years we have operated a differential rent scheme which ensures that the rents charges are proportionate to the Tenants' incomes. Thus no-one in housing need is too poor to accept an offer of accommodation., whilst those who can afford to pay a higher rent do so. Thus no ratepayer's money is wasted.

MORTGAGES

Despite the recurring financial crises caused by the sheer incompetence of the Labour Government, every effort has been made to help those wishing to own their own homes and we shall continue our policy of providing mortgages wherever possible.

PARKING

The first parking scheme has been in operation for 4 months and has proved itself a complete success. The next scheme will cover the Kensington High Street area and will begin to operate later this year. Progress will be continued, to the great benefit of all residents.

REFUSE AND LITTER

A twice weekly refuse collection has, for many years, operated throughout the Borough, but every effort is made to improve the service provided. Extra sweepers are employed whenever possible and we shall continue to do everything in our power to keep the Borough clean and tidy.

AS
CONSERVATIVES
WE INTEND

★ **to get maximum help** for slum clearance in the North of the Borough and to ensure, that despite the Government's sharp cut back in its housing targets, more homes are provided.

★ **to extend home improvement grants.**

★ **to provide more play space** for the children of North Kensington and so reduce accidents, particularly by using the land under the Western Avenue Extension.

★ to spend the ratepayers' money **wisely.**

★ **to put North Kensington's problems FIRST.**

HOUSING

Our priorities are slum clearance, redevelopment wherever extra accommodation can be achieved, modernisation of old Council property, and aid to bona-fide Housing Associations. Our differential rent scheme not only ensures that tenants pay only the rent they can afford, but also that subsidised housing is made available to those who really need it.

OUR SOCIAL SERVICES

The new Royal Borough has far greater control of Health, Welfare and Children's Services. We aim to make services for the elderly, sick, disabled, handicapped and for deprived children increasingly personal and part of the whole life of the Borough. We have maintained our level of welfare expenditure in spite of current restrictions.

RESIDENTIAL AMENITIES

Where change becomes inevitable we aim to control it as far as possible in a manner which preserves local amenities. We work closely with local amenity and architectural societies, and we took the lead in establishing car parking priority for residents. Two-thirds of the cost of the parking scheme—already operating successfully in East Chelsea—is borne by commuters.

An incentive to the production of appealing party programmes lies in the situation of electoral marginality, and although the Conservative majority is secure, in a number of wards there is a close contest with no real certainty as to the election outcome. Does this prompt the majority party councillors there to bring forth more specific programmes geared to what they feel would appeal to the electorate and so gain votes? The short answer to this question is that marginality does not lead to the production of appealing party programmes.[10] The typical method of improving electoral prospects lies in the development of intensive campaigns of voter mobilisation – campaigns that are really devoid of any policy content but aim at locating support and then ensuring that there is a full turnout on polling day. In a situation where only a small percentage of the eligible electorate vote,[11] the party that locates and mobilises support is, other things being equal, in a more favourable position to win (Bochel & Denver, 1971). It might be argued that this preparedness to put effort into canvassing in the marginal wards reflects well on the process of democratic elections, for even if party programmes are not drawn up to appeal to the electorate, at least candidates are out in the wards discussing local issues and policies with electors before trying to convert them and win their support. In fact such a view misrepresents and romanticises the reality of canvassing which is simply designed to locate support with the minimum of debate and discussion; the good canvasser is the man who knocks on many doors, not one who engages in persuasive discussion on just a few doorsteps. A chairman made the situation clear: 'The main function of canvassing is to establish who your support is, and people should realise that they can help by voting early in the day so that later in the day knockers-up have fewer people to go and get out to vote. It's a very secondary function to try and persuade people to vote for you: nine-tenths are unpersuadable anyway since they are clearly aligned to one party or another . . . I advise the canvasser that if he gets into an argument he should stop at once, for while you're arguing with Snooks you could have called on five or six people. I believe that it's Socialist policy that if a Conservative canvasser knocks on your door you invite him in for tea and keep him as long as you can.'

In the section I have set out a model which still sees the electors as critical actors in the policy process, but in a way which is potentially of more use in enabling me to make sense of my case because it displays a greater

10. Even if majority party candidates from the marginal wards were to bring forth appealing programmes and gain election they would not be able to put their plans into effect as they are invariably in a position on the council where they lack influence in policy matters. Council leadership is in the hands of the long-serving councillors, and they, by definition, come from the safe seats.
11. In the three wards that were regarded as marginal in the 1968 local elections, the turnouts were as follows: St Charles, 24·6%; Norland, 31·8%; and South Stanley 31·9%.

realism than the Electoral Chain of Command Model. However, looking at the model alongside the situation in Kensington and Chelsea forces me to conclude that the fit between fact and theory[12] is poor and in consequence the model cannot be used as a basis for discussing and explaining the policy process in the Royal Borough.

The Doctrine of Responsible Party Government represents one attempt to come to terms with fact that political parties serve as crucial mediators in the translation of electoral support into public policies; the Theory of Competitive Leadership represents another, and although the former theory considers that the electorate have the opportunity of choosing between competing slates of policies the latter theory restricts the role of the electorate to one of choosing between competing teams of rulers.

III. THE THEORY OF COMPETITIVE LEADERSHIP

Schumpeter (1954, pp. 269–85), points out that in the classical theory of democracy, 'the selection of the representatives is made secondary to the primary purpose of the democratic arrangement which is to vest the power of deciding political issues in the electorate.' He suggests, 'suppose we reverse the roles of these two elements and make the deciding of issues by the electorate secondary to the selection of the men who are to do the deciding. To put it differently, we now take the view that the role of the people is to produce a government.' According to Schumpeter, 'voters do not decide issues,' and democracy 'means only that the people have the opportunity of accepting or refusing the men who are to rule them'. He calls this view of the electoral and political process 'the theory of competitive leadership' (Schumpeter, 1954, pp. 284–5).

It may well be that this theory provides a more realistic view of the role of the electorate in the policy process, but the cost of this greater realism lies in the fact that in reducing the role of the electorate in the determination of public policies, it demands that more research attention be paid to the forces within government, and if this research is to be undertaken then no clues are provided in the two theories which have been the central concern of this chapter.

The two theories which have formed the core of this chapter have seen the ordinary citizen as a central and influential figure in the policy process, able to gain policies which meet with his approval through participation in regular elections. Both the theories have been developed with only scant

12. I have not dealt with the internal cohesion of the parties in Kensington and Chelsea (Requirement Two), since in the context of the model this is but a means of ensuring that the electoral programme is actually put into effect. Since I have argued that programmes are not really put before the electorate in Kensington and Chelsea such cohesion as does exist serves ends other than that of ensuring that parties will actually develop and implement popular policies.

regard to the facts of electoral politics; they are mechanistic and deterministic and are based on assumptions as to the behaviour of the electors and the elected which have rarely been checked out against the available evidence. Information on the way in which both electors and the elected relate to the electoral process will enable us not only to assess more fully the utility of the theories I have laid out, but will also form a clearer impression of the actual part which elections and the electorate play in the process of public policy-making. In the next two sections I will deal with the elected and the electors.

IV. THE POLITICIAN'S THEORY OF VOTING BEHAVIOUR

Once it is remembered that elections are first and foremost choices for incumbents of particular roles, it then becomes vitally important to see how those subject to elections relate to them. This need is all the greater in situations of one-party dominance where elections do not even serve as a vehicle for team change. In these circumstances elections really can determine nothing except in so far as the ruling team allows this to be the case. Whether there is congruency between constituents' views on policies and the policies of the government is dependent on the anticipations of decision-makers and on their attempts to reach out and search for electorate opinion. Maybe the fact of elections encourages this behaviour, but whether this is so will depend on the politicians' beliefs about voters and on the assumptions which they make as to the factors which shape the voters' decision.

In this section I will report on a research study which argues that election winners have a theory of voting behaviour which serves to constrain their policy-making activity to working within the framework of what they consider to be the wishes of their constituents. I will go on to suggest that election winners in the governing party in Kensington and Chelsea do not hold similar beliefs and so are less constrained by their perception of their constituents' policy preferences when they develop their pattern of public policies.

Kingdon argues that the 'freedom' of a representative 'may vary according to his theory of voting behaviour' and 'the representative who believes that voters pay attention to election issues probably is less free of his constituents than one who does not' (Kingdon, 1967, p. 144). He accounts for the different beliefs of winners and losers in Wisconsin elections in terms of the 'congratulation–rationalization effect' – 'winners develop complimentary beliefs about voters and losers develop rationalizations for their losses simply by virtue of the outcome of the election' (Kingdon, 1967, p. 142) – and he concludes that 'by virtue of his electoral victory, an office-holder and specially a marginal winner believes that the eyes of the public are on him, that voters cast their ballots according to his actions and characteristics, and that they are comparatively well-informed about the issues of an election. If the incumbent thinks the electorate is watching him, whether they are or not in fact, he will attempt to anticipate their reactions to his decisions' (Kingdon, 1967, p. 145. For a British politician's view, see Macmillan, 1969, p. 33).

Before looking at the theories of voting behaviour held by winning councillors from the majority party in Kensington and Chelsea, it is important to note that a politician who considers that constituents pay close attention to his policy-making activity may nevertheless still not aim to develop policies which satisfy the majority of his electors because his seat may be so safe that he has no need to behave in this way, or alternatively he may have so little regard for his position of elected power that he shows no concern to secure his victory if this involves comprising his independence. I have already pointed out that the majority of seats on the council are safe for the Conservatives, but in the marginal wards candidates are often asked to stand and in several cases those who have been elected neither expected this to be the case nor really wanted this to be the case. More important, even if a politician is eager to develop policies which will win the approval of the majority of his electors this does not mean he will be successful in this endeavour, for he can only respond to what he thinks are the wishes of his electorate. When I consider the councillors' use of information in Chapter 9 I will suggest that their selectivity is such that they are only likely to come into contact with those who are in agreement with their own views. In other words, holding the belief that the electors' assessment of the legislative stance of the candidate will affect the election outcome may not result in a candidate developing policy positions which are any different from those which he might develop in the absence of this belief. Notwithstanding the fact that knowledge of politicians' beliefs about voters in isolation from hard facts about their information sources is only a limited clue to understanding their success in developing popular public policies, what are the beliefs held by winning councillors from the majority party in Kensington and Chelsea?

I have already answered this question indirectly when, in assessing the utility of the Responsible Party Model as a description and explanation of the policy process in Kensington and Chelsea, I noted that the typical response of councillors to electoral marginality involved the development of intensive campaigns of voter mobilisation. This strategy was based on the councillors' theory of electorate voting behaviour, for they did not consider that the policy stance of the local parties was likely to have much effect on the election outcome. This is shown in Table 2. Instead they stressed the importance of the electorate's relatively stable identity with a political party, noting that change was occasioned not by local matters but by the impact of national political events. The following statements made by councillors make their views clear: 'The result of an election is usually decided by feeling in the country as a whole and is based on general issues

C

quite unconnected with local government. What we do as a council or what happens in the council chamber has very little bearing on the result. For example, at the last election [1968] the feeling in the country was one for a big swing and this happened in Kensington despite the fact that for many months previously there were questions and attacks on the majority by the opposition often going on till 11.30 or midnight. The tenor of the opposition was that we were breaking faith, and that we were showing no interest in what was happening in the borough. The local press gave all this wide coverage and yet I doubt if it made any difference either way.' 'We didn't win a sweeping victory because of any local issues – any more than in any other London Borough. . . . People vote in local elections, especially in the large authorities of London, on the basis of their view of national politics as a whole.' 'If you put up a slate of poodles, if they had blue labels round their legs then they'd get in here. It's not a bad thing, and it doesn't distress me that it's this way; it's inevitable as local government goes with

TABLE 2.

'When you stand for election* do you think that the policies of the local party you support are important in determining the election outcome?'

Yes	9	20%[13]
No	35	76%
Other	2	4%

*Includes 8 aldermen who were asked, 'When councillors . . .'

the political barometer and follows the fortunes of the parties at the national level.'

Although Kingdon found that politicians in Wisconsin held beliefs about voters which were such as to constrain their freedom, councillors in Kensington and Chelsea held very different beliefs. Their belief that electors had little interest in, or knowledge of, their activity, and voted on the basis of party label or an assessment of national politics, was one which allowed them very much more freedom from constituents.

V. THE VOTER

Both the Electoral Chain of Command Model and the Responsible Party Model give the ordinary elector an influential role on the policy-making process, for he is at the start and finish of that process, choosing candidates and programmes and therefore initiating government action, but also

13. Respondents who attributed significance to the policy stance of the parties were drawn disproportionately from the ranks of the aldermen and the newly elected councillors from the marginal wards. Aldermen were in effect stating what *should* be the case, and the new councillors more than stressing the importance of their policy stances stressed the importance of personal contact with the electorate, so justifying their own expenditure of effort in this direction.

assessing retrospectively the past performance of candidates and parties so somehow vetoing or setting the seal of approval on established policy. Understandably, much was expected of the ordinary citizen. He was to be interested and informed about the activities of those in government and opposition, and was to vote, not on the basis of habit or whim, but as a result of a mature reflection on the alternatives before him, paying particular regard to the policies espoused by candidates and parties. However, one of the interesting developments in the past century has been the 'full-blown contrast that has arisen between the assumptions of the older democratic theorists and what now appear to be the actual facts of political life' (Dahl, 1961*a*, p. 406). Nowhere is this contrast more striking than in the case of the elector, for 'it is abundantly clear that the voter of today does lack both high political interest and an urge to participate in the political discourse' (Burdick, 1959, p. 139).[14] How does this information lead us to assess the adequacy and realism of the models I have set out in this chapter, and what are the facts about the voter in local elections in Britain?

When I outlined the various requirements of the Responsible Party Model earlier, like most writers I only dealt with what was required of the parties. 'What the conception of government by responsible parties requires of the general public has received much less attention', and yet as Stokes and Miller go on to point out, 'a necessary condition of party responsibility to the people is that the public have basic information about the parties and their legislative record. Without it, no institutional devices can make responsibility a fact' (Stokes & Miller, 1962, p. 532). If public policy is to be popular then the electorate must have information on party programmes and public policies and give the parties 'programmatic' support. If this is not the case, then it cannot be said that the voters have endorsed the programme of the winning party (even supposing one is put forward) so that public policies result which are congruent with the wishes of the majority of the electorate.

'Surprisingly little evidence is available' on the connection between voting and the policy preferences of British voters, 'perhaps because it has been so commonly taken for granted that every General Election in Britain constitutes an electoral mandate or at least an unfavorable judgment on past policy performance' (Wahlke, 1971, p. 276). However, Benewick has suggested that 'opinions about questions of policy are not closely related to voting behaviour . . . [and] only a minority of voters appear to have party policies uppermost in their minds when they go to the polls', for 'between 40 and 50 per cent of the voters at a general election vote for the party of

14. The response to this 'gap' has often involved a redefinition of democracy. See, Berelson, Lazarsfeld & McPhee 1954 esp. p. 312; Janowitz & Marvick, 1964; McClosky, 1964, and Morris-Jones, 1954. For critical comments on this development, see, Walker, 1966; Bachrach, 1967; Davis, 1964; and, Duncan & Lukes, 1963.

their choice either in spite of its policies or in ignorance of them' (Benewick, Birch, Blumler & Ewbank, 1969, p. 178). Birch, after a careful review of the secondary sources dealing with the question, concluded 'that the majority of electors do not make up their minds how to vote on the basis of the policies outlined in the election manifestoes' (Birch, 1964, p. 121), and other evidence[15] we have on the voting behaviour of electors means that we must 'doubt the applicability of the responsible party model even in Great Britain' (Wahlke, 1971, p. 276).[16]

When we look at voting behaviour in local elections, then we find, contrary to the expectations implicit in the Electoral Chain of Command Model and the Responsible Party Model that there is no real evidence to suggest that local experience of local services has an influence on behaviour at the polls so that electors give programmatic support to the parties.[17] Turnout at local elections is low,[18] and the overwhelming impression derived from research studies is that electors are ignorant of quite basic facts of local political life (N.A.L.G.O. Survey, 1957; Griffith, 1963; and, Bonnor, 1954), and vote, not on the basis of local issues, policies, and candidates,[19] but on the basis of a strong orientation to national politics. (Bealey *et al*, 1965, pp. 239–46; Sharpe, 1960; and, Richards, 1968, p. 155). The most impressive confirmation of the importance of national events and parties affecting the local election results was provided by a study of the 1964 elections in eleven boroughs. Fletcher, in analysing the results, noted: 'It was not merely the influence of "party" that dominated the elections, however, and determined the result in the vast majority of cases where change took place. More specifically, it was the influence of *national* party-political trends. . . . Throughout the period of the study, change in party fortunes in the local elections followed the same *general trends* as voting intentions recorded in the Gallop Poll' (Fletcher, 1967, p. 319–20, original emphasis. See also, Rees, 1968, p. 136; Butler & King, 1965, p. 340; and, Sharpe, 1962b, p. 7).

Findings like this must challenge from another side, the extent to which either the Electoral Chain of Command Model or the Responsible Party Model can be seen as a realistic picture of the political process at the local level in Britain.

15. Benney, Gray & Pear, 1956, pp. 139–54; Milne & MacKenzie, 1958, pp. 108–27; Abrams & Rose, 1960; and, Butler & Stokes 1969.
16. Key (1966, p. 59), has suggested that, contrary to established orthodoxy, for 'large numbers of persons' the 'vote is instrumental to their policy preferences'. For a critique of this study, see Barry, 1970.
17. Though for a contrasting view, see, Budge, 1965.
18. In Kensington and Chelsea turnout has steadily fallen throughout this century. In the 1909 elections almost 50% of the electorate voted, whereas in the elections since 1960, only about 25% of the electorate have gone to the polls.
19. For a contrasting view, see Painter, 1969; and, Birch, 1959, pp, 73, and 114.

VI. CONCLUDING REMARKS: THE SYMBOLIC FUNCTION OF ELECTIONS

'Most people today shrink from believing that the vote is not an effective instrument of citizen policy making, for such a conclusion would seem to strike at democratic beliefs' (Lindblom, 1968, p. 46). Certainly students of politics have rarely seen elections just as devices to select and reject people for political office, but have instead probed behind the simple and the obvious to argue that they serve as vehicles to enable the public to control government and shape public policy to their will. Theories of the policy process have been centred on the base of elections and the electorate, and in this chapter I have laid out two such theories which have been used by political scientists to make sense of the local policy process in Britain and to explain councillor behaviour. In addition I have attempted to assess the extent to which the Electoral Chain of Command Model and the Responsible Party Model are adequate to the facts of local government in general and my case in particular. I have been forced to conclude that they represent an idealised picture of the situation which bears little relation to the hard realities of electoral and governmental behaviour in Kensington and Chelsea, where the party system does not conform to the requirements of the Responsible Party Model, where winning councillors do not hold beliefs about voters which serve to constrain their activity, and where the electorate do not give programmatic support to parties and candidates.

This conclusion does not mean that elections and election campaigns are unimportant, 'it is rather that the functions they serve are different and more varied than the ones we conventionally assume and teach' (Edelman, 1964, p. 3). Participation through the vote is 'participation in a ritual act ... only in a minor degree is it participation in policy formation' (Edelman, 1964, p. 3), and in order to assess the function of elections in Western democracies we need to see them not just as devices for making demands on government but also as devices which secure public support for government. Elections are one device among many[20] which cement the loyalty of subjects to a particular regime. Yet if they are to ensure that the public support the system, and are compliant to the decisions made by government then it must be believed that elections secure governmental responsiveness. In this sense, 'every electoral system is a sort of confidence trick ... elections only work because we believe they are going to work' (MacKenzie, 1954, p. 69). The myths about representative and responsible government have to be believed, and to the extent that they are shown to be myths which bear little relation to the realities of public policy-making and governmental responsiveness then they fail.

20. On this question see Max Weber's work on legitimacy, Bendix, 1960. For an interesting discussion of the ways in which obedience was secured in the British system in the nineteenth century, see Bagehot, 1867.

Only scant attention has been paid to this symbolic function of elections, (Edelman, 1964; Rose & Mossawir, 1967; and, Wahlke, 1971), and yet voting 'contributes to the development or maintenance of the individual's *allegiance* to the existing constitutional regime' (Rose & Mossawir, 1967, p. 175, original emphasis. See also MacKenzie, 1957, esp. pp. 255–6), and mobilises the periphery into accepted and safe methods of participation (Mackenzie, 1954, pp. 56–7. See also the work of Stein Rokkan, for example Rokkan and Valen, 1962). Moreover, they also anoint elected representatives with a specific prestige (Loewenstein, 1965, pp. 261–2) which, far from facilitating public involvement in government, may lead to politicians attempting to insulate themselves from more direct forms of demand presentation by claiming that the fact of their election gives them a particular insight into the public will which transcends narrow sectional advantage. I will return to this theme in Chapters 8 and 9.

The object of this chapter has not been to assert that elections are totally unimportant in enabling the electorate to secure public policies in accord with their views. My argument has been that the theories which have been used to make sense of the policy process in local government have exaggerated the importance of the electorate and have failed to see elections as devices for mobilising public support for government and regime. A more accurate assessment of their role can only be provided if close attention is given to the part which parties actually play, and if we take into account the orientations of both candidates and electors. When information relevant to these questions is assembled from the facts of the situation in Kensington and Chelsea, reinforced by more general information on the nature of the local electorate, then we must recognise that the key to explaining the development of public policy in my case will not be provided by seeing the local council as an institution of representative and responsible government and anchoring research around the study of elections and the electorate. If we are to explain public policy, we must begin by setting aside the traditional study of elections, and in the next chapter I look to theories and ideas which have seen in pressure groups a key to understanding and explanation.

3 The importance of pressure groups

For the decisions of government, political pressure groups are of equal if not greater importance than the agencies of government themselves and the political institutions of the parties, the electorate, and public opinion.

> D. C. Blaisdell, *American Democracy Under Pressure* (New York, The Ronald Press Co., 1957), p. 27.

The last chapter pointed to the danger of attributing descriptive validity to the normative literature of our culture, and so highlighted the fact that a crucial 'dilemma for political behavior research is the apparent and oft-berated contrast between observable behavior patterns and the heritage of democratic belief' (Garceau, 1951, p. 70). At the turn of this century the fit between American political fact and normative democratic theory was so poor that hard-boiled observers found it necessary to make sense of the policy process by discovering 'invisible government,' pointing to 'patterns of influence beyond the prescriptions of the democratic institutions and the philosophical texts' (Garceau, 1958, p. 105). Reform journalists and muckrakers[1] were in the vanguard of this discovery of pressure groups, and political scientists were slow to study the part which they played, for it 'was not until the Twenties that any scholarly studies of pressure groups were made in the United States' (Eldersveld, 1958, p. 175), with Odegard claiming that his study of the Anti-Saloon League, *Pressure Politics*, published in 1928, 'gave its name to the whole process' (Odegard, 1967, p. xxxii).

At first pressure groups were seen as a peculiarly American institution, and as late as 1956 Beer could note that 'when an American looks at British politics, one of his first questions is likely to be, "Where are your pressure groups?" Since the subject has hardly been studied and most works on British government largely ignore it' (Beer, 1956, p. 1). Although

1. For a selection of these magazine articles, see Weinberg & Weinberg, 1964. See also, Steffens, 1904.

there have since been numerous studies of the part played by pressure groups in national political life in Britain (Eckstein, 1960; Beer, 1965; Self & Storing, 1962; S. E. Finer, 1958; Stewart, 1958; Potter, 1961; H. H. Wilson, 1961; and, Wooton, 1963), the initial resistance to noting their importance was bound up with the extent to which the emphasis on responsible party government and strong party discipline was seen as leaving little room for their involvement in the policy process. Finer observed that 'party is too strongly in control of English politics for members to be liable to influence by lobbyists. . . . There is hardly a loophole between the constituencies and Parliament through which the lobbyist can slide to extort concessions' (H. Finer, 1961, p. 463). After a careful study, Beer concluded that 'not only are British parties strong, but so also are British pressure groups' (Beer, 1958, p. 131. See also, Beer & Ulam, 1962, p. 170), Few writers now choose to account for pressure group power and influence by arguing that they are the 'children of neglect' (Schattschneider, 1948, p. 18), and are strong when parties are weak, although this was once an explanation which was widely used to account for the major role they were said to assume in the policy process.

In spite of the increasing attention which has been paid to the role of pressure groups in a whole variety of political systems (Ehrmann, 1957, 1958; La Palombara, 1964; Weiner, 1962; and, Skilling & Griffiths, 1971), there have been no systematic attempts to explore the part which they play in influencing the decisions of local authorities in Britain: 'there activities on the local level appear never to have been studied,' and 'we have no systematic treatise on . . . local pressure groups' (Birch, 1959, p. 165; and, Sharpe, 1967a, p. 1).[2] It would be comfortable to suppose that they do not exist at the local level, and although it may well be that a "whole new range of local pressure-groups have emerged in the last ten years' (Sharpe, 1967a, p. 3. See also, Broady, 1968, pp. 34–5), this does not alter the fact that groups have long been involved in local politics.[3] The fact that they have not been studied reflects more on the orientations and assumptions of those studying local government than it does on the reality of the political process at that level. The preoccupation with the study of law and the obsession with the extent of central control meant that local authorities themselves received only scant research attention, and then, when they were studied, the assumption that the local political process would conform to the Electoral Chain of Command Model meant that attention naturally centred on elections and formal processes of citizen involvement. There

2. Brief references to interest groups in local government appear in the following studies: *Planning*, 1947; Broady, 1968; Royal Commission on Local Government in England, Research Studies, 1, 1968, esp. pp. 22, and 23; Bealey, Blondel & McCann, 1965, pp. 379–82; Sharpe, 1960, 1966; Richards, 1968, p. 154; Hampton, 1970, pp. 214–45; Adeney, 1971; Beetham, 1970; Godfrey, 1968; Peterson, 1969; Brier & Dowse, 1966; and, Hill, 1970.
3. Chaloner (1950), for example, notes how from 1885 to 1891, Crewe was ruled from the offices of the railway company.

was not the expectation that pressure groups would be involved in local government.

Although there have been no significant studies of interest groups in the local policy process in Britain, this does not mean that we should not consider the part which they play. Indeed the established literature on interest groups suggests that if we wish to understand and explain public policy-making then it is vitally important that we pay particular attention to the role which these groups assume in relation to government. It would of course, be wrong to argue that because studies in other contexts have found interest groups to be important there, then they must be important in Kensington and Chelsea, but at the same time it would be foolish to try to assess the part which interest groups play in any particular political system without being mindful of the established literature which exists on this subject. Even though the *conclusions* in other studies may not hold elsewhere, if the *explanations* sustaining the conclusions are cogent, then they could be used to assess the role of interest groups in other contexts. The important point to bear in mind is that even though the majority of studies have been 'primarily descriptive' (Eldersveld, 1958, p. 184), and based on a relatively 'inarticulate' conceptual scheme (Ehrmann, 1958, p. 8), they do not just provide us with a *description* of the place of these groups in the policy process, for there has been an incredible amount of 'implicit' *theory* in this work (Garceau, 1958, p. 106; Monypenny, 1954, p. 183. But see La Palombara, 1960), and this 'definite undertone of . . . causal theory' (Eldersveld, 1958, p. 184) constitutes the most self-consciously developed body of empirical political science concerned with making sense of governmental behaviour and explaining how and why public policies are made.

My concern in this chapter is restricted to empirical studies which have seen in the study of interest groups a key to the explanation of public policy.[4] I have already mentioned that my interest lies in the explanations rather than in the conclusions of these studies, and in consequence the bulk of the remainder of this chapter will be devoted to a consideration of the explanations used to account for the dominant role which interest groups are seen as assuming in the policy process. If the explanations are cogent

4. I will not, therefore, be discussing 'group theory' and the work of A. F. Bentley, since I consider that it has little to tell us about the activities of pressure groups, and still less to tell us about the making of public policy. I agree with Eckstein (1963, p. 391) who, after sketching out the rudiments of group theory suggests that 'the next question which would seem to arise is what it has to do with the comparative study of pressure groups, It should be apparent from its outlines that the theory is not concerned solely, or even primarily, with the masses of activity we generally call "pressure groups".' For those interested in the 'group approach', see work by Bentley, 1908; Latham, 1952*a*, 1952*b*; Hagan, 1958; and, Golembiewski, 1960. For critical discussions, see, Odegard, 1958; Rothman, 1960; R. S. Parker, 1961; Stedman 1953; and, Hale, 1960.

with respect to the cases with which they are concerned, then they are of potential utility in differing contexts, and I will see how far they are adequate to the facts in Kensington and Chelsea. However, if the explanations are considered inadequate with respect to the cases they purport to explain, and if they ignore crucial areas relevant to a full understanding of the relationship between interest groups and government, then we must not only question the validity of the conclusions in these studies, but we must also avoid using the 'explanations' in any attempt to make sense of public policy in Kensington and Chelsea. Before I do this, in the first section of this chapter, I will briefly look at the conclusions which students of interest groups have reached regarding the respective roles of interest groups and governments in the policy process.

I. THE CONCLUSIONS: STRONG GROUPS, WEAK GOVERNMENT

Students of interest groups present information which is rather ambiguous as to the respective parts which governments and groups play in the making of public policy, but they nevertheless conclude that government is a fairly passive responder to group demands and so they regard interest groups as the real motive-force and cause of particular policies. In this bald form this assessment is just an assertion, and although its full substantiation demands a documented review of the literature, this lies beyond the scope of this section where only limited evidence is assembled from some of the classic studies.

Odegard's study pointed out that Prohibition laws 'did not spring full-blown from the . . . Anti-Saloon League', but he nevertheless argues that 'moral and economic beliefs are not crystallised into law without the backing of a considerable constituency and the existence of a pretty well-defined opinion' (Odegard, 1928, p. 78). His general comment on the nature of the policy process denies that politicians and governments have much of a role: 'The final form of a tariff bill is more frequently determined by the pressure organizations that influence the politician than by the economic and political beliefs of the politician himself. . . . Legislation frequently finds its source, not in the brain of an independent, courageous statesman, but in the devious channels of pressure politics. The history of any law carries with it, in large part, the history of the organized groups whose wishes and wills it embodies' (Odegard, 1928, p. 104).

Schattschneider considered that 'the nature of public policy is the result of "effective demands" upon the government' (Schattschneider, 1935, p. 4). He argued that 'the protective system can be accounted for *only* by the partial, irregular, and biased activity of economic interests', suggesting that 'the central problem of the politics of the tariff is, why were pressures so unequal and distorted as *to bring about* the regulations as it was finally written?' (Schattschneider, 1935, pp. 122, and 109, my emphasis). Notwithstanding this explicit stress on the causal importance of pressure groups and the bias of input activity, Schattschneider nevertheless hints at the bias of Congress and their crucial role in the policy process: 'The bill was a Republican measure written by partisans, thinking in terms of the slogans of the party, for people whose political response was invited with the whole force of the organised publicity of the party. . . . Potentially interested groups could scarcely have been under the illusion that, as between the proponents and opponents of the legislation, the committees, and the Congress behind them, were neutral' (Schattschneider, 1935, p. 99).[5]

Latham is perhaps the master of ambiguity in the way in which he assesses the respective roles of groups and governments in the policy process. At one time he gives the legislature a limited role, lacking in any policy initiative, when he argues that it 'referees the group struggle', but on another occasion he asserts that it 'does not play the inert part of cash register' (Latham, 1952a, pp. 35, and 37). Lindblom rightly suggests that 'it is their role as referee, however, that is conspicuously played up' (Lindblom, 1968, p. 80).

If Latham has been accused of giving the structures of government too small a role in the policy process, then Banfield gives them a still further reduced role, for he does not see them as 'referees' but as 'ratifiers' of the compromises devised by the large formal organisations which exist in Chicago. 'The political head, . . . neither fights for a program of his own making nor endeavors to find a "solution" to the conflicts that are brought before him. Instead, he waits for the community to agree upon a project. When agreement is reached, or when the process of controversy has gone as far as it can, he ratifies the agreement and carries it into effect' (Banfield, 1961, p. 253. See also, Banfield & Wilson, 1963). Although Banfield stresses that politicians assume this passive role, he nevertheless argues that they have the *potential* to act more decisively (Banfield, 1961, pp. 266–7), and at times suggests that they *actually do* move well beyond the ratification of compromises (Banfield, 1961, p. 250).[6]

Truman, in the most comprehensive and important study, gives interest groups a crucial role in the policy process, and since he argues that governmental decisions are the resultant of effective access by various interests' (Truman, 1951, p. 507), in order to account for public policy it is necessary for him to outline the factors which allow groups to gain differing amounts of access to government. Access is the intervening variable linking group demands to policy outputs. He summarises these 'complex of interdependent factors' in three 'somewhat overlapping categories: (1) factors relating to a group's strategic position in society;

5. In a later study, Schattschneider (1960) attributes rather more importance to the bias of Congress. See esp. pp. 41–3.
6. Banfield (1961) also points to a very different relationship between the politician and the 'civic leaders' from that which he notes when he argues that the politicians assume a ratifying role (p. 278). In addition (on p. 288), Banfield argues that it is 'above all' the chief elected officials who are the most influential in Chicago politics.

(2) factors associated with the internal characteristics of the group; and (3) factors peculiar to the governmental institutions themselves' (Truman, 1951, p. 506. See also pp. 264, 164, 159, and 269, for propositions which fill out this rather bald statement).

Since I have argued that students of interest groups are rather uncertain as to the part which government plays, but tend to conclude by denying it any active role, it is particularly important that I see how Truman explores the third factor, which he amplifies by noting that he is concerned with 'the operating structure of the government institutions, . . . and the effects of the group life of particular units or branches of the government' (Truman 1951, p. 507). The first point is the long-standing one about the importance of weak parties and the federal system, but the second point is more novel and anticipates later work which I will introduce at the end of this chapter. Truman's reference to the group life and 'the influence of office', with the suggestion that 'the fact of holding public office is itself a significant influence upon the relative access of the groups', amplifies his suggestion that 'government is not simply a neutral force' and the politician not 'equivalent to the steel ball in a pinball game, bumping passively from post to post down an inclined plane' (Truman, 1951, pp. 346–50, 106, and 332). However Truman develops this point in such a way that he tends to deny that government is anything other than a responder to outside influences, because the standards, or rules of the game, which define the legislator's role and shape group life are set not by the legislature itself, but are 'prescribed for him by the society' (Truman, 1951, p. 347). In other words, although Truman points to the importance of the group life of Congress it is a group life the norms of which are set from outside, and although he argues that Congress cannot be regarded as a purely neutral force in policy-making, its activity is such as to ensure that all the interests outside of government gain a fair and measured public response. At any event he devotes only two chapters to a consideration of the legislative process, and then only to consider how groups influence it, for as Scott and Hunt suggest, 'presumably, when one has dealt with the pressures exerted on Congress, there is not much left to say about that body. Congress is not presented as an active, moving, decision-making body but as primarily a recipient of external influences' (Scott & Hunt, 1965, p. 10).

The ambiguity in these studies as to the respective roles of governments and groups in the policy process should alert us to question the conclusion about the dominance of interest groups and the weakness of governments, but notwithstanding this, what explanations are offered to sustain the conclusion, and, if cogent, how far are they adequate to the situation in Kensington and Chelsea?

II. THE EXPLANATIONS FOR STRONG GROUPS AND WEAK GOVERNMENTS[7]

Power at the Polls

Truman reminds us that 'the standard popular statement of the role of organised political interest groups is that because they constitute highly disciplined blocks of voters who will do the bidding of their leaders at the ballot box, they are able to bend elected officials to their wills' (Truman, 1951, p. 314). Odegard, for example, urges that 'it should be kept in mind that whatever power or influence the League developed in legislative lobbies is attributable to the votes of the people back home who take their political advice from the League' (Odegard, 1928, p. 105). Similarly, Herring claims that 'the lobbyist in Washington is ready to guarantee almost any result' if he has the financial and moral support of a group with a large and widely distributed membership, as the 'timid' representative sees interest groups as a 'great threat' and 'many an able public servant has been defeated because of his opposition to such a group' (Herring, 1929, pp. 244–6).

Key (1961, pp. 518–24; and 1943), Zeigler (1964, pp. 240–7), and Truman (1951, pp. 314–20. See also, Gilpatrick, 1959), however, all emphasise that the power of interest groups at the polls has been grossly exaggerated, and, in suggesting this, they question the adequacy of the popular explanation for group influence. In fact, more important than the objective situation is the politicians' subjective assessment of the influence of groups at the polls, since if they think that certain groups are influential, and if they are concerned to maintain their position of elected power, then they may be prepared to accede to the demands of those groups irrespective of their real capacity to affect an election result. Consider the case of Hounslow Borough Ratepayers Council, and the Councillors for the Greater London Borough of Hounslow. In 1965, a Mr G. Kirby held a meeting at Chiswick Town Hall in which he asked people to come forward to form a ratepayers association. Unfortunately no one did, but Mr Kirby was not deterred by this and he proceeded to have headed notepaper printed and sent regular reports of large 'meetings' to the press together with resolutions to the local council, eventually letting it be known that some 26 candidates would stand in the local elections in the name of the Ratepayers Council. Like all good things, this did not last but until 'the staggering truth' was uncovered in the local newspaper, 'the council was one of the best organised and most powerful ratepayers associations in the country – or so

7. Lesser studies of interest groups often fail to account for the major role which these groups are said to assume in the policy process because their use of the term 'pressure' inhibits and blocks the search for adequate explanations. The term pressure is rarely defined by those who use it; it is assumed that it both defines itself and explains the success of the particular group under study. For a similar comment, see Scott & Hunt, 1965, pp. 8–9.

everyone thought . . . [and] members of Hounslow Council started seriously to consider resolutions put forward by non-existent branches . . . [and] the politicians, thinking that Mr. Kirby had powerful support from the ratepayers were . . . left wondering if they were due to be defeated in the next election' (*West London Observer*, 10 November 1966).

In the previous chapter I noted that in general the reality of local elections in Britain was such that interest groups had no decisive effect on the results. I also showed that councillors in Kensington and Chelsea held beliefs about voters and the causes of local election results which allowed no room for pressure group influence at the polls. If we are to account for the influence which interest groups exert in Kensington and Chelsea then little is to be gained by relying on those theories which refer to group power at the polls.

The Power of the Purse

In many political systems, elections and campaigning are extremely costly enterprises for the serious contender, and if there are no tight legal restrictions on the use of funds in an election, then a candidate is going to be open to 'assistance' from a variety of sources. Interest groups are often in a position to offer this assistance and this 'may establish a strong obligation on the part of the legislator toward an interest group' (La Palombara, 1964, p. 207). In other words, even though groups may not be able to mobilise numbers of voters at the polls, their influence may be explained by arguing that politicians respond favourably to the demands of those groups that provide finance and campaign assistance.

In spite of the fact that this explanation has not been well-developed by modern political scientists who (in noting the supposed passing of the 'old lobby') have tended to see interest groups as a channel of general citizen influence, there is no doubt that money, whether in the form of campaign assistance or more direct and subtle gifts, is a resource of major importance in most political systems. However, notwithstanding this, the situation in Kensington and Chelsea is not one where an interest group could gain leverage by the offer of campaign assistance: local elections involve a very limited expenditure, and adequate resources are available from within the political parties themselves. In the period before the Second World War, a number of interest groups in the area were active in the nomination and selection of Conservative councillors, at least in so far as they would 'endorse' certain candidates and secure 'pledges' from them that they would take a certain stance on an issue, but in the more recent past there is no evidence to suggest that interest groups have any involvement or influence in the nomination, selection, or election of Conservative councillors. Of course it is always difficult to uncover evidence as to the existence of bribery in politics, and because of this there is tendency for observers either to ignore or exaggerate its importance depending on their level of confidence in any governmental system. I have no evidence of bribery in Kensington and Chelsea, and neither have radical groups from that area been able to point to instances of this even though they have kept a close ear to the ground for a number of years.

Explanations for interest group influence in the policy process which centre on the importance of groups giving money to election campaigns and politicians, are at best not proved to be true in Kensington and Chelsea, and in all probability they give a false picture of the relationships between groups and councillors and of the factors which account for group success.

Structural Factors and the Weak Party
Schattschneider points to the importance of weak parties when he argues that 'the effectiveness of pressure groups in American politics is related directly to the condition of the parties. . . . Since the parties do very little to discipline or defend their members in Congress, . . . the pressure groups are able to trade on the fears and confusion of individual members of Congress' (Schattschneider, 1948, p. 18. See also, Blaisdell, 1957, p. 218; Truman, 1951, p. 325; and, Buchanan, 1963). The theme is familiar, with the absence of responsible disciplined parties, government is said to become a 'vast arena in which group interests and personalities struggle for power', producing 'the politics of "boodle" and accommodation' (Bailey, 1959, p. 10). The cogency of the explanation which suggests that interest groups are strong where parties are weak has been challenged by Beer's work on British interest groups, by the wider international study of groups, and more recently, Teune's interviews with candidates for the Indiana legislature led him to conclude that 'strong parties do not lessen the ties with interest groups' (Teune, 1967, p. 504). The fact that parties are disciplined and strong in no sense means that interest groups must be correspondingly weak and unimportant in policy-making, but rather suggests that we can expect to find a stable pattern of relationships between a party and interest groups, a pattern which will be based on the views of the party leadership as to what are good and reliable groups. In Chapter 8 I will show that this is the case in Kensington and Chelsea.

The structural form of American politics, with the separation of powers, the federal system, and many elective offices, is seen as providing 'multiple foci of decision-making' (Macridis, 1961, p. 34), and this is said to enable groups to gain particularly effective access to governmental decision. However although the existence of a large number of access points provides groups with openings, this is no guarantee that groups will be effective in dealings with government. The opportunity for groups to contact those in government does not explain why public policy-makers respond favourably to the demands of some groups but unfavourably to the demands of others.

Notwithstanding the deficiency of this explanation for interest group influence, in a general sense it is probably correct to assume that 'open' political structures and multiple access points are indicative of a participatory political culture which will be sympathetic to the activity of interest groups. Although it would be a mistake to elevate indications and expectations as to patterns of behaviour into causal explanations for the power of interest groups and the responsiveness of governments, in any research context it is nevertheless important to note those features of government structure which ease or impede interest group involvement in the policy process. A recent study submitted to the Royal Commission on Local Government in England looked at this question and argued that there were certain factors which served to 'hinder' the development and growth of 'specialised pressure groups,' and make it difficult for them to gain access to local councils: 'First, the multiplicity of areas and the division of functions between them makes the organisation of such groups difficult; secondly, many existing local authority areas do not in any way correspond to communities . . . [and]; thirdly, the way in which a great many local authorities run their affairs through elaborate committee and sub-committee structures does not make it easy for the views on the development of services as opposed to particular cases or issues to be voiced and properly considered' (Royal Commission on Local Government, Research Studies, 1, 1968, p. 32).

Structural factors and the weak party do not explain why governments are receptive and responsive to interest group demands, and although the structure of government is important in providing opportunities for groups to gain access, certain factors do not facilitate this in the context of British local government. When I deal more directly with Kensington and Chelsea in Part Two of this study, I will outline in more detail those features of government structure which serve to inhibit a responsiveness to demands of certain groups.

The Characteristics of Interest Groups
Accounting for group influence in the policy process is not easy, and writers aware of this point note how 'we must content ourselves with a general statement of the factors which appear, in one measure or another, to affect the influence of groups' (Keefe & Ogul, 1964, p. 357). The list of factors which they point to as of importance is usually dominated by reference to the characteristics of interest groups. Keefe and Ogul recognise that 'the structural peculiarities of the government and of the political parties will tend to affect the access of certain groups to centers of power', but they go on to note the importance of: '(1) the size of the group, (2) its prestige, (3) the cohesion of its membership, (4) the skills of its leadership, (5) the distribution of its membership, (6) its ability to rally both widespread support and the assistance of other groups, and (7) its resources, especially financial' (Keefe & Ogul, 1964, pp. 357–8. See also, McKean, 1938, pp. 218–36; and, Monsen & Cannon, 1965, pp. 10–17).

The characteristics that writers identify in fact represent a checklist of the resources that may be available to groups. In essence we are told that big, wealthy, groups will be successful, and it is precisely because these observations appear so obvious that writers feel no need to go on to suggest why the resources are of importance, or how they enable groups that possess them to gain favourable governmental decisions. Explanations which concentrate on the resources and characteristics of interest groups are little other than descriptions of successful groups, and they leave us without any appreciation of the linkage between groups and governments. They cannot be regarded as adequate.

The Bias of Inputs

Schattschneider argues that 'pressures are formidable and overwhelming only when they have become unbalanced and one-sided. As long as opposed interests are equal or nearly equal, governments can play off one against the other', and 'no extensive legislation would be probable' (Schattschneider, 1935, pp. 288, and 122).[8] He explains the success of interest groups in the issue of tariff reform by noting that not all interested parties were equally engaged in the process of making demands, and this bias of inputs meant that it was politically feasible for the legislature to accede to the demands and embody them in law. Schattschneider does not only refer to the bias of inputs, for he also notes a bias within the dominant party in Congress which was such that it was predisposed to favour the demands which were directed to them. There is no doubt that he makes very good sense of his case, and we need to look to the situation in Kensington and Chelsea to see whether the bias of inputs reinforces the bias of the majority party, so leading to public policies which embody the interest group demand.

There is certainly a bias in terms of the demands that are directed to the council, since, by and large, they press for either change or innovation in the established pattern of public policies. In other words, the bias of inputs does not serve to reinforce the bias which exists within the governing party, but on the contrary represents a direct challenge to that bias. The bias within the majority party is such that the interests of certain categories of the population are built into government and public policies without the necessity of their organising into a demanding group. In Kensington and Chelsea the restricted source of demands is an indication of the political weakness of those sections of the population whose interests are embodied in the demands. Instead of a harmonious relationship between demanding groups and the authority structure, which existed in Schattschneider's case, the situation in Kensington and Chelsea is one of conflict, with the council resisting the majority of demands directed to them and refusing to embody them in the policies which they develop. How and why this is done will be discussed later in this study, but for the moment it is simply necessary to note that the bias of inputs does not lead

8. For a similar comment, see, Bauer, Pool & Dexter, 1964, p. 398; and, Edelman, 1964, pp. 22–43.

to public policies which embody those demands; it does not account for the development of public policy in Kensington and Chelsea; and it does not serve as a satisfactory basis for making sense of the relationship which exists between groups and the council in the policy process.

The Rules of the Game

Explanations for interest group influence which centre on the capacity of groups to pressure government have been subject to increasing criticism over the past two decades, and more recently students have sought to account for the major role which groups are said to assume in the policy process by referring to the rules of the game, arguing that these are such as to ensure that groups can gain a favourable hearing at the hands of government irrespective of their capacity to exert any pressure.

Truman considers that society sets certain rules and that these constitute a 'generalized attitude favoring fair play' which serves to define the appropriate behaviour of legislators and ensure that the broad interests of society, whether organised or merely existing as 'potential groups', meet with favourable governmental decision. He argues that 'in the great majority of instances the successful legislator has so learned his role that groups whose demands clearly require the forbidden behaviours will get a cold reception' (Truman, 1951, pp. 232, and 349–50).[9] Similarly, Key argues that groups assume a role of major importance in the policy process because of the 'expectation that all entitled to play the game will get a fair deal,' but unlike Truman, he does not consider that society sets the rules, for 'the manoeuvers of pressure group politics . . . come ordinarily to occur among those highly involved and immediately concerned about public policy; the connection of these manoeuvers with public opinion and even with the opinions of mass-membership organizations tends to be tenuous' (Key, 1961, p. 526).

The rules of the game are the rules of access: they allow some groups to be involved and to be influential in the policy process gaining public policies which they favour, while denying others a part. If we are concerned to categorise interest groups according to the extent of their access and rapport with government then we need to identify these rules, and to undertake this research task it is necessary at the outset to specify just who sets and enforces these rules. Truman considers that they are set by society. Key takes the view that they are set by a much smaller group of political activists. I suggest that they are set by the governmental decision-makers themselves, operating in most cases against a backdrop of apathy, ignorance and powerlessness which prevents rival rules gaining authority and effect. This suggestion leads in to the concluding section of this chapter.

9. See also Banfield & Wilson (1963), who argue in similar vein that the politician assumes a passive role, allowing groups to take part in the policy process, because 'the public' takes the view that this is the way public policy should be developed. For a similar comment with respect to British politics, see Rose, 1965, p. 44.

III. CONCLUDING REMARKS: THE IMPORTANCE OF GOVERNMENT

In the previous sections I set out the different ideas which aimed to explain public policy-making by accounting for the supposedly dominant role which interest groups assume over weak and passive government prepared simply to do group bidding. I suggested then that several of the explanations lacked cogency, and others, though relevant in some contexts, did not fit the facts of the situation in Kensington and Chelsea. More important, however, all these explanations pay scant attention to those in government, in spite of the fact that it is their response which is critical to the success of group demands since groups themselves do not directly make public policies. Wahlke, for example, makes the point that 'much research on pressure politics attempts to explain the actions of supposedly "pressured" legislatures and legislators by looking not at them but at the pressuring groups. Little is said about how or why the legislator is influenced by the supposedly critical characteristics of pressure groups' (Wahlke, Eulau, Buchanan & Ferguson, 1962, p. 312).

To assess and adequately explain the influence which interest groups have in the making of public policy, we must not only study the groups doing the talking, taking 'for granted the persons they press upon' (Wahlke, Buchanan, Eulau, & Ferguson, 1960, p. 204), but we must also actively study 'who is listening' (Scott, & Hunt, 1965, p. 11) in order to understand better the basis on which they selectively respond to group demands. Zisk rightly argues that 'the predispositions of policy-makers act as filters through which interest group efforts to influence policy outcomes must pass. The accessibility of public officials to groups, and the degree to which they accommodate group requests, depends in part on these predispositions' (Zisk, Eulau, & Prewitt, 1965, p. 619).

In the past decade there has been an increasing recognition of the need to study the subjects of group demands (Zisk *et al*, 1965; Wahlke *et al*, 1960; Scott & Hunt, 1965; Bauer *et al*, 1964; Huckshorn, 1965; Longley, 1967; Crane, 1960; Garceau & Silverman, 1964; Teune, 1967; and, La Palombara, 1964). These studies have taken up the hints in earlier work,[10] and have started to explore this subject systematically, as I do in Chapter 8, when I outline the rules of access developed by councillors in Kensington and Chelsea to assess group demands.

There is little doubt that a legend of pressure group potency has grown up which, until recently, prevented the search for systematic explanations of their part in the policy process. The influence of interest groups on public

10. Truman (1951) has pointed to the importance of the 'group life of the legislature'; Latham (1952a, 1952b) has a brief discussion of the importance of 'officiality'; and Schattschneider (1935) has pointed to the necessity of noting the bias of government.

policy can only be properly assessed if particular attention is paid to the subjects of group demands. Although this change of research emphasis does not necessarily mean that interest groups will be assigned a less important place in the policy process, it does mean that we can less usefully see the study of interest groups as providing the key to the explanation of public policy-making. Public policy cannot be regarded as 'the resultant of a parallelogram of organised interest group forces,' and 'the simple pressure-group theory of politics is no more adequate than was the ideal of direct majoritarian democracy or the neatly ordered responsible two-party system' (Garceau, 1958, p. 106).

4 The demographic approach

a devasting set of findings . . .
Robert Salisbury, 'The analysis of public policy: a search for
theories and roles', in Austin Ranney, *Political Science and
Public Policy* (Chicago, Markham, 1968), pp. 151–78, p. 164.

'Political science', we are told, 'has been guilty of viewing political life as
a closed system. Specifically, political scientists have developed modes of
analysis which lead them to account for what happens in the political
system solely in terms of its internal activities' (Dye, 1966, p. 299).
Recently writers have argued that in order to explain public policy it is
necessary to note not only the influence of the political environment on
government, but also the influence of the socio-economic environment. 'In
recent years a growing body of research has used multivariate statistical
techniques to examine the relationship between aggregate environmental
characteristics and the public policies of state and local governments.
This research has been concerned primarily with isolating or demonstrating
the social, economic, and political correlates of either public policies (e.g.,
expenditures, revenues and referenda issues) or governmental structures
(viz., form of government, size of election districts and type of ballot)'
(J. W. Clarke, 1969, p. 1172).

This work has been mainly centred on the public policies of the fifty
American states,[1] but similar investigations have examined urban policy
outputs,[2] and these have sometimes been buttressed by the 'ethos theory'
of city government.[3] Work of this kind has spilled over from America,

1. Dawson & Robinson, 1963; Dye, 1965, 1966; Froman, 1966; Fry & Winters,
1970; Hofferbert, 1966a, 1966b, 1968; Jacob, 1964; and Sharkansky, 1967a, 1967b,
1968a, 1968b, 1968c, 1969, 1970a, 1970b.
2. Clark, 1971; Cutright, 1963; Dye, 1964, 1967; Dye, Liebman, Williams &
Herman, 1963; Froman, 1967; Hawley, 1963; Kessel, 1962; Lineberry & Fowler,
1967; Masotti & Bowen, 1971; Williams, Herman, Liebman & Dye, 1965;
Wolfinger & Field, 1966; Schnore & Alford, 1953; and, Sherbenou, 1961.
3. Banfield & Wilson, 1963; Wilson & Banfield, 1964; Wolfinger & Field, 1966.
For a critique and a bibliography of this work, see Hennessy, 1970.

61

for there is at least one international study (Cutright, 1965), and a number of studies have been completed using data on British local government (Alt, 1971; Boaden, 1971; Boaden & Alford, 1969; and, Davies, 1968).

The last few years has witnessed the rise of what one critic has called the demographic approach' (J. Q. Wilson, 1968, p. 4), and judging from the burgeoning number of critical review articles[4] it is an approach which has aroused the wrath of many students of politics. The sheer volume of this work; its self-consciousness in attempting to explain public policy; and the fact of its extensive, and probably increasing, development in the area of British local government, are all reasons which are such as to demand that we pay it particular attention.

The literature I am reviewing has its roots in a short article by Dawson and Robinson (1963), which was important, partly because it synthesised two earlier traditions of work by political scientists and economists,[5] but largely because it represented a self-consciously theoretical search for explanations of public policy, and this involved the explosion of ideas 'long a part of the folklore of political science' (Jacob & Lipsky, 1968, p. 519). Before that date, political scientists had argued that features of state political systems had an important effect on public policies. Key (1949) and Lockard (1959) noted the importance of party competition affecting the form of state welfare policies; Adrian (1960, pp. 306–7. See also Grant & Nixon, 1963; and, Jewell, 1962) suggested that malapportionment 'has serious effects upon governmental policies'; and there were good reasons for supposing that voter participation levels influenced policy choices (Dawson & Robinson, 1965, pp. 406–7).

Dawson and Robinson challenged these research findings for failing to control for the impact of socio-economic variables, and in their study set out to 'discover the relationship among the extent of inter-party competition, the presence of certain economic factors, and the extent of nine public welfare policies, using American states as units for investigation' (Dawson & Robinson, 1963, p. 265). Dissenting from Key and Lockard, they suggested that 'inter-party competition does not play as influential a role in determining the nature and scope of welfare policies as earlier studies suggested. The level of public social welfare programs in the American states seems to be more a function of socio-economic factors, especially per capita income' (Dawson & Robinson, 1963, p. 289). Hofferbert (1966a, p. 73) and Dye (1966, p. 258), have also rejected the proposition that party competition is related to the level of governmental activity, and studies have concluded that legislative malapportionment is not related to a distinctive pattern of policy putputs (Jacob, 1964; and, Dye, 1965). Estab-

4. J. W. Clarke, 1969; Hennessy, 1969; Jacob & Lipsky, 1968; Rakoff & Schaefer, 1970; Salisbury, 1968; and, J. Q. Wilson, 1968.
5. On this point, see Rakoff & Schaefer, 1970. Examples of political science work in this field would include, Key, 1949; and, Lockard, 1959. An example of work by economists in this field would be, Fabricant, 1952.

lished ideas have been knocked down, the importance of political factors in explaining policy outputs has been questioned,[6] and in their place increasing importance has been assigned to the socio-economic environment of government. The position is perhaps best summed up by Dye, when he states: 'Economic development shapes both political systems and policy outcomes, and most of the association that occurs between system characteristics and policy outcomes can be attributed to the influence of economic development. Differences in the policy choices of states with different types of political systems turn out to be largely a product of differing socio economic levels rather than a direct product of political variables. Levels of urbanization, industrialization, income and education appear to be more influential in shaping policy outcome than political system characteristics' (Dye, 1966, p. 293). The implication of the research work in this tradition is that 'political processes function as secondary or neutral mechanisms which transform demands arising from the socio-economic environment into public policy' (Hennessy, 1969, p. 9).

Dye (1966, p. 297) rightly suggests that 'political scientists may feel uncomfortable with our findings that certain political variables do not count for much in shaping public policy', for if government was given a weak role in the theories I reviewed in the last two chapters, then it is now pushed into a position of irrelevancy. The set of findings 'cannot be dismissed as not meaning what it plainly says – that analysis of political systems will not explain policy decisions made by these systems' (Salisbury, 1968, p. 164). Unless political scientists take exception to this work and point to gaps in the explanations, then our distinctive claim as a separate discipline concerned with political behaviour can hardly be countenanced. Instead, we may only need technicians collating and quantifying increasing numbers of political and environmental varables and feeding them into these models, to provide us with explanations of public policy of still greater precision and exactness.

There are two ways in which this work [7] can be critically assessed. First, one

6. Although two studies in this research tradition do point to the importance of political variables affecting the form of public policies. See, Fry & Winters, 1970; and, Lineberry & Fowler, 1967. See also, J. W. Clarke, 1969, esp, p. 1181.

7. Three diagram ssum up the various facets of the demographic research orientation to public policy. In this chapter I am confining my attention to those studies which attempt to explain public policy by considering the part played by both socio-economic conditions *and* political variables, even though they may conclude that political factors are really of no importance. I am not looking at studies which deal with only aspects of this, either by pointing to an association between certain socio-economic variables and particular forms of governmental structure, while ignoring the further question of public policies; or by pointing to a relationship between socio-economic conditions and public policy, this time ignoring the part which political variables play in the process. In particular I will centre the bulk of my attention on Thomas R. Dye's book-length study, *Politics, Economics, and the Public.*

may admire the general approach and concentrate upon deficiences in the *details* of its application, arguing that if more variables are included and if those that are included are better conceptualised then this will provide us with a comprehensive and adequate explanation of public policy. This line of criticism is accepted by many writers within this research tradition who do themselves note problems of this kind and suggest ways in which the models can be improved. Second, and of greater importance, one may stand back from the details in order to point to *ommissions and problems* which cannot be met by particular and specific improvements because certain questions which relate to important areas of public policy just cannot be asked, let alone answered, within the terms of the framework that is offered. From this perspective one questions whether anything is really explained by those who rely on this approach. In other words, one can, so to speak, play the game and suggest improvements in the rules, or one can question the whole basis of the game and whether it is worth playing or is even capable of any real improvement. I will advance each of these lines of criticism in the next two sections.

I. THE MINOR CRITIQUE

Dye (1966, pp. 3–4) considers that 'a model for the explanation of public policy outcomes . . . may describe relationships between socioeconomic inputs (forces), political systems characteristics (systems), and policy outcomes (responses)', and he goes on to note how 'these relationships can be diagrammed', as in the figure.

For Dye (1966, p. 7) 'economic development – urbanization, industrialization, wealth and education – is viewed as the crucial input variable which shapes the character of political systems and the kinds of policy

A model for analysing policy outcomes in American state politics (after Dye, 1966).

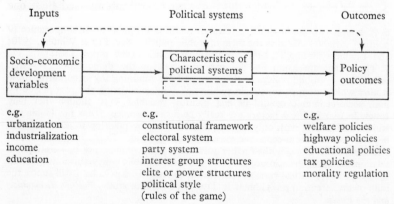

outcomes it produces' but as just about all the critics have noted, it is hardly appropriate to call these 'socioeconomic development variables', 'inputs'. 'The level of industrialization does not make demands' (Rakoff & Schaefer, 1970, p. 56), and the measures which Dye offers have little substantive relationship to the phenomena they are supposed to represent. This line of criticism is of no great moment, and in many ways it is rather hair-splitting to pay overmuch attention to the fact that sometimes certain socio-economic conditions are called 'inputs', as there is little doubt that this term is often chosen as a shorthand expression,[8] albeit one which is designed to suggest a causal link between environmental conditions and public policies which is more substantive than that which is conveyed through correlations.

Critical attention has been paid to the conceptualisation of the political system. Again, nearly all critics are in agreement in deploring the fact that only three or four variables are considered,[9] and these they regard as an 'inadequate' and 'primitive' characterisation (Hennessy, 1969, p. 12; and, Jacob & Lipsky, 1968, p. 515). They suggest that the model could be much improved if there were measures of interest group activity and a considera-tion of the organisation of the legislative and executive branches of government. They come close to suggesting that if only more political variables were included, then the political system would again be given pride of place in any explanation of public policy. In fact it is easier to argue that additional variables should be considered than to suggest how they could be conceptualised and measured for inclusion in the model. Indeed, one reason for the crudity of the conceptualisation of the political system is because the method itself limits attention to those variables that can be easily obtained and manipulated by multivariate analysis, and 'while census bureau data are available for a variety of variables . . these data obviously are silent on such matters as the distribution of power and the attitudes of community elites' (Bonjean, Clark & Lineberry, 1971, p. 264). Dye (1966, p. 296) is well aware of these limitations, and he admits that: 'It may be that the measures we have employed are too crude to reveal the real impact of political variables on state activities. Perhaps the effect of politics on policy outcomes is too subtle to be revealed in quantitative analysis.' He is likewise aware of the need to consider the part played by additional political variables,[10] but as he says even though. 'the list of both obvious

8. For example, at one point, Dye (1966) hints that economic development is *not* itself an input but in fact serves as the major force which 'generates' inputs (p. 282). Dye is never explicit whether he is using the term 'inputs' to cover 'demands' and 'supports', but it is difficult to see how his variables could be measures of support.
9. Dye 1(1966) takes two characteristics of the party system (level of inter-party competition, and party in control), and two characteristics of the electoral system (level of voter participation and degree of malapportionment).
10. The suggestion of what else needs to be considered is rather limply phrased as 'differences among state populations in their political values and attachments' (Dye, 1966, p. 297).

and subtle differences in politics among the fifty states is boundless. Yet only a limited number of political variables can be systematically investigated at any one time' (Dye, 1966, p. 48). Much of this criticism of the conceptualisation of the political system is unfair, for the political variables which are most often used have long been regarded as of importance in affecting the form of public policy in the American states, and it is wrong to claim that Dye and others have only put up political straw men which could be easily knocked down (Dye, 1966, p. 297).

So far I have pointed to some of the criticisms which have been directed at this model with respect to the measurement and conceptualisation of socio-economic 'inputs', and political system variables, but what of their handling of the 'dependent variable', public policy? One line of criticism again admitted by many of the practitioners of this approach, is to note that this too has been poorly conceptualised, with confusion surrounding the boundaries which distinguish one policy from another. Sharkansky notes that, 'the unfortunate use of the term has led . . . writers to lump all kinds of government activity – and some private activity – into one shapeless category' (Sharkansky, 'Problems of theory and method: Environment, policy, output and impact', paper delivered at the Conference on Measurement of Public Policies Ann Arbor, 1968, cited in Hennessy, 1969). Levels of expenditure have been the most frequently used measure, but contrary to assumptions which conceptually equated spending and services (Dawson & Robinson, 1963; Dye, 1965; and, Hofferbert, 1966a). Sharkansky has questioned whether measures of expenditure can properly be taken to refer to services performed (Sharkansky, 1967a). There is another conceptual weakness which surrounds their use of the term public policy and its measurement, for as Hennessy points out, 'the majority of the output indicators reflect the combined activities of state and local units, while some refer to state activities alone and others are not clearly labelled. At the same time political measures refer only to state affairs. In short, the measures of politics refer to a different area of behavior than the measures of output' (Hennessy, 1969, p. 11).

This consideration of the three static 'boxes' of the model does not reveal any particularly insurmountable problems; more variables here, better conceptualisation there, and all is well and can be vastly improved. However when we look to the dynamic in the model and consider the relationships and linkages between socio-economic conditions, political system variables, and public policies, then we are inevitably forced into a more major critique of this approach.

II. THE MAJOR CRITIQUE

If political science is to develop, then it must be concerned not just with description, but with the construction of models and theories which relate together the differing facets of social and political relationships that are of importance in leading up to particular public policies. Certainly the literature we are discussing in this chapter abounds with 'hypothesised causal models' (Lineberry & Fowler, 1967, p. 714), and there is no doubt that there is an overt interest in 'explaining' relationships between the 'independent variables' (the socio-economic conditions), and the 'intervening variables' (the political system characteristics), as they both come to affect public policy, which is regarded as 'the major dependent variable which political science seeks to explain' (Dawson & Robinson, 1963, p. 266).

The most fundamental feature of the conceptual and theoretical underpinnings of this public policy research is the reliance on the ideas of David Easton: 'Recently a number of scholars have accepted the challenge formulated by David Easton to systematically investigate the linkages between socioeconomic environment, political system characteristics and the content of public policy. Researchers in American state politics have undertaken to study the relationships between environmental inputs, system characteristics and policy outcomes in a systematic and comparative fashion' (Dye, 1968, p. 1). The problem is that Easton's model of the political system is quite incapable, as it stands, of serving as a basis either to guide the collection, or to aid the interpretation, of data. The model offers only a symbolic representation of the process leading up to authoritative decision; the ingredients of the model are ill-defined and developed, and we are provided with only very general preliminary hypotheses as to the linkages which may exist between the structures and processes relevant to an understanding of the policy process. The nominal designations offered by Easton cannot be measured and correlated to provide an explanation for public policy, and yet, in their haste to collect and measure data, students in this research school have failed to go back a step behind the operationalisation of concepts to undertake the crucial preliminary work involving both the discussion and clarification of concepts, and the elaboration of reasons, or hypotheses, which suggest *why* we might expect certain relationships to exist between them. Dye (1966, pp. 282–3) might well question this assessment, since he claims: 'Our model hypothesized several explanatory linkages. First of all, it posits that socioeconomic conditions help to shape the character of state political systems. Secondly, it suggests that socioeconomic conditions help to determine policy outcomes in the states. Finally, it raises the question of whether or not political system characteristics in the states independently influence policy outcomes.' In this bald and general form we are told very little. We are told something of what to expect, but not why to expect it. These hypotheses can hardly be expected to satisfy our interest in the causal relationships that lead up to particular public policies. Jacob and Lipsky are surely not being over-harsh, therefore, when they suggest that, 'Dye . . . leaves unexplored the nature of the linkages that he asserts exist between economic development and programmatic outputs. We conclude from reading his analysis that by some magic a high level of economic development becomes transformed into high levels of expenditure. The processes by which this transformation takes place remain in the shadows' (Jacob & Lipsky, 1968, pp. 516–17). The fact is that Dye cannot deal with this sort of question; his method does not allow it, and he lacks a causal theory and explanatory hypotheses.

A major deficiency of this research lies not only in the fact that we are provided with only a few general hypotheses, for with the hypotheses, which are suggested there is still the problem of their verification. Dye (1966, p. 24) admits that there is 'a serious gap between the language of correlation and regression analysis and the language of explanation ... statistical associations can at best tell us only how close the association is between variations in economic development and variations in public policy outcomes. It is quite clear that the causal language of our model is not the same as the relational or associative language of correlation analysis.' Dye, then, is aware of the jump from correlation to explanation; from the language of research operations to the language of explanations, but it is precisely this which constitutes a major problem for, as Wilson asks, 'in what sense have we "explained" a public policy by observing its association with certain population characteristics? That such characteristics are relevant is beyond much doubt, but how or why are they relevant?'[11] (J. Q. Wilson, 1968, p. 4).

The 'linkage problem', and the deficiencies of the demographic approach in handling this, really lies at the heart of the limitations of this work, as is admitted by Hofferbert. He rightly suggests that his work and other studies in the tradition have given a 'clear indication that there is a relationship between environment and public policy', but, as he goes on: 'Remaining to be studied is the specific manner in which environmental forces are translated into policy. To investigate this will require more intensive examination than has so far been conducted into political interest formulation (or evolution) and aggregation. It will also be necessary to conduct careful studies of political communication and leadership processes. In summary, the chief challenge for inquiry is to specify the factors which link environment and public policy in the American states' (Hofferbert, 1966a, p. 82).[12]

11. There is an additional problem, for Dye (1966, p. 26) admits: 'Correlations do not tell us whether system characteristics produce policy outcomes, or policy outcomes produce system characteristics. The direction of causality is a product of our model and not of research operations.' For a suggestion that the direction of causality may be the other way around, see, Eulau & Eyestone, 1968; and, Williams & Adrian, 1963.

12. It would be a mistake to exaggerate the extent to which there has not been an attempt to spell out some of the causal links. Lineberry & Fowler's work (1967) is of mportance in this respect, and, so too, the 'ethos theory' does suggest some sort of inking mechanism between socio-economic conditions and the form of govern-

Until Hofferbert's research prescription is undertaken, perhaps all we have in these studies is a *description* of differences in policy outcomes in selected governmental areas, together with statements as to the associations which exist between those outcomes and certain socio-economic conditions. We are not really offered hypotheses which suggest *why* we can expect these associations and neither are we told just *how* it is that certain socio-economic conditions are translated into public policies by the structures of government which, statistical analysis or no statistical analysis, have a part to play. These explanations for public policy are rather like the 'social determinism' of the electoral studies which explain voting behaviour by pointing to associations between the direction of a vote decision and the social situation of groups of voters. In that case it is fairly easy to conceive of the linkage, but when we turn to public policy it is harder for us to imagine the factors which account for the linkage between policies and environments. It is one thing that the study of elections has been made apolitical, it is quite another thing when public policy analysis is treated in the same way, and yet, as Dye (1966, p. 300) admits, his study 'does not in itself increase our understanding of the functioning of political systems: we still want to know *how* a political system goes about transforming socioeconomic inputs into policy outcomes'.

III. CONCLUDING REMARKS

Anyone starting to read the vast volume of work of the demographic approach, could feel overawed by its apparent completeness and sophistication and consider that here at last is the way forward to providing really testable explanations to account for the form of public policy. On the surface it presents a great deal: a model with inputs, outputs, and feedback, and data that are rigorously quantified and manipulated by statistical techniques. But when it comes down to it, we really have learnt very little of interest as a result of this work. Certain socio-economic conditions are associated with certain types of public policies, and certain crude political variables (supposedly characterising the political system) are less important than has been thought in affecting the nature of public policies.[13] These

13. Interestingly, studies which have used this approach in the analysis of public policies in English local authorities have invariably found political variables to be of importance in accounting for differences in local policies. See, Alt. 1971; and, Boaden & Alford, 1969.

ment. There is the idea that the social and ecological structure of a city will largely determine which view as to the proper role of government will prevail. In cities where there is a large percentage of the population which is of foreign stock then it can be expected that a 'private regarding' ethos will prevail which will favour a machine style of politics. In more affluent, better-educated, homogeneous, middle cities, however, a 'public regarding' ethos will prevail which will favour reform oriented government.

findings point to a close relationship between certain socio-economic conditions and the form of public policies but they provide no clues as to why or how this relationship exists. If we are to deal with these questions (questions which lie at the heart of what most people understand by the term 'explanation'), then we need to move outside the framework offered by these models.

5 Overview: organisations and environment

[We need] to correct a tendency in some contemporary political science to underplay the role of high-level leadership in democratic policy making.

C. E. Lindblom, *The Policy-Making Process* (Englewood Cliffs, N.J., Prentice-Hall, 1968), p. 106.

In this chapter I want to take up the important task of explaining the necessary relationship between the preceding chapters, with their emphasis on theory, and those which follow, with their emphasis on the situation in the Royal Borough of Kensington and Chelsea. One aim is to assemble some of the points which I made in criticising the theories reviewed in Part One so that I will be in a position to outline ideas and approaches which I will use in my analysis of the factors affecting the development of public policy in that Borough.

My reason for adopting this procedure and for including a lengthy section on established theory is because I do not consider that the facts of my case-material could speak for themselves and this being the situation there is a need for a deliberate discussion of my theoretical position before I move on to the situation in Kensington and Chelsea. In my view, the facts only come to mean something when ascertained and organised in the frame of a theory. 'Theory, therefore, must always be *a priori* to the empirical observation of the facts' (Myrdal, 1957, p. 160), and so to avoid the dangers of the case approach and the tired, unthinking use and acceptance of established theories, I have tried to stand back from my case and give careful attention to existing theories and hypotheses in order to see how far they contain cogent explanations which are of potential use in making sense of the case under scrutiny (Waldo, 1962, p. 61).

In the three substantive chapters that make up Part One of this study, I have identified what I consider to be the major bodies of writing in political science which have offered explanations for public policy and the behaviour of government. Of course, only a limited amount of this work has been specifically developed to explain the process of public policy-making in British local government, but I have not restricted my attention solely to these studies, but have instead also looked to other theories which have been used to explain the policy process in Western democracies because they may suggest useful methods and approaches for my case even though their conclusions need not hold with respect to the situation in Kensington and Chelsea. In the three chapters I have offered a partial review of each of these bodies of theory: I have assessed the general cogency of the explanations; and I have given an indication of the extent to which they assist in ordering the facts of my case. In this chapter I want to draw together a more general critique of this work, for these differing theories have methods of research and conclusions in common, display certain common deficiencies which limit their general use in any explanation of public policy, and are especially deficient as explanations in the context of politics in the Royal Borough of Kensington and Chelsea.

I. SIMILARITY OF THEORIES

One common feature of the theories is their conclusion that the impact of the environment is of overwhelming importance in accounting for the form of public policy and the making of policy decisions, and they deny that government assumes an autonomous or major role in the process. They also share a similar research focus, for scant attention is paid to government itself. (For a similar comment, see Marvick, 1961, p. 15.)

Theories which have emphasised the part which elections play in the policy process, usually rest upon a strong prescriptive and normative base, accept much of the political folklore of Western democracies, and point to what is recognised as a formal and quite legitimate means of influencing government, suggesting that the real influentials in the process are the ordinary citizens whose will is translated into public policies through the mechanism of free and frequent elections. Increasing attention has been paid to the part which collectivities of men organised into pressure groups, and operating partly outside the formal rules of representative democracy, are supposed to play in influencing the decisions of government. In part the rise of this group view was a specific reaction to the deficiencies of the electoral theories and at first it appeared as if work on the role of pressure groups would challenge the accepted orthodoxy which saw government as responsive to the ordinary citizen. In fact, political scientists have done much to tame the supposed excesses of this work, for they have more often than not seen these groups as contributing to the health of representative democracy by providing yet another channel for citizen participation which fills out the opportunities for influence through the ballot box. However, even when they recognise that the interest group chorus sings with an upper-middle-class voice, this still does not alter the fact that they view government simply as a responder to environmental demands. In both these bodies of theory, government itself is seen as passive and weak, responsive and open to external influences, so that it simply referees or ratifies group demands, or else serves as a sort of automatic transmission belt converting vote inputs into policy outputs. The independent and autonomous role of government is played down, for its role is effectively limited to responding to pressures and influences from outside. Hawley and Dexter remind us that 'students of legislation or legislative bodies think almost automatically in terms of pressure politics, power, influence or social recruitment. . . . [These] studies of legislation for the most part neglect to consider the process of deliberation and legislative decision which can be studied as such rather than as mere concomitants of pressures and influence' (Hawley & Dexter, 1952, pp. 478–9).

Theories of this kind may have moved away from a consideration of factors internal to government, but they nevertheless still emphasise the importance of overtly political structures and processes. The demographic approach moves further down the road laid by these earlier writers, but instead of pointing to the importance of the political environment of government, and instead of arguing that government is weak and responsive, they point to the importance of the socio-economic environment, and argue that government is really quite irrelevant in affecting the form of public policies.

When I discussed the demographic approach in the last chapter, I pointed out that it was grounded in the work of David Easton, and this should alert us to the fact that the ideas about the policy process which I have discussed in the last three chapters have not simply been contained in studies of relatively low-level theory, but have been caught up and developed by the major proponents of behavioural political science. (For contrasting views, see Storing, 1962; Ranney, 1962*b*; Eulau, 1963; McCoy & Playford, 1968; Dahl, 1961*c*; and, Easton, 1969.) Although those in the vanguard of this movement have frequently underestimated the amount of empirical theory which exists in the literature of political science, and have given the impression that their attempts in this direction represent a radical departure away from a fact-gathering and reforming discipline concerned with value theory (Easton, 1953), it is significant, not only that we already have a considerable amount of empirical political theory, but more important, the recent attempts to construct explanatory theories have involved essentially a continuation and clearer articulation of the ideas which I have already outlined in this part of my study. In the work of both David Easton (1953, 1957, 1965*a*, 1965*b*) and Gabriel Almond (1960, 1965), as in the earlier, less theoretical work on elections and pressure groups, there is a tendency to focus on inputs and to ignore the part played by the structures of government which are seen as fulfilling a limited transmission and conversion role.

All the theories I have reviewed here, have in common the fact that they

D

regard government as weak in the face of environmental forces. Government is characterised as an insecure institution in which the governors are concerned, first and foremost, to maintain their own positions of power, and this they do by exchanging public policies for the support of the politically relevant sections of the environment. Public policies are regarded as the resultant of a process of bargains and exchanges (Downs, 1957; Dahl & Lindblom, 1953; Catlin, 1964, esp. chap. 2; and, Beer, 1965): they are the outputs which result from the pressures and sanctions mobilised against the government by the active and all-powerful input structures. This conception that government is responsive to its environment, and assumes a small role in policy-making, is one which sits comfortably within the framework of myths which sustain the system of representative democracy, and represents a Conservative view of the proper role of government (Oakeshott, 1962, pp. 168–96, esp. p. 187; Lewis, 1968; and, Utley, 1949). In fact these 'input–output' models of the political system are the political science equivalent of the 'stimuli–response' theories of learning developed by psychologists. If they have tended to ignore the importance of individual creativity (Chomsky, 1959), then we have tended to ignore the independent role which government may enjoy in the process of policy formation in favour of limiting its role to the making of predictable responses to demand stimuli.

What is noticeable in all these studies, is not simply that government is given a small role in the policy process, but that it is not really made the subject of any serious research attention. Indeed Almond is candid in admitting that his functional approach 'underplayed' the part taken by the governmental structures, and he considered that 'their neglect in the development of the theory of the functions of the polity represents a serious shortcoming in the present analysis', justified only by what he saw as the need to wrest comparative politics away from its almost exclusive concern with governments and constitutions (Almond, 1960, p. 55). The trouble is that the general failure to study government means that the explanations for governmental behaviour given in the theories I have set out in Part One are mechanistic and deterministic, and are based simply on assumptions as to the motivations of the governors which centre on their supposed desire to gain security in the face of a pressuring and sanctionful environment.

II. THE PROBLEM OF APPROACH AND METHOD

Now it must be admitted that a very real merit of the work which has formed the subject matter of this part of my study lies precisely in the fact that it has recognised very explicitly that it is not possible or adequate to consider the making of public policy simply by discussing the activities within the formal structures of government as if they operated in isolation, unaffected by influences from outside. I do not wish to suggest that the influence of environmental forces should be ignored, and that research should instead concentrate solely on the internal mechanics of government, for I accept the view that governments only have a relevance in the context of their wider social and economic environment, and it would be a retrograde step to study the activity of these structures as if they were in a vacuum. The question is not one of deciding whether or not we should study the impact of the environment on government, rather it is one of deciding *how* we should study and assess that impact, and *what* we should consider to be the relevant environment.

I suggest that the established theories which I have considered have adopted a research approach to these questions which is deficient because they have failed to pay adequate attention to those in government, the subjects of, and the responders to, environmental influences. They have failed to distinguish between the operational and psychological environments of political decision-makers, and in ignoring those in government, they have dealt only with the operational environment, and this is not the environment which directly impinges on governmental decisional activity. Harold and Margaret Sprout (1965, pp. 206–7, and 224, original emphasis) argue that 'environing conditions and events can affect decisions . . . *only* by being perceived and reacted to *psychologically* in the light of the environed individual's felt needs and previous experience. What an individual perceives and how he reacts to it (that is, the composition of his psycho-milieu) may or may not correspond closely to his operational milieu. . . . But it is his percepts and reactions thereto, not the milieu as it is, or as someone else apperceives it, that determines what is to be undertaken.' They go on to note that 'from the perspective of decisions and decision-making, what matters is how the individual or group imagines the milieu to be, *not* how it actually is.'[1] Dexter clearly has a distinction of this kind in mind when he makes the point that, 'we talk frequently of a Representative or Senator "representing" or "failing to represent" his constituents. This is shorthand. The fact is the congressman represents his image of the district or of his constituents', and this being the case Dexter argues that it becomes critically important to direct our attention to answering such questions as 'how does he get this image? Where does it come from?' (Dexter, 1957. p. 2).

The truth of the matter is that a research approach is inadequate if it assesses the impact of environmental forces on government by noting just the inputs that are directed to government together with the reinforcing rewards and sanctions, while making crude assumptions as to the governmental response in the absence of any systematic research enquiry. Silverman (1954, pp. 180, and 190) makes the point that 'many fingers attempt to reach into the pie of the legislative process', and 'the views of

1. For other references to the terms 'psychological' and 'operational' environment, see, Frankel, 1964; Gore & Dyson, 1964; Simon, 1957; and, Snyder, Bruck & Sapin, 1954.

the legislators themselves about the place each factor in the process to some extent define the nature and role of these various elements.' He concludes by suggesting that 'to a large degree, the ways in which these forces enter the legislative process are dependent upon the extent to which they are considered useful, proper, or desirable by the legislators themselves.' In other words, it is vitally important to note, not so much the inputs directed to government, but the '*imports*' (Rice, 1963) selected by government. Even where inputs or demands are sent to government – and this is often less frequent than we are led to suppose – then they still have to penetrate the perceptual screen of governmental decision-makers if they are to have an effect on public policy (Milbrath, 1960). Whether they are allowed to have this effect depends more on factors internal to government and on the decision-maker's rules of selection and attention, than it does on anything which is inherent in any demand. This stress on the idea of imports does not mean that the consideration of environmental influences on public policy is narrowed, for instead of simply considering what is directed, or sent, to government, we are now in a position to see the basis of a decision-maker's response to inputs, and to note how decision-makers reach out to groups and other environmental structures in such a way that it might be quite unnecessary for those groups ever to direct demands to government.

This suggested emphasis on imports, and on the way those in government develop rules to handle the inputs and demands that are directed to them, in a sense involves a complete reversal of the way in which the relationship between governments and their environments has usually been studied. Although in Chapters 2 and 3 I pointed out that some writers have recognised the need to pay special attention to the reception and processing of demands by government, and the views of those subject to election, until recently these few writers have been a distinct minority swimming against a tide of input and stimuli studies. The stress on inputs directs the attention of the researcher away from government to environmental structures, whereas the idea of imports directs research attention to the structures of government themselves in order to see the way in which those in government select from a whole mass of potentially available environmental stimuli. An interest in public policy-making and the response of governments means that we need to pay especial attention to the way in which governmental structures select and search and exclude certain environmental factors from impinging on their decisional activity, while giving sympathetic consideration to others.

III. THE PROBLEM OF GENERALISATION

It is no part of my critique of these theories to argue that their conclusions as to the respective roles of governments and environments in the making of public policies are wrong, since the correctness of the conclusions depend upon the facts of any particular situation, and as such they defy general refutation. However, I do wish to suggest that it is wrong to generalise, and to assume that all governments are weak, responsive, and open to an ever-pressing and all-determining environment, so that they lack any autonomy to develop their own pattern of policies. This suggestion does not mean that I am rejecting the view that governments are 'open systems' (Parsons, 1951; J. G. Miller, 1955; and, Trist, Higgin, Murray & Pollock, 1963), and neither am I arguing that governments do not need environmental support in order to secure their survival (Presthus, 1965, esp. pp. 74–5). The crucial question, however, is how far does gaining this support involve costs for government which are such as to restrain their decisional activity and limit their autonomy. Certainly in the theories I have set out, support is anything but cost-free, for it has to be exchanged for agreeable public policies and this has the effect of reducing government to a weak and passive force responding to environmental power and initiative. In fact, notwithstanding the prevalance of this view, governments are in different positions of strength relative to environmental forces, and differ in their need to incur the cost of reduced decisional autonomy to secure their own survival. This being the case, it is important to specify the variables, or special circumstances, which are such as to lead to some governments being in a weak and controlled position. If we can do this then we can roughly categorise any government in terms of the extent to which it is able to enjoy autonomy from environmental influences in policy-shaping activity. I will look at studies of two 'weak' organisations where decisional activity was critically shaped by the impact of environmental forces, and I will note the circumstances which account for this state of affairs. This will serve as a foil against which to look at the situation of the majority party on the council of the Royal Borough of Kensington and Chelsea. I will first consider Phillip Selznick's study of the Tennessee Valley Authority, and then Robert Michel's study of the Socialist Party of Germany at the turn of this century.

Selznick considers that organisations develop patterns of behaviour in response to particular needs, and one such need he identifies as the necessity of obtaining 'the security of the organization as a whole in relation to social forces in its environment' (Selznick, 1966, p. 252). In the case of the Tennessee Valley Authority, Selznick considered that the mechanisms of ideology and co-optation met this need (Selznick, 1966, p. 259). The official TVA doctrine of 'grass roots administration' served to adjust the organisation to its area of operation as the 'idea of taking account of, or working with, or otherwise accepting the existing social institutions of the Valley is clearly consonant with the iron necessities of continuing to exist and work in that area' (Selznick, 1966, p. 55). Co-optation (the 'process of absorbing new elements into the leadership or policy-determining structure of an organization as a means of averting threats to its stability or existence' (Selznick, 1966, p. 13)), serves to secure three needs which an organisation has of its environment; first, it gives an organisation legitimacy so that it is publicly accepted; second, it establishes reliable channels of communication by which it can reach down to its clients; and finally, it enables an organisation to come to terms with specific centres of power. This latter type of co-optation involves drawing powerful institutions into the organisation and 'results in some constriction of the field of choice available to the organization or leadership in question' (Selznick, 1966, p. 16), because it 'results in an actual sharing of power' (Selznick, 1966, p. 260). The TVA was able to gain a certain security within its area of operation but only at the cost of compromising its own autonomy, by accepting a more restricted range of activities which did not challenge local power centres which were of necessity drawn into the body of the TVA itself.

Michels noted how the Socialist Party of Germany (SPD) moved away from their radical objectives of social and political transformation to being primarily concerned with the maintenance of the organisation: 'The external form of the party, its bureaucratic organization, definitely gains the upper hand over its soul, its doctrinal and theoretic content, and the latter is sacrificed whenever it tends to involve an inopportune conflict with the enemy. The outcome of this regressive evolution is that the party is no longer regarded as a means for the attainment of an end, but gradually becomes an end-in-itself' (Michels, 1911, p. 358). Michels mainly accounts for this change in organisational activity by pointing to the importance of the 'technical' and 'psychological' factors internal to the party. However, although these factors explain *how* party leaders are able to emancipate themselves from rank and file control, they do not suggest *why* this should result in a change in the direction of organisational activity. To account for this it is necessary to note the effect of the hostile environment: 'The forces of party, however well-developed, are altogether inferior and subordinate to the forces of the government, and this is especially true in a country such as Germany. Consequently one of the cardinal rules governing the policy of the Socialist Party is never to push its attacks upon the government beyond the limits imposed by the inequality between the respective forces of the combatants' (Michels, 1911, p. 358).[2] In other words, when a relatively weak organisation is set within a hostile environment, then in order to survive it must accept external constraints on its decisional activity and compromise its original objectives.

Each of the two organisations accommodated itself to environmental forces in different ways, but both were open and responsive to environmental influences, and any explanation of their policy-making activity which failed to pay especial attention to the impact of the environment would be hopelessly deficient. The leaders of the SDP anticipated the possible sanctions which could be imposed on them from outside and they

2. Incidentally, the chapter from which the reference is taken – 'Party life in wartime' – was not part of the original manuscript, but was specially written for the English edition.

drew back from their original objectives. In the TVA, there was an initial recognition of the likelihood of considerable opposition, and the style of the organisation – the grass roots approach – was designed to minimise this. However, the actual pattern of organisational activity was transformed because the imperatives of organisational survival meant that the power centres from within their environment had to be co-opted into the organisation. The result of this was that the TVA lost control of the determination of its own policy, and the distinction between organisation and environment became increasingly blurred.

Both the SPD and the TVA were open and responsive to environmental influences to the detriment of their decisional autonomy; this is a descriptive statement. But what were the special circumstances which accounted for this state of affairs? Why were these organisations in a position where they could gain their survival and security only at the cost of accepting massive restraints on their freedom of action?

Two features of the organisational situation of these groups are of central importance. First, the original objectives of both organisations were radical and far-reaching, and their attainment would have adversely affected a number of well-established and powerful surrounding groups.[3] Second, the organisations did not possess sufficient resources under their own independent control to achieve their objectives without massive outside help and assistance.[4] In this situation, there is either an early recognition that the objectives are unattainable, or else there is an attempt to strengthen the organisation by recruiting additional resources. But precisely because the original objectives are injurious to those outside, additional resources are anything but cost-free, and they can only be gained by accepting restraints on decisional autonomy and shifting organisational commitments in a direction which is such as to gain the sympathy and support of environmental power centres. Both groups were 'weak' organisations which were operating in 'hostile' environments.

Political scientists in their explanations of public policy have paid particular attention to the structures and processes which surround government, and have argued that the sanctions and rewards which environmental structures have at their availability are such as to ensure that governments are responsive to their interests and wishes. They have, in other words, given the impression that governments are 'weak' organisations operating in 'hostile' environments. How far is this a reasonable characterisation of the situation in Kensington and Chelsea? To what extent does the majority party on the council of the Royal Borough have to incur the cost of restricted decisional autonomy in order to secure

3. David E. Lilienthal regarded the TVA as a 'pioneer undertaking of government' as 'for the first time a President and Congress created an agency which was directed to view the problems of a region as a whole' (quoted in Selznick, 1966, p. 12).

4. Selznick (1966, p. 12) makes the point that the 'power granted to the Authority was not sufficient fully to execute that broad responsibility' of unifying the various governmental activities within the area of the Valley.

support and survival? The lessons of the two cases I have just reviewed suggest that if the majority party does not have policy objectives which pose a threat to powerful groups in Kensington and Chelsea and, more important, if it has resources under its independent control or can secure cost-free resources so that even if its objectives do challenge established interests its position can be maintained, then it is in an organisational situation in which it need not be open and responsive to environmental demands in the determination of public policy in order to secure support and its own survival. In other words, if the majority party is a 'strong' organisation in a 'passive' environment then it is in an organisational situation where it can enjoy extensive decisional autonomy.

When I outline the ideology of the Conservative councillors in Chapter 10, it will be clearly demonstrated that the policy objectives of the majority party do not pose a threat to established private interests within the Royal Borough. I will not, therefore, dwell on this question here, but instead I wish to suggest that even if the governing party were to challenge established interests, this would not place the party in a vulnerable position, because it is able to secure support and resources without the necessity of incurring any restraining costs, in spite of the fact that the literature of political science suggests that governments can only secure support by accepting massive restraints on their decisional autonomy. In fact the language of political science in stressing the ideas of support and exchange creates a quite misleading impression of the basis on which governments survive and operate. In hard reality most governments rest on a bed of apathy and acquiescence rather than on anything as active and enthusiastic as is suggested by the term 'support'. The situation in Kensington and Chelsea is no exception to this general rule, and the majority party is in an exceptionally strong position. In that authority elections serve only to legitimise a well-established and almost traditional system of rule, for the majority party's position is secure, and the non-programmatic nature of public support means that councillors do not incur any restraining costs in order to ensure their continued position of dominance. Men and money are recruited to service the objectives of the majority party in such a way that the environment which supplies them can exert little control over their use. The product of an old penny rate is over £100,000, and in reality, the public who pay are in no position to use this as a sanction or reward to bend the council to their will. The council does not need to rely on outside organisations to reach down to a client public for it has within its own employ a corps of full-time officers. Co-optation may have been a major feature of the experience of the TVA but it is little used in Kensington and Chelsea.

If we are to begin to understand the factors affecting the development of public policy in the Royal Borough of Kensington and Chelsea, then we need to recognise that the majority party, and the local authority as a whole, is in a position of strength; it is a power centre in its own right (D.

C. Miller, 1958*a*, 1958*b*; B. S. R. Green, 1968; and, Newton, 1969), and it has no need to compromise its decisional autonomy in order to be assured of support and survival.

IV. WHAT IS TO BE DONE?

In Part One of this study I have laid out three bodies of theory which constitute the core of political-science writing concerned to explain public policy and the behaviour of government in Western democracies. I have drawn two major lessons from this literature, and an awareness of these serves to guide the selection of information for the more empirical part of this book.

First, as I have pointed out, the theories reviewed in Part One about the influence upon government policy of elections, pressure groups, and the general socio-economic environment share a common assumption that external pressures have a direct relation to the actions of government, if they do not indeed determine them. The *methods of enquiry* based on these theories are, however, inadequate, for research workers have gathered material on inputs, pressures, and lines of communication centring on government, without examining systematically the prior questions about whether the government is indeed open to those lines and lacking in means of controlling and regulating its external relations. If we are to assess adequately the impact of environmental forces upon the decisional activity of those on the council of the Royal Borough, then we must pay particular attention to those *in* government, noting the way in which they relate and respond to external influence attempts. This need to adopt an 'import approach' is especially pressing where the organisational situation of a government is secure so that there is no real possibility of its being replaced. In these circumstances, environmental influences can only effect public policy if they penetrate the perceptual screen of those in power.

Second, merely reassessing the *way* in which we take account of the likely impact of the environment on the policy-shaping activity of governmental decision-makers does not go far enough. It is important to realise that not all governments are in an organisational situation of weakness where they need to be open and responsive in order to secure support and their survival. Although the literature I have considered has been grounded in the assumption that governments in Western democracies can best be viewed as representative institutions, and has *concluded* that they are relatively weak organisations operating in hostile and demanding environments, this is certainly *not* an adequate characterisation of the position of the governing party in Kensington and Chelsea, which is better typified as a strong organisation in a passive environment. In this kind of organisational situation, it becomes utterly impossible to understand the policy activity of government if we are only going to discuss how it does or does not respond to environmental influences, as it is in a position when it enjoys substantial freedom from those forces and so can shape public policies with only limited reference to external considerations. We are, therefore, confronted with the problem of deciding just what factors need to be taken into consideration if we are to make sense of, or account for, the development of public policy in Kensington and Chelsea.

In many ways, the development of the dominant explanatory theories for public policy has involved an increasing movement away from government, for attention has shifted from elections, to pressure groups, to the socio-economic environment of government. The functional approach is the latest intellectual embodiment of this move away from the institutions of government, and although it has been a necessary corrective to the unrealities of an excessive formalism, there is a need for 'the reconsideration of the cruciality of institutions and structures' (Braibanti, 1969, p. 52. See also, R. E. Jones, 1967, esp. p. 92) for the 'institutional structure of a system is of paramount importance in political life' (W. C. Mitchell, 1967, p. 17). There is no doubt that the rise of behaviouralism made the study of the institutions of government appear a reactionary and old-fashioned research interest, and although the behavioural and the institutional approaches were seen as contradictory and dichotomous ways of understanding the political process, the dichotomy is a false one (Truman, 1955. See also, Huntingdon, 1965; and, Jouvenel, 1965), and there is an increasing recognition of the necessity of paying particular attention to the part which government *itself* plays in the development of public policy. However, this recognition has not carried with it any clear research prescription as to what is to be done.[5]

There are three sections in Part Two of this study, and they each represent a response to what I have seen as the problems and inadequacies of the theories I have reviewed, both generally and more particularly as they fit the facts of the situation in Kensington and Chelsea.

The first lesson I pointed to was a general one of method. I argued that in order to assess the impact of environmental forces upon public policy it is necessary to appreciate the way in which those in government relate and respond to their environment. This theme is developed in Section B, on 'The external relations of the council'. In Chapter 8 I identify the rules of access developed by councillors to handle interest groups and their demands, and in Chapter 9 I identify the information sources which they look to, avoid, and resist, and this knowledge enables us to form a picture of their psychological environment.

The second lesson I pointed to was of more specific relevance to my case. I argued that the organisational situation of the governing party of the Royal Borough was one where it enjoyed considerable decisional autonomy from environmental forces, and as such, in order to explain

5. Although Blondel *et al* (1960, p. 68) argue that government 'must be studied from a "decision-making and not a legalistic point of view"'.

adequately the development of public policy, it was not enough simply to reassess the way in which we studied external relations, it was also necessary to include other factors within the ambit of analysis.[6] The additional factors which I consider need to be taken into account are set out in Sections A and C. In Section A, I deal with 'The internal regulation of council activity', noting how the leading councillors can control and shape the behaviour of council members and so have a crucial effect upon the development of council policy. In Section C, I outline the ideology of the leading councillors; I outline, that is, their views as to the proper role of government. Councillor ideology is of particular importance when the council is involved in the making of policy decisions which involve change or innovation in the established pattern of resource commitments.

The emphasis in Part Two is on the freedom and autonomy of government (see also, Bauer, Pool & Dexter, 1964, esp. Part Five; Lindblom, 1968; Wahlke, Eulau, Buchanan & Ferguson, 1962; and, Eckstein, 1962), and on the capacity of the majority party to control disturbance which may require the taking of policy decisions. In other words, the emphasis is on the *maintenance* of public policy and on the forces which are such as to enable the council to avoid and resist change and innovation in the established pattern of public policies. There will not be any discussion of dramatic cases of council action and decision, but instead there will be a consideration of the structured context of council activity.

6. Bailey (1950, p. 218) makes the point that 'in a study of policy-making it is not enough that we understand the forces external to the policy-maker.'

Part Two
PUBLIC POLICY-MAINTENANCE: THE CASE OF THE ROYAL BOROUGH OF KENSINGTON AND CHELSEA

Section A
The internal regulation of council activity

I concluded the first part of my study by suggesting that a dominant tradition of political science writing provides an inadequate explanation for the development of public policy in my case. This does not mean that I must immediately devise my own idiosyncratic ideas to make sense of policy-shaping behaviour in Kensington and Chelsea, rather it suggests that I should look to other bodies of writing to see whether they have greater potential to enable me to deal with the facts of my situation.

I do not deal centrally with my case until Chapter 7, for in Chapter 6, I outline the literature on the conventions of British government, and the rules of the game of American legislatures – a literature which represents the application of simple role theory. Although the limits of such an approach should be recognised, I consider that the concepts and ideas from role theory can be used to make sense of councillor, and council, behaviour in Kensington and Chelsea. I will argue that the chairmen are the authoritative councillors who have the power to establish and maintain standards of conduct for the various positions on the council, and I will identify the behaviour rules which they uphold. In addition, I will also identify the recruitment rules used to fill positions within the council. I will argue that the rules for recruitment and behaviour represent different ways in which councillor behaviour is controlled so that it does not challenge the maintenance of established council policies.

6 Conventions, rules and role theory

The unwritten rules of the game in legislative bodies provide an almost virgin field for empirical research.

> J. C. Wahlke, H. Eulau, W. Buchanan, and L. C. Ferguson, *The Legislative System* (New York, Wiley, 1962), p. 168.

An author who writes a book about roles does not start with a clean sheet. Other writers have ventured into the field before him and he is under obligation either to build upon their contributions or to explain why he rejects their definitions and theories.

> M. Banton, *Roles* (London, Tavistock, 1965), p. 21.

I. CONVENTIONS

A student of British politics will not have to sit through many classes before his attention is directed to the 'conventions' of the constitution. Britain, we are told, is a country without a written constitution, and although there is flexibility in the way the affairs of government are conducted, there is nevertheless an order and predictability which is explained by the critical importance of the 'unwritten rules' which have grown up over the years to 'provide the flesh which clothes the dry bones of the law' (Jennings, 1959, p. 81). In Britain there exists 'a whole system of political morality, a whole code of precepts for the guidance of public men, which will not be found in any page of either the Statute or the Common Law, but which are in practice held hardly less sacred than any principle embodied in the Great Charter or in the Petition of Right' (Freeman, 1890, p. 114).

Writers who point to the importance of these precepts[1] are aware that they exist in all political systems, but they are seen as especially important in Britain precisely because there is so little regulation of political life by formal law. Conventions determine not only the 'mode in which the

1. Or, as they are otherwise called, 'maxims' (Mill, 1861); 'conventions' (Dicey, 1959); 'customs' (Anson, 1922–35); 'obligations' (Wade & Phillips, 1960); or, 'tacit understandings' (Low, 1904).

discretionary power of the Crown (or of Ministers as servants of the Crown) ought to be exercised' (Dicey, 1959, pp. 422–3), involving such customs as those relating to ministerial responsibility and collective responsibility, but they also guide the behaviour of those in Parliament, ensuring, for example, that Members sit when the Speaker stands, that there are arrangements for 'pairing', and that in the Lords, lay peers do not participate in legal proceedings. Conventions not only guide the *behaviour* of public men, but they also specify what *attributes* qualify a person to hold a particular office. It is, for example, now well-recognised that membership of the House of Lords disqualifies a person from assuming the position of Prime Minister, and this convention is enforced because it is argued that 'if the Prime Minister were chosen from the Lords, it could easily be represented as undemocratic, and a Government supporting it would lose votes at the next election for offending public opinion' (Harvey & Bather, 1963, p. 515).

Writers who point to the importance of these conventions usually argue that they developed first for largely practical reasons, but have gradually grown into 'obligatory rules', ensuring that there is scope for 'common action' (Jennings, 1959, pp. 72, 82, and, 102). However (and as I suggested in Chapter 2) these writers also suggest that the conventions ensure that there is a system of Government which is truly responsible to the people. Even though most writers recognise that the conventions are not enforceable in the courts,[2] they still argue that they are 'followed as consistently as the rules of law' (Jennings, 1959, p. 80), because they are sustained by the 'weight of public opinion, which expects politicians to behave in the true spirit of the constitution' (Harvey & Bather, 1963, p. 515). 'There is in fact a standard of political authority which commands obedience. Those who govern submit to the judgement of public opinion, which they may seek to influence, but cannot ultimately control' (Wade & Phillips, 1960, p. 91).

Conventions have generally been seen as developing because of the incomplete and inadequate specifications for behaviour contained within formal law. In Chapter 1, I outlined the extremely prevalent view which suggests that local authorities are mere administrative structures which have to work within the highly restrictive framework of law and central control. The widespread acceptance of this view has meant that there has been a tendency not to look for such unwritten rules, or even worse, to assume that there are no rules of this kind of relevance to the student of political behaviour at the local level (Hart, 1968, p. 120). MacKenzie (1951, p. 346) noted this deficiency in 1951, when he attempted to deal in general terms with the conventions of local government, a term which he used generally to cover 'all general statements or rules about government

2. Dicey (1959, pp, 445–6) does in fact suggest that if conventions are breached then this would bring the offender into conflict with the courts and law of the land.

which are true, or at least might be true, and yet are not statements about law'. More recently, Maddick and Pritchard (1958, 1959) in their study of the conventions of local authorities in the West Midlands used the term to mean 'practices which are added to those prescribed by law, and are adopted simply because they are found useful' (Maddick & Pritchard, 1958, p. 145). Their finding that there was 'variation rather than similarity' (Maddick & Pritchard, 1958, p. 155) in the practices adopted by local authorities pointed to the necessity for closer studies of the unwritten rules of particular local authorities, but this has not been done. (But see Burkett, 1960.)

I argued in Chapter 1 that those writers who assert that local authorities are simply administrative structures ignore the considerable autonomy which local authorities enjoy, and this being the case their behaviour cannot be understood simply by a consideration of formal law alone. Indeed, if we look more specifically at the position of the local councillor, one authority on local government law has noted that 'there is little statute or common law regarding individual members of local authorities. . . . The principal legal rights relate to the inspection of documents, and to the payment of allowances for loss of earnings, travelling and subsistence. The principal duty consists of an obligation to disclose any pecuniary interest a member may have in a matter before the council' (Cross, 1966, p. 51). This recognition that formal law does not closely define the behaviour of either the council or the individual councillors; the realisation that the theories I reviewed in Part One do not adequately make sense of council behaviour; and the fact that discussions about conventions have been seen as useful in explaining behaviour at the level of central government, all suggest that a study of the conventions of local government in Kensington and Chelsea may provide us with a way of understanding councillor behaviour, so enabling us to make sense of council activity with respect to the making and maintenance of public policy.

Before I turn to my case, it is important to look to more theoretical studies which have used the language of conventions, or unwritten rules, in order to see how these writers have handled problems I may well encounter. First, I will discuss the literature on the folkways, rules of the game, or norms of American legislatures. Second, I will suggest the similarity between these ideas and those of simple role theory. Third, I will suggest a research exercise which utilises the language of role theory to make sense of social behaviour, but which comes to terms with some of the problems I will have pointed to in my review of the literature on the rules of the game. Finally, I will outline an aspect of this exercise which I consider can be used to define and identify the rules which set the boundary on the patterns of behaviour displayed by councillors in Kensington and Chelsea. These ideas will be used to guide the selection of material in the other chapter of this section.

II. RULES

Legislatures are institutionalised groups; they are 'clubs' and the people in them share a certain 'group life' (W. S. White, 1957; and, Truman, 1951). This means that when anyone enters such an organisation they are not able to behave completely as they might wish because there are certain norms, or rules of the game, which serve to regulate the behaviour of members. 'There are unwritten rules of behavior, which we have called folkways, in the Senate. These rules are *normative*, that is, they define how a senator ought to behave. Nonconformity is met with moral condemnation, while senators who conform to the folkways are rewarded with high esteem by their colleagues' (Matthews, 1959, p. 1086, original emphasis).

One group of writers which has pointed to the importance of these norms has argued that they apply to *all* members of a legislature; are set by *society*; and have a profound influence on the *behaviour* of those within legislatures.

Wahlke and associates in their study of four American state legislatures argued that the rules are 'considered legitimately binding on every member of the group', and 'all [the legislators interviewed] accepted without any question whatsoever the belief... that rules of the game are the same rules for every one in the chamber' (Wahlke, Eulau, Buchanan & Ferguson, 1962, pp. 141, and 148–9). Matthews similarly found, in the case of the Senate, that the informal rules there were 'generally accepted' and widely shared by the membership as a whole, and although he argued that their 'origins are obscure' (Matthews, 1959, pp. 1064, and 1088), other writers have suggested that the particular norms which serve to define acceptable legislative behaviour are, in fact, set by society. Truman (1951, p. 347), for example, noted that 'when a man enters a legislative position he takes on a new role that is prescribed for him by the society', and Wahlke and associates (1962, p. 9), although rather less specific, do not see the norms as set by the legislators alone, but argue that 'the office of legislator is a clearly recognisable position in the four states studied, [and] ... legislators and many other persons in those societies associate certain norms of behavior with those positions'. These writers who study the legislative rules of the game are aware that 'the folkways are no more perfectly obeyed than the traffic laws' and are 'not invariably adhered to,' but they nevertheless argue that they are important in shaping and guiding the behaviour of legislators (Matthews, 1959, p. 1086; and, Truman, 1951, p. 348). It is this conclusion that makes these studies of particular interest to the student of public policy, since if we accept the ideas and methods which sustain it, then it is appropriate to identify normative rules in other decisional contexts, as in doing this we are making sense of decisional behaviour by providing a statement of the structured context within which it takes place.

What then are the reasons that are given for suggesting that the rules of the game shape the actual behaviour of elected decision-makers?

First, the writers usually argue that the norms are shared and *accepted* as legitimate by all members. Second, although 'not all the behavioral norms are unambiguous . . . many of the norms defining the legislator's role are relatively unambiguous' (Truman, 1951, pp. 347–8). These 'set the approximate limits within which . . . discretionary behavior may take place' (Truman, 1951, p. 349), and provide a *tight framework* within which the individual legislator has to behave. Finally, even if it is the case that all the members do not accept the rules, then they can still have an effect upon legislative behaviour, because they can be *enforced* by a whole system of rewards and sanctions which are adequate to bend erring legislators back to the 'proper' behaviour. Wahlke and associates suggest that the 'rules of the game are no pious platitudes about good behavior. They are rules enforceable by clearly recognized sanctions which all members have in their power to impose on errant members' (Wahlke *et al*, 1962, p. 168). These sanctions can range from a vote of censure, through obstruction of a member's bill, to the quiet 'cold shoulder'. Rewards, on the other hand, can range from the granting of 'legislative effectiveness' through favourable committee assignments (which Masters (1969, p. 352) notes go to the responsible member who has a 'basic and fundamental respect for the legislative process and understands and appreciates its formal and informal rules'), to the reward of gaining the respect and friendship of legislative colleagues.

So far I have been selective in identifying studies which have discussed the norms of legislative life, in order to highlight what is a widely accepted view of the nature and importance of these normative rules. In fact, other studies have challenged this position, as some writers have argued that the same rules do *not* hold equally for all members, noting that different rules apply to the various positions that exist within any legislative body (Bauer, Pool & Dexter, 1964, p. 460; Huitt, 1961, 1957; Patterson, 1961; and, Barber, 1965). Other writers have suggested that the rules are set, *not* by society, but by influential members within the legislature itself (W. S. White, 1957). Criticisms of this kind enable us to refine a model centring on legislative rules, but there is a more far-reaching criticism which challenges the utility of searching for explanations of behaviour by looking at legislative rules. Some writers take the view that the rules do *not* provide a tight framework to guide behaviour, but allow considerable scope for idiosyncratic behaviour and are poorly enforced.[3] Notwithstanding this last criticism, I will be suggesting a way in which I feel we can usefully

3. W. S. White (1957, p. 122) argues that in the Senate, 'the great ones do about as they please'; and Huitt (1961, p. 573) argues that a new Senator 'selects' the role which he wishes to play, and he notes that there are few sanctions in this body which are used to discipline members, for 'the Senate is not a body disposed to impose sanctions on any behaviour but the most outrageous'. For a critical review article on the subject of 'rules of the game', see Price & Bell, 1970*b*.

study normative rules to make sense of councillor behaviour in Kensington and Chelsea, but in undertaking this exercise it will be necessary to bear in mind that the rules may not be the same for all councillors, and I must be careful in specifying just who prescribes the behavioural standards.[4]

For the moment it is interesting to note that in many ways the explanations for individual behaviour contained in discussions of rules of the game, or conventions, are similar to the explanations for public policy-making – or governmental behaviour – which I discussed in Part One. In both bodies of literature there is a reluctance to focus on the particular position or structure under examination. Instead attention centres on surrounding structures or individuals and on the pressures or sanctions which are said to determine the behaviour of either government or individual legislators so that it is in accord with the demands or expectations of others.[5] The problems and deficiencies which I highlighted with respect to the 'impact of environment' theories apply with equal force to simplistic discussions of normative rules. Just as a consideration of environmental forces should not allow us to ignore government, so too a consideration of normative rules should not allow us to ignore those who are subject to those rules.

III. ROLES

Explanations for legislative behaviour which centre on the importance of unwritten rules not only have much in common with other sorts of political science explanations for public policy-making, but have even more in common with explanations for 'status' or 'position' behaviour which have been developed in the disciplines of anthropology and sociology where writers have been particularly self-conscious in developing models of society based on role theory. The fact that many of the writers who discuss the rules of the game in legislative bodies acknowledge a debt to those writers from other disciplines who have been in the forefront in developing and using the concept of role, suggests that it is worthwhile to move away from the political science literature to the original work. In this section I will indicate the similarity between early work on this subject and the later political science work on conventions or folkways. Both bodies of literature share common problems and deficiencies. In the next section I will look to the more recent literature of role theory which avoids some of the pitfalls and problems I have already noted when I discussed the literature on the legislative rules of the game. This will serve as a basis to enable me to outline a model which can be used to identify those normative rules which shape councillor behaviour in Kensington and Chelsea.

4. Huitt (1961, p. 566) makes the point that 'it is essential to identify *whose* expectations are meant – who, that is, prescribes the appropriate behavior'.
5. See Eulau & Hinckley, 1966, and note their discussion of the 'inside' and 'outside' models of legislative behaviour.

Linton was by no means the first social scientist to use the term role, but his ideas have been particularly influential, for not only did he provide the classic distinction between status and role, but his idea that positions and attending roles were elements of societies and that individual behaviour could be construed as role performance implied that role linked individual behaviour to social structure. Linton (1936, pp. 99, 114 and 102) argued that there are 'more or less conscious patterns of what the behavior of individuals in certain positions should be', and the occupancy of a particular position 'at once limits and defines his activities and establishes a minimum of things which he must learn'. 'Behavior in all relationships is strongly influenced by the ideal patterns' which are defined by 'society' and 'shared by many members'. The similarity between this, and the discussions of legislative folkways which I have already outlined is clear enough. But it is not only 'anthropological conventions [which] have required that cultures should be described in terms of norms of behavior without reference to either deviations or individuals' (Linton, 1945, p. x). Sociologists have also often postulated that there is societal consensus around normative expectations for position behaviour with behaviour in close conformity to those expectations because of the existence of reinforcing sanctions. Inkeles (1964, pp. 57 and 80) makes the point: 'Sociologists have traditionally explained the fact that most people fulfill their major social obligations by referring to the system of sanctions imposed on those who fail to meet, and the rewards granted to those who do meet, the expectations of society. Performance is thus seen as largely dependent on factors "outside" the person. The only thing that need be posited as "inside", in this view, is the general desire to avoid punishment and gain rewards. . . . In trying to develop a "model" of any society, the social scientist almost inevitably gives a simplified picture which gravely underestimates the variety and diversity of attitude and behavior found in most societies.'

IV. A RESEARCH EXERCISE

The recognition that there are particular problems and difficulties associated with explaining legislative behaviour by using the idea of normative expectations, and the fact that these difficulties have much in common with those which we might encounter in other disciplines which have discussed roles and norms, does not mean that I must abandon the idea of discussing and explaining councillor behaviour in the light of the normative expectations which surround those positions. Indeed, if I were to do this it would almost be to deny that there is any predictability and regularity in behaviour, or that there is any organisation and informal structure. I would inevitably be left to discuss behaviour on the basis of observing (where possible) day-to-day activity which I would have to construe as entirely idiosyncratic and unpredictable. Such a course of action is not necessary, however, for

I can still fruitfully use the idea of norms or expectations as a useful explanatory device, but in doing so I must take into account some of the critical problems which I have identified in the studies which I have so far considered.

First, I recognise that within any organisation there are likely to be a *number* of official and unofficial positions and it is important to identify those positions. Moreover, I should not expect that behavioural expectations will apply *equally* to all those positions. For example, in the context of local government, councillors occupying the formal position of committee chairman may be expected to behave in quite a different way from those councillors who occupy the unofficial position of 'new' councillor.

Second, I cannot avoid the necessity of discussing just *whose* expectations define the appropriate standards of behaviour for the particular positions I am studying, and *how* I identify those expectations. Neither can I continue to assume that there is *consensus* (rather than conflict) as to those expectations and standards.

Finally, and this will be discussed later, it is not adequate just to outline norms and reinforcing sanctions and then to assume that behaviour will be in conformity with their requirements. I must study the *incumbent* of any particular position in order to appreciate his orientations to the expectations which are likely to surround him. The recognition of these problems and difficulties must inevitably mean that a more complicated research exercise is necessary than those which have been undertaken by students of conventions or folkways.

In much of the literature which I have so far considered in this chapter, the behavioural expectations for any position are said to be set by 'society', and it has often been argued that there is consensus around those expectations. Society is an abstraction, however, and it is necessary to break this down into statements about what different collectivities of people expect any particular position to be doing. 'In order to demonstrate what "society" or a "group" expects, we must ask its members what they expect. Asking many different individuals the same question seldom results in a single answer. Thus, by seeking an empirical demonstration of the expectations held for an incumbent of a specified position by a population of a role definers, we are led to expect not a single expectation, but a number of expectations that may or may not be the same' (Gross, Mason & McEachern, 1958, p. 5). In other words, for any particular position which we might identify, and whose behaviour we might be concerned to explain, we must recognise that the position-incumbent could be subject to a whole range of quite different expectations which may impose pressure on him toward different kinds of behaviour. In other words, incumbents of most social positions experience 'role conflict'.[6] But this is not all, as in many cases people may hold expectations for a particular position but may not

6. For a discussion of differing types of role conflict, see Kahn, Wolfe, Quinn, Snoek & Rosenthal, 1964.

communicate them, or even if they do communicate them they may not be able to reinforce their expectations with sanctions or rewards to encourage behavioural compliance. This question of communication in particular is of central importance in modern society, since the situation of many people in organisations is one of 'role ambiguity'.[7] Many position-incumbents do not know what is expected of them, and they often lack the information which they need in order to behave in a way which will fulfil those expectations which they wish to satisfy.

The recognition that conflict and ambiguity are likely to typify the situation of most positions, makes it particularly vital to appreciate the way in which any position-incumbent relates to expectations, and defines appropriate behaviour for himself. But even where there is a clear and communicated consensus as to the proper behaviour for a particular position we still need information on the knowledge and orientations of a particular position-incumbent if we are to satisfactorily account for his behaviour. The fact is that much of the work which has used the idea of role has paid only scant attention to the incumbents of social positions and has emphasised 'the social determinants of behavior' (Biddle & Thomas, 1966, p. 5), mixing 'norms and actual behavior together in a shapeless mass' (Homans, 1951, p. 125). All too often there is the assumption that there are the norms for a position, and it is further assumed that these are known and accepted by the incumbent of a particular position so that his behaviour is almost automatically in conformity with their requirements.[8] For example, Wahlke and associates, in what is one of the most influential studies of legislative behaviour, argue that 'the concept [of role] postulates that individual legislators are *aware* of *the* norms constituting the role and consciously *adapt their behavior* to them in some fashion' (Wahlke *et al*, 1962, p. 9, my emphasis). In other words, the three differing phenomena of behavioural expectations; the individual position-incumbent's definition of his situation; and his actual behaviour, are equated one with another prior to research, when in fact their equation can only be demonstrated by the observation of particular situations and cannot be assumed in advance.

Raising these problems which lie in the way of explaining the behaviour of social positions by referring to the expectations of others, and noting the deficiencies of studies which have dealt with this subject, is not to say that expectations of this kind are unimportant. On the contrary, it must be recognised that most behaviour occurs with respect to others and is affected by the expectations of others, but a full discussion of the behaviour of a particular position-incumbent must involve the following research steps:

7. Kahn *et al* (1964, p. 24) make the point that 'all too often people are unclear about the scope of their responsibilities; they simply do not know what they are "supposed" to do. When people know what to do, they do not always know how'.
8. Gross *et al* (1958, p. 4) make the point that one task for role theorists is, in fact, to 'account for the variability of the behavior of incumbents of the same position'.

A specification of the range of expectations that are held for the behaviour of the position by other positions.

An assessment of the extent to which those expectations conflict one with another in terms of their requirements for behaviour.

An analysis of the communication of various expectations to the particular position-incumbent, and an assessment of the extent of role ambiguity.

An analysis of the sanctions and rewards which may be available to reinforce some of the expectations.

Now it is important to realise that not all expectations are communicated, still less are all expectations reinforced by rewards or sanctions for conformity or deviance from their requirements. These two variables are of critical importance in affecting the likelihood that particular expectations will come to guide and restrain the behaviour of a particular position. It is, therefore, especially important to identify those persons who hold expectations for the behaviour of the particular position under study which they both communicate and can reinforce by the application of rewards or sanctions.

So far, this research proposal has ignored any consideration of the position-incumbent himself. Before we can begin adequately to discuss the impact of expectations on behaviour it is, however, necessary to deal with factors which are 'internal' to the individual whose behaviour we are concerned to explain. We need to know the knowledge which he has of the expectations that are held for him. He may gain this knowledge by receiving and understanding those expectations that are communicated to him, or by searching out expectations and cues which are not sent to him. In addition, we need to appreciate the extent to which he regards the various expectations as suitable guides for his behaviour, either because he considers that they are legitimate, or because he is mindful of the sanctions which can be applied should he deviate from their requirements and is keen to gain the rewards associated with compliance. This means it is particularly important to identify those persons who are regarded by particular position-incumbents as authoritative and legitimate role definers.

A research exercise which took all these dimensions of enquiry into account for all the positions that were involved in any organisation would be an immense undertaking, the scope of which lies well beyond the bounds of this study. At the same time, too much detail of this kind would mean that the imperatives of organisational life for particular positions could easily be overlooked, and there would inevitably be too great a concentration upon the idiosyncratic nature of social behaviour. In other words, although a full consideration of behaviour would involve the collection of information and an analysis of all the dimensions which I have outlined above, it is my intention to whittle some of this away in order to concentrate attention upon identifying those expectations for behaviour which are likely to have a particularly important effect on the behaviour of positions within the Council of the Royal Borough. This means that I must identify those expectations which are likely to be *communicated* to councillors and which are capable of *reinforcement* by the application of rewards or sanctions. This will necessitate the identification of those positions which are recognised and *accepted* by councillors as having the right or ability to hold behavioural expectations for them to which they are prepared to comply, or to which they recognise they have to comply.

V. RULES FOR RECRUITMENT AND BEHAVIOUR

So far I have made no attempt to identify those positions which can be regarded as holding expectations which are likely to be particularly important in affecting the behaviour of the various positions on the council; I have merely pointed out that expectations may be held by an infinite range of persons, both from inside and outside of the council, and that there is no likelihood that there will be consensus in all their behavioural prescriptions. In fact, in the rest of this section there will be no reference to the expectations that are held for councillor behaviour by 'society' or those *outside* of the majority group on the council. In Section B I will give some indication of the extent of communication between councillors and their locality, but as far as the present section is concerned it is only necessary to note that there is restricted interaction between councillors and their public. Comparatively few behavioural expectations are communicated to councillors by people from outside of the council, and such communications as are sent are frequently regarded as quite unacceptable guides for the behaviour of either individual councillors or the council as a whole. Moreover, in Part One, I dealt with the point that in the organisational situation of the Council of the Royal Borough it really is not the case that the 'environment' (or 'society' or the 'public') is in a position where it is able to impose sanctions upon either the council as a body, or upon the vast majority of the Conservative councillors. The recognition that few expectations are communicated to councillors from outside of their group on the council, and the recognition that such communications as they do receive are often unacceptable and unreinforced by rewards or sanctions means that these expectations cannot be considered as of particular importance in affecting the likely behaviour of councillors, and for this reason they will not be considered here. If we are to consider those expectations which are most likely to affect the behaviour of the various positions on the council, then we must see people *within* the council as being the persons who hold those expectations. Not only are the sanctions of councillor on councillor stronger and more immediate than the sanctions of society on councillor,[9] but within the restricted context of a face-to-face group both the extent of communication and the acceptability of communicated expectations is vastly increased, for as Homans points out, 'the more frequently men interact with one another, the more alike they become in the norms they hold' (Homans, 1951, p. 126).

9. W. S. White (1957, pp. 153–4) makes a similar point: 'While the pressures *on* Senators are well known . . . the pressures *from* Senators are in fact more intensive, more effective, and far less recognized by the public for what they are.'

Even though we can recognise the basic irrelevance of society as the crucial definer of behavioural standards for the various positions on the council, it is not adequate simply to state that the 'council' are the definers, as there may not be consensus within the group, and neither is it the case that all the councillors will be of equal importance in this process of setting and upholding effective and enforceable standards. We need in other words to identify those councillors who are recognised and accepted as authoritative; who have the resources at their disposal which enable them to uphold and enforce behavioural standards; and who, therefore, are likely to communicate their expectations to other councillors. In order to identify the authoritative councillors in Kensington and Chelsea, I asked thirty-nine Conservative councillors and four Labour councillors, the following question:

> 'Now I'd like to change the subject and ask you about how policies are decided here in the council. Obviously not everyone is of equal weight when it comes to making decisions in the sorts of issues we've been discussing.[10] Generally speaking, who would you say are the members who stand out as being particularly important in the decision-process? Please don't just consider your own party members, but include councillors from the other party as well if you feel they are relevant.'

Baldly stated,[11] it is reasonable to conclude from the responses that the chairmen were regarded as the authoritative councillors, and in the context of an on-going group[12] this means that they are not just particularly influential in making and maintaining public policy, but they are also the councillors whose views as to appropriate behaviour for other positions set the norms,[13] or behaviour rules, for those positions. Many councillors will hold expectations for the behaviour of other positions on the council, but only a limited number of councillors are in this position of being recognised as authoritative, and it is the behavioural expectations of these people which are particularly decisive in affecting the actual behaviour of other position-incumbents.

Identifying behaviour rules involves a consideration of only part of the

10. The issues that were discussed with councillors ranged from questions of play provisions to questions relating to council housing policy and the building of the new town hall. Although this question restricted attention to the identification of those of *general* influence, this does not mean that it is not possible to identify those of *particular* influence within more restricted spheres of council activity. For a study which does identify those of general *and* specific influence, see Francis, 1962.
11. For a fuller discussion of the identification of the authoritative councillors, see Dearlove, 1972, chap. 10.
12. For a discussion of the differences in leadership patterns in experimental and on-going groups, see Verba, 1961.
13. I am adopting the standard usage of the term 'norm' (Verba, 1961, p. 192; and, Homans, 1951, p. 123), but I am making it clear just *who* within the group has the sanctions and the authority to enforce their standards. Contrary to the suggestions in much of the literature, not all group members are in this position.

normative framework which will enable us to predict and anticipate the likely behaviour of the various positions on the council. There are not just 'expectations for behaviour' – some of which will constitute behaviour rules – but there are also 'expectations for attributes'. Gross and associates point out that 'most authors have restricted their treatment of expectations to those in the first category, for behaviour', but they go on to note that it is important to specify not only 'what incumbents of positions *should do* . . . [but also] what incumbents of positions *should be*, or the characteristics they should have' (Gross *et al*, 1958, p. 63, original emphasis). Here again, just as with expectations for behaviour, not all expectations for attributes, or 'qualities' (Sarbin, 1954, esp. pp. 227–9), will be of equal importance. But with the expectations for attributes, however, the situation is immensely simplified, as *only* those who are actually recruiting or selecting people for incumbency of positions are able to put their expectations into effect. A knowledge of the criteria which the recruiting and selecting structures use when filling particular social positions; a knowledge, that is, of the attributes which they see as suitably qualifying a person for office, is crucially important to anyone interested in understanding the likely pattern of behaviour which will be later displayed by those filling the positions. It may well be that these 'recruitment rules' which guide the selectors in filling particular positions are consciously constructed by them with the specific intention of ensuring that the position-incumbents will behave in a known, predictable, and acceptable manner. However, even if these rules are not consciously constructed with a view to creating the likelihood that certain behaviour patterns will follow, we can still analyse the implications of these rules for behaviour, as they will have an effect whether or not this is in the mind of the selectors and recruiters.

In the next chapter I will identify the recruitment rules and the behaviour rules for the various positions on the council. In addition I will deal with the expectations for the behaviour of the various positions held by the non-authoritative councillors, and I will also discuss the acceptability of the behaviour rules to the particular position-incumbents. Finally, I will consider the relationship between the recruitment rules and the behaviour rules and the implications which they have for the likely direction or council activity with respect to the making and maintenance of public policy.

7 Rules for recruitment and behaviour

> While the Devonshire Committee was concerned primarily with training, it was demonstrated again, as with the Fisher Committee, that the subjects of selection and training were essentially inseparable.
>
> Robert Heussler, *Yesterday's Rulers: The Making of the British Colonial Service* (London, Oxford University Press, 1963), p. 183.

This chapter applies the ideas I developed in the last chapter to the situation in Kensington and Chelsea, and consists of three sections. The first two sections are essentially descriptive. In Section A I will identify the recruitment rules used in filling certain positions on the council, and in Section B I will identify the behaviour rules for those positions, and the behavioural expectations held by the non-authoritative councillors. In Section C, however, I move beyond description to consider the relationship between rules for recruitment and behaviour, and the implications of these rules for the behaviour of individual councillors and for the collective activity of the council as a whole as they affect the likely development of council policy.

It is possible to identify a number of positions on the council. There are the official council positions of councillor and aldermen, mayor and deputy mayor, and chairman and vice-chairman of the standing committees; there are the positions within the majority party of leader, deputy leader, and party whips, as well as similar positions within the minority party; and there are the unofficial positions of new councillor and senior councillor. In this chapter I will not consider the recruitment and behaviour rules for all these positions, for I will confine my attention to the ordinary councillor (and in particular the new councillor), the chairmen, and the leader of the council. The concentration on these positions is justified because this study is concerned with the making and maintenance of public policy. The chairmen and the leader must be considered as they are recognised as assuming an influential role in this process, and the ordinary councillor should be considered since he is the raw material for all the other positions on the council. On the other hand, the minority party and the mayor and deputy mayor are really outside the decisional process; the alderman is not in practice a distinct position on the council; and the vice-chairmen and the majority party whips, although distinct positions on the council, were not regarded by most councillors as influential and important in the policy process, and neither do they constitute a threat to the established leadership group in the same way as that which may be posed by the new councillors.

I. RECRUITMENT RULES

> There arises in the leaders a tendency to isolate themselves, to form a sort of cartel, and to surround themselves, as it were, with a wall, within which they will admit those only who are of their own way of thinking.
>
> Robert Michels, *Political Parties*, 1911 (New York, Free Press, 1966), p. 126.

For purposes of analysis, the process of recruitment can be explored by asking questions about the supply of applicants for a position, and by asking further questions about the control of recruitment and appointment by those with the authority to decide between rival applicants.

The first set of questions would have to cover a wide range to provide a full explanation, but three enquiries in particular would have to be made. (Barber, 1965, esp. pp. 10–15). We would need to know how many people were actually attracted to the position, and of those that were attracted we would need to know how many people felt they were capable of assuming that office, and thought that they had a chance of being accepted.

The selection side of this process is less complex, and this section deals mainly with the methods of recruitment and selection used in filling the three positions which form the subject of this chapter. Of course, it is not really possible to consider either aspect of this process in isolation from the other. People will only offer themselves for selection if they consider that they have a chance of being chosen – that is they consider they possess the qualities which the selectors are looking for. Moreover, from the selectors' side, it is important to consider the supply of people for any position as the volume of applicants has a critical effect on the role which the recruiting and selecting structures perform and on the rigour with which they can develop and apply their recruitment rules to those in competition for selection. If few people put themselves forward then not only do the selectors have to look for recruits but they may have to modify their criteria of suitability for office, and lower the standards which they usually apply to candidates. In a situation of shortage the selectors face the choice of recruiting a full complement by lowering standards, or of engaging in extensive recruitment activity.

The fact that the supply of candidates has implications for the role which the recruiting and selecting structures assume, means that this aspect cannot be ignored, but I am more concerned with the structural side, and so although there will be brief references to the supply side (in so far as it has a direct bearing on the role which the structures assume), this aspect will not be fully discussed. I will point to those structures which have the responsibility of finding suitable candidates for the positions on the council which I am considering, and I shall identify the criteria which they use to guide their activity and choice. In particular I am interested in identifying the 'basic' attributes which the selectors consider recruits should have in order to be considered as potential office-holders, but in addition I will also note some of the additional 'peripheral', or 'optional' (Nadel, 1957), attributes which the selectors like position-incumbents to possess, but which they do not regard as so critical in affecting candidate suitability.[1] It is these attributes which the selectors look for in potential position-incumbents that I call the 'recruitment rules' (Valen, 1966; Morris-Jones, 1969, 1971; and, Etzioni, 1961, esp. pp. 153–7).

The Councillor
The right to stand for council is not seriously limited. A person wishing to become a councillor must be a British subject, be of full-age, and possess a 'positive qualification serving to identify ... [him] with the area in question' (Hart, 1968, p. 100), which means that he must either own property in the area, be registered as a voter in the area, or have had a year's residence in the area in the twelve months preceding the selection.[2] By these criteria, many people could run for council, and the legal disqualifications are not restrictive. In practice, however, any discussion of the recruitment and selection of councillors for urban local authorities demands a consideration of the role of the political parties, since they dominate the pre-selection of candidates for the local elections (Committee on the Management of Local Government, 1967, vol. 2).

In Kensington and Chelsea the main electoral contest is between Conservative and Labour candidates. The Liberals also present a fairly full slate of candidates, and a number of Communists usually stand, but no candidate from these parties has ever been elected to the council. The constituents select candidates by their votes, but in practice the parties severely filter the supply of candidates. Moreover, in Kensington and Chelsea, Conservative pre-selection is most important since in all the wards of South Kensington and in all but one of the wards in Chelsea adoption and selection by the local Conservative associations automatically means

1. Seligman (1961) makes the point that there are two stages in the process of recruitment: 'certification', or the screening of people for eligibility for candidacy; and 'selection', of the actual choice of candidates.
2. The property qualification was abolished by s.15, Representation of the People Act, 1969. For a full catalogue of the qualifications and disqualifications, see Local Government Act, 1933. For a summary, see Hart, 1968, pp. 102–5.

that the candidates will become councillors. These wards provide thirty-nine of the sixty councillors. In Kensington and Chelsea, not only are the majority of councillors (and aldermen)[3] Conservative, but also all the leadership positions within the council are filled by Conservatives. In this discussion, therefore, I will only consider the recruitment and selection of Conservative councillors, and I will not deal with the recruitment and selection of other party candidates.

The recruitment and selection of Conservative candidates takes place at intervals, and the three local Conservative associations do not have to find sixty candidates every three years, but only candidates for those wards which they do not hold, and for those wards where a sitting Conservative councillor chooses to retire, and at any one time most sitting councillors seek re-election and it is extremely rare for a sitting councillor to be asked to stand down. In the case of the first council of the Royal Borough (elected in 1964 but not coming into official service till 1965), of the fifty-three Conservative councillors and aldermen only nine were in fact serving for the first time and had no experience on either the council of Kensington or of Chelsea. Indeed, the creation of the new London borough involved a reduction in the number of councillors from ninety-six to sixty[4] and so in some cases there was an over-supply of sitting candidates who wished to continue on the new borough. The rule of 'last on – first off' was used to eliminate the surplus. In 1968, retirements meant that fourteen new candidates were required to fill positions on the council, and, in addition, the fact that the Conservatives won three wards from Labour meant that there were a total of twenty-six new Conservative councillors, which as I will suggest in the last section of this chapter, posed a particular problem of control for the more senior councillors. In 1971 there were only nine new Conservative councillors elected to the council.

Candidate selection is organised differently in each of the three constituencies that make up the borough. In both South Kensington and North Kensington, selection is centrally organised by the local Conservative associations, whereas in Chelsea the process is centred more in the hands of the wards and the ward committees. In fact the role which the recruiting and selecting structures assume in each of the constituencies varies, and depends on the supply of candidates, and on the rigour with which the selectors seek to apply demanding standards when screening potential councillors.

Not surprisingly the supply of people offering themselves to the Conservative party for consideration as local councillors has been affected by

3. There are 60 councillors in the Royal Borough and 10 aldermen. Aldermanic seats are divided between the two parties represented on the council on a basis proportional to their councillor strength. In the 1964 aldermanic elections, 8 Conservative, and 2 Labour aldermen were elected.
4. There were 60 councillors in Kensington and 36 councillors in Chelsea.

the extent to which particular wards are safe for the party, and in North Kensington (where there are really no wards which are safe for Conservative candidates) the local association has had great difficulty in finding adequate numbers of candidates. This shortage has meant that sitting councillors and the Selection Committee of the local association have had to recruit people to stand.[5] Two councillors from North Kensington, first elected in 1968: 'I'd been a member [of the Conservative party] for about six months and was then approached as to whether I'd stand for [names ward]. I said O.K., as long as I wouldn't win, but of course I did.' 'I was asked to stand, begged in fact, in January [1968] and at the time I never thought I'd win, although by February I realised there was a chance. . . . I never went through any selection procedure or questioning.' In this situation, it has been difficult for the selectors to demand that all their candidates have all the attributes which they consider ideally fit a person for the office of councillor. Two members of the association involved in the selection process: 'Most of our councillors don't live in North Kensington, and few have local interests except on the council. . . . The difficulty is finding good councillors.' 'If one is to be a satisfactory councillor then I feel you must live and belong in the area you're elected from. It's a problem that some of the Conservative councillors don't live in their ward, but what can you do? You have to get someone to stand, and you're restricted to party members.' In this situation of shortage, where even active recruitment fails to draw in candidates with the required attributes (and on occasions the North Kensington selectors have approached people active in local organisations who are *not* Conservatives to request them to stand in the name of the party), then it is not possible for the selectors to be as selective as they might wish. The 'less suitable' candidates will stand in the wards that are usually held by Labour, but on occasions these wards are won by Conservatives – as in the 1968 elections – and so people are drawn into the council (usually for only a three year term) who may have little desire to be a councillor and who are likely to fit-in rather badly with the majority group. Two North Kensington councillors first elected in 1968: 'I regard myself as a leaseholder rather than a freeholder. I have no political ambition, and to tell the truth I really had very little desire to be a councillor.' 'So far (and as you know I've only been on a short while) I don't really feel that I belong. I feel left out of things, and I don't seem to have much in common with the senior councillors who all seem rather old and stuffy.'

One 'safe' way round this problem of a shortage of candidates has been for the North Kensington Conservative Association to 'import a lot of candidates from South Kensington'. A senior South Kensington councillor:

5. Committee on the Management of Local Government, 1967, vol. 2 (Table 2.10, p. 64) makes the point that in the Metropolitan Boroughs, 83 % of councillors said that they were asked to stand, and in the majority of cases they were asked by a political party.

'We used to have a tradition, and still do to a certain extent, whereby young South Kensington people earn their spurs in North Kensington. This is good because it sorts out those people who are keen and have staying power.' This practice is not popular with many of those responsible for selecting Conservative candidates for North Kensington, but they recognise that in a situation of shortage they have little choice.

The problem of the supply of potential Conservative candidates is not restricted to the wards in North Kensington since it is also a problem – albeit of a lesser and different kind – in other parts of the borough where the seats are safe for Conservative candidates. Understandably, party leaders were reluctant to talk about the problems which they faced in attracting an adequate supply of persons willing to stand as candidates, but there is little doubt that although there is a surfeit of candidates in both South Kensington and Chelsea, it has been rather more difficult to attract suitable candidates in South Kensington, partly because the selectors have been rather more demanding as to the attributes which they expect their candidates to possess. A senior Chelsea chairman: 'At the Joint Committee[6] I remember Kensington saying that they had recruitment problems, but this isn't a problem in Chelsea where we have a waiting list and really do have to choose.' In South Kensington, then, there is a certain amount of activity in actually recruiting people to stand for the council. A South Kensington councillor first elected in 1968: 'I was asked to stand. It's not easy to get people to stand and it's bloody hard work. In fact even if I hadn't been asked I would probably have offered myself as I was told that I was just what they were looking for.' An alderman recalled the process of his selection in 1949: 'The [South Kensington Conservative] Association was very run-down after the war. I joined, and I think after my first ward meeting I found myself as treasurer. A few old boys had managed to keep the thing going through the war and they wanted someone else to have a go. After a little while someone said, "Have you thought of being a councillor?", and I said "No", and they said, "Would you consider putting your name forward?", and I was elected in 1949 – there was a big turnover then."' In Chelsea, on the other hand, the active recruitment of Conservative candidates is regarded with disfavour, but the agent considered that if they were to recruit then it would be possible to boost the number of candidates 'four or five fold'.

In South Kensington and Chelsea, the selectors have to reject half of those who are available to serve as councillors as there are not enough council seats for all those who have volunteered, or have been recruited to stand. The existence of this surfeit of candidates reveals the need for choice, and the existence of active recruitment by the South Kensington selectors reveals the need for the recruiting structures to have criteria by

6. The Joint Committee refers to the meetings that occurred between senior members of the Metropolitan Boroughs of Kensington, and Chelsea, prior to the official merger and creation of the new London Borough in 1965.

E

which they decide to approach some potential candidates rather than others. In other words, the choice involved in recruiting and selecting candidates for the council suggests the need for what I have called recruitment rules.

In normal times, the bulk of the Conservative councillors come from South Kensington and Chelsea.[7] Moreover, precisely because of the electoral uncertainty in North Kensington, Conservative councillors from these wards cannot be assured of a period of continued council service. In this situation it is difficult for the council leaders to make plans which involve the grooming of these councillors for positions of leadership, and in the period 1965–70, no councillor from North Kensington was a chairman of a standing committee. If plans are made for the promotion of North Kensington councillors then these can be upset by electoral reversals. For example, in 1970 two North Kensington councillors were promoted from vice-chairmanships to chairmanships on two of the more minor committees, but their period of office was cut short as a result of their losing the 1971 elections.[8] The fact that the North Kensington Conservative councillors are usually a small or non-existent group on the council, are rarely in positions of leadership, and are in practice a *self*-selected group, means that I will not be considering their selection in this section; indeed, there are really no recruitment rules to consider. I shall concentrate on the structures and processes in South Kensington and Chelsea, noting the attributes which are seen as fitting a person for the office of councillor.

First, I shall consider South Kensington, the constituency which provides twenty-three safe Conservative seats on the council.[9] The rules of the South Kensington Conservative Association provide that: 'A Standing Committee for the purpose of selecting and recommending to the Executive Council suitable candidates for election to the Borough Council shall consist of the Officers of the Association, the Branch Chairmen, one other representative of the Young Conservative Organisation, the Leader and Chief Whip of the Conservative Party on the Borough Council, if members.

7. In 1964 there were 6 Conservative councillors from North Kensington; in 1968, there were 16, and in 1971 there were none.
8. Cllr Mrs Coleridge was made chairman of the Childrens Committee, and Cllr Miss Weatherhead was made chairman of the Libraries Committee. Cllr Michael Cocks was made chief whip in 1968. All these councillors were first elected to the council in 1964.
9. Prior to the merger there were five wards in South Kensington for the local elections; Queens Gate, Redcliffe, Earls Court, Holland, and Brompton. The position of the Brompton ward was rather strange, however, for although it was part of Kensington for the purpose of local government, in parliamentary elections it was part of the Chelsea constituency. With the merger of the two boroughs the selection of candidates for this ward was organised by the Chelsea Conservative Association, but even so in the 1964 and 1968 elections, two of the four Brompton representatives had served on the old Kensington council.

... The Chairman of the Association shall be Chairman, and the Committee shall meet from time to time to interview and select suitable applicants.' There are six Officers (President, Chairman, Deputy Chairman, two Vice-Chairmen, and the Honorary Treasurer), and six Branch Chairmen (there are two branches in Redcliffe and Earls Court wards, and one branch in Holland and Queens Gate wards), and so with the other three representatives the Committee consists of fifteen members. On the surface only two of the fifteen members of the Selection Committee are also on the Borough Council, but in fact the overlap between formal office-holding in the South Kensington Conservative Association and membership of the Borough Council is such that usually just over half the Committee will be senior councillors of the Royal Borough.

The process of councillor selection starts with the drawing up of a list of potential candidates which will then be considered by the Committee. The agent and the chairman will meet to discuss the likely number of vacancies that can be expected at the next election, and then a list will gradually be drawn up. The Agent: 'It's a bit mixed up how they get onto the list in the first place. Earlier I will have warned all the Branch Chairmen, and the Chairman will have warned other people. . . . Also people will write to me once the word gets round that the Selection Committee is likely to be sitting and people will come forward. The leader [of the Council] could also well ask people to put their names forward.' There are no restrictions on who is eligible to put himself forward for selection, though self-selection will mean that only Conservatives will come forward, and even then individual selectors may advise a prospective candidate that he is unlikely to be selected, which could deter some potential candidates.

Nearer to the time of election, when there is a clearer idea of the number of councillor retirements, and, therefore, of the number of vacancies that need to be filled by new recruits, the Selection Committee will meet to interview each of the candidates on the list for about twenty minutes. Once the required number is selected (and a list of reserves drawn up for unforeseen by-elections) then the Chairman of the Association will decide where they are to stand: 'as far as possible it's in the wards where they live, and this is the criteria that's been adopted here as the opposition is always ready to make a song and dance over this. The Chairman doesn't really have to look to anything else except this, unless there are "rogues" – that is the vacancies in their own wards don't exist' and where this is the case then the Chairman and the Agent will meet to decide where the candidate should stand. The role of the Executive Council (an unwieldy body of over fifty members) is invariably limited to the ratification of the Selection Committee's choice.

What does the Selection Committee look for when deciding which prospective candidates to select for official council candidature for the Conservative Party? What are the criteria which guide their selecting and recruiting activity and which result in their eventually eliminating half of those on the list from a place on the council? In fact, one person intimately involved in the selection process argued: 'What you're trying to get me to say is that there is some rationale in all this and that there is some logical plan. But I am prepared to tell you, even though it's on tape, that there is nothing. . . . You're dealing with a bunch of amateurs where anything can guide their choice.' Notwithstanding this statement it is possible to suggest that there are certain basic attributes which need to be possessed by potential candidates if they are to be sure of selection and, in addition, there are a number of more optional attributes, which are in no sense as fundamental, but they may favour a candidate who possesses them over others who similarly conform to the basic rules. The statements cited below (all of which, unless otherwise stated, were made by selectors) represent the recruitment rules used to choose South Kensington Conservative candidates for the borough elections, which means in effect the rules to select the borough councillors. I start by identifying the more basic attributes, but as I move down the list so the attributes can be regarded as increasingly optional.

1. 'In this constituency it is part of the rules of the Association that every councillor shall automatically be a member of the ward committee [and] they wouldn't get a chance of being selected unless they were on the ward committee. Suppose someone came to me and said "I've moved into the area and I've been chairman of the so-and-so parish council", I would have to say to them "You wouldn't have a hope in hell if you'd been chairman of the Rutland County Council unless you serve on the ward committee".'[10]

2. 'You have to be known and on the ward committee, and the more people who know, and like you in the Association the better, as you're not going to have to sit an exam.'

3. 'First, you want someone who is genuinely interested in local government, and can say how long he is prepared to be doing it. You don't want someone using it as a stepping-stone to a higher career after three years,[11] as then they are just beginning to be of use to the council. We have to look to the chairmen and the vice-chairmen in a few years time. It is only after three years that anyone is of any use to the council, so we want to know if they are going to stick at it, and that means that we're interested to know if they are planning to go on living in the borough.'

There are, as one selector put it, no real 'statutory' questions which will

10. Bochel (1966, p. 364) notes, in the case of the selection of Labour candidates in Manchester, that 'undoubtedly, office-holding in the party is a considerable advantage, and may even be a necessity, for many of those seeking to be councillors.'
11. There was not unanimity on this point, as a minority of selectors took the view that it was desirable to select councillors who would become 'rising politicians' as it gave prestige to their council, and was a testament to the quality of their councillors.

be asked of prospective councillors, but there are, nevertheless, a number of 'stock' questions which feature in the interview.

4. 'Someone will always ask if you have attended meetings of the council, and if you say "No", someone will always say "If you haven't found time to attend in the past, how can you attend once every six weeks?" I personally resent people coming to the Selection Committee time and time again who have never been near a council chamber.'

5. Candidates are likely to be asked if they have been co-opted onto the council or have served on any other public body: 'If you have two people who've both been on the ward committee, then the sort of thing which will sway them [the Selection Committee] is whether they have any past connection with local government – been a school governor, attended a local government course, or something. If you have three people all quite good on the ward, then these other things can make you stand out. One chap got on who wasn't a particularly nice character, not really well-liked, but the feeling was his regular attendance of council meetings gave him a right to stand.'

6. Other questions seek to identify the interest and the knowledge of prospective councillors in local government: 'Someone on the Committee is likely to ask "Do you have a particular interest in local government, and if so what field?" and if someone says "Housing" then they will be sure to ask your views on this just to see if you're putting it on. The view you give will carry weight. One candidate got adopted, who I didn't think would in the face of better-known people, but it was because he knew about local government.'

7. A councillor first elected in 1968 stated: 'The first question I was asked, was asked by an old colonel, and it was, "What would you do to reform the council?" I said that as I hadn't been on the council, it was really too soon to form an opinion. Some of the young candidates fired-off with ideas, but they weren't selected.'

8. At the end of the interview the leader of the council will state: 'You realise that there's a party system in operation on the council and that the party group makes decisions, and that subject to conscience you will be expected to abide by the decision of the party?' Members of the Selection Committee 'have to know if the candidate will support the party on all issues which are not those of conscience.'

Earlier I mentioned that the forced retirement of sitting councillors was an infrequent occurrence, and although I know no case of this in either North Kensington or Chelsea, it has happened in South Kensington: 'The last time [the 1971 election] the Selection Committee had the names of all the councillors from South Kensington, and in effect they decided whether they were going to re-adopt or not. There was a terrific argument about four of them, which revolved more around their work in the ward than their work on the council, as the Branch Chairmen were asked if they were satisfied with their councillors. Anyway they decided to interview two of them and they rejected one. . . . Although this doesn't happen often, it was designed to show that no councillor has a right to a seat in perpetuity.' In fact this particular practice did not meet with the sympathy of all the Selection Committee, and 'The Chairman said he didn't really hold with this, and he said that if the Finance and General Purposes Committee didn't object he felt that they should all continue to serve if this is what they wanted.'

In Chelsea, the selection of Conservative candidates is not organised centrally by the Association, there is much less of a stress on recruitment, and sitting councillors are not involved in the process.

Candidates are adopted at ward meetings and although their choice has to be approved by the Executive Council of the Association, in recent years there has been no case of the Council failing to endorse ward nominees. In 1970, the rules of the Association were changed, and a list of candidates is now drawn up by the Finance and General Purposes Committee. Selection is still in the hands of the ward committees, however, and they are free to select from candidates on the list, or they can put forward 'their own particular favourite'. The final approval of the Executive Council is still needed.

Precisely because there is no one structure involved in selecting Conservative candidates for the local elections, it is much more difficult to provide a definitive statement of the attributes which are looked for by the many persons involved in the selection process. Indeed, although it was possible to provide *the* view of *the* selectors in the case of South Kensington it is much less likely to be the case that there is such a consensus in Chelsea. In spite of this, however, there is little doubt that in Chelsea they are not only looking for a councillor with rather different attributes from those which qualify a South Kensington applicant for office, but they are also (and not surprisingly in view of the process which they use to select and adopt candidates), rather more catholic in terms of whom they are prepared to admit would be a good and suitable councillor.

Understandably in view of the extent to which the selection process is centred at the ward level, there is the expectation that candidates should live in the ward which they represent, but there is little expectation that they should take an active part in the activities of the Chelsea Conservative Association. Indeed, although 'they must know what's going on, it's not good for them to be an officer [in the Association] and a councillor. There's a conflict of loyalties and a conflict of time required and one or the other should go. We prefer them not to be in the hands of the same person.' This is in marked contrast to the situation in South Kensington, where as I mentioned, there is a considerable overlap between membership of the council and activity at the officer level in the local Association. The reluctance in Chelsea to contemplate councillors holding other political positions extends also to activities which lie outside of the Association: 'In Chelsea, there is a clear feeling that people do not wish to have as their representative people who are going to be a representative on the GLC [Greater London Council] or anywhere else. It's O.K. if they are a candidate, but that's as far as it goes; they shouldn't run alongside each other, and if a councillor does stand for the GLC and is successful then he should give up his councillorship here.'

In South Kensington, I suggested that there was a concern to select active Conservatives, and the questions asked by the selectors sought to elicit their views on political issues and party discipline. A concern with these matters is much less evident in the selection of Chelsea candidates: 'I don't think the question of the whip concerns the wards to the extent that you would think. I think that they leave it to the councillor although always with the proviso that they should represent the ward and speak up.' 'I don't think the candidates' political principles enter into it at all. Nominally they are Conservatives, but we could accept an independent if he were particularly meritorious. . . . Throughout the Association as a whole some people would not be happy to see independents, but many would.' The fact that selection is not in the hands of the people closely associated with the council means that there is much less cognisance of the need to select councillors who will fit-in with the existing group on the council. Even so there is at least a recognition of the need to select candidates who will be prepared 'to do at least three terms' on the council and 'will carry the thing through', and there is a suspicion of 'professional politicians': 'We look for someone to represent Chelsea and not an aspiring M.P. or something like that.' 'We don't really like the thought of someone who has been standing as a councillor somewhere else coming to stand here. To us it savours of professionalism.' In South Kensington there was little indication in the questions asked of potential candidates that they would be expected to assume an active role in the ward, outside of the context of the political work of the ward committee, but in Chelsea there does seem to be more of a concern to select candidates who can be expected to undertake a certain amount of constituency work: 'He has to be a nice chap for he has to put up with an enormous amount of endless talk. He has to be prepared to climb six flights of stairs to see an old person who may just want to chat. He has to be a gentle sort of person and be able to talk to every sort of person and have the patience to listen to people. The ward expect them [their councillors] to get out and about, and so they are known, and this is reflected in the voting figures.'[12]

So far I have given no indication of the importance of a potential candidate's class in affecting his chances of selection, and I have omitted this because it

12. Certainly in the 1964 and 1968 elections the turnout was some 4% to 5% higher in Chelsea wards than in the South Kensington wards.

is not a factor of any importance since all those who offer themselves for candidacy are (or have been) in white-collar occupations or are married to people in that position, and so a certain class background can be taken for granted. Some selectors and councillors expressed the view that it would be desirable to have some working-class councillors within the majority group, but most considered that the group was a good cross-section, and those who recognised that this was not the case did not consider that it mattered. Two South Kensington councillors: 'We have a good cross-section of people here, solicitors, barristers, hoteliers, architects, women, councillors who have lived abroad, retired people and people of independent means who have lived in the borough and who have always been active here and in local societies.' 'The council isn't a cross-section of society in Kensington and Chelsea, but I don't think you'll get other people to do it. I don't think this matters anyway. It might if one was in a different, smaller society, but not here.'

Although I have just suggested that the occupational background of a potential candidate is not a factor of importance affecting his chances of selection, the fact that many of the senior councillors see local government as essentially a manager of certain services, and above all as a spender of ratepayer's money, means that there is a certain preference for people with a professional or financial background. This preference is in fact reflected in the composition of the council, for if we look at the composition of the Conservative group in the council for the period 1968–71,[13] we find that there are eleven barristers or solicitors, and sixteen councillors who are either accountants, Members of Lloyds, Members of the Stock Exchange or in insurance or banking, as well as six who are company directors and at least ten who are in some administrative occupation in business. One chairman much involved in the selection of councillors pointed out: 'What we need is a mixture: rising young politicians from the Young Conservatives; people with local interests like Brew [director of a large local garage, "Brew Brothers"] – and there are not enough of these; people in commerce and the professions, like stockbrokers; people who can give time in the day, women and retired people. .... You want a cross-section of the borough, but you aim for the better people. You want people with connections outside the borough who can help it. People of importance; a few prestigious persons who can link into other groups and so on. .... Yes, you are right we don't tend to have working-class people, and of course we only have Conservatives. I can't think of one Conservative councillor who is what you would call working class.'

13. This information on the occupations of councillors and aldermen is taken from the 'descriptions' which they offered of themselves to the Returning Officer at the 1968 elections. Although ideally information on the social, educational, and economic characteristics of the councillors should have been gained by interview, I considered that questions of this kind could well antagonise respondents and so result in the loss of other information, and interview contacts.

The Chairman

All local authorities may appoint such committees as they think fit, although in certain cases the appointment of a particular committee is obligatory. Local authorities are left free to determine the composition of the committees they appoint, and (with the exception of the Finance Committee) they are able to include persons not members of the council provided that their number does not exceed a maximum of one-third of total membership. Despite the importance of committees in the working of a local authority, there is only a limited legal specification of their formal structure and powers, and there is no reference in law to the position of chairman or vice-chairman.

The Standing Orders of the Royal Borough provide that: 'At the first meeting of a newly appointed Committee and at the first meeting of a Committee after the Annual Meeting of the Council, the first business shall be to appoint a Chairman and Vice-Chairman for the ensuing year. . . . The Mayor or Deputy Mayor shall preside during the appointment of Committee Chairman. If neither the Mayor nor Deputy Mayor is present, the election of Chairman shall be conducted by the Town Clerk.' In addition to prescribing the method of appointment, Standing Orders also impose certain limitations on chairmen and vice-chairmen: 'No member shall hold the office of Chairman or Vice-Chairman of any Standing Committee for more than two years in succession. No member shall be Chairman of more than one Standing Committee at the same time. A member who has served for two years as Chairman of a Standing Committee shall not be eligible for election to the office of Chairman or Vice-Chairman of the same Committee until after the expiration of one year. In the case of an appointment to fill a casual vacancy the period of two years in the Standing Order shall commence to operate from the next annual appointment of Committees.'

In fact the Standing Orders provide neither a full, nor accurate picture of the appointment and tenure of chairmen and vice-chairmen. Chairmen and vice-chairmen are not elected by the committee (they are appointed by the leader); incumbents of those positions need to possess attributes which are not outlined in Standing Orders; and the two year rule has been broken on a number of occasions.

A chairman pointed to the manner in which the chairmen are selected: 'The chairmen are elected by the committee, but in fact they have little choice. It's laid down by the party on the advice of the leader. I suppose the committee could refuse to ratify, but there would be an infernal row if this did happen, but it would just not happen in a well-run party group. I've never known it happen in my twenty or so years of public service.' Although the leader appoints the chairmen he does not have complete freedom of choice in this for there are a number of 'traditions' which he has to follow if his appointments are to be acceptable. Indeed if the leadership of the party changes (as happened in 1968) then 'it is understood that when he

TABLE 3. *Chairmen and Vice-Chairmen of the Standing Committees of the Royal Borough of Kensington and Chelsea, 1965–71*

Committee	Chairman and Vice-Chairman	1965–6	1966–7	1967–8	1968–9	1969–70	1970–1
Public Amenities	C	Fisher	Hulme	Fisher	Gumbel	Gumbel	Piper
	V.C.	Townend	Gumbel	Gumbel	Piper	Piper	Hopkins
Libraries	C	Thackway	Thackway	Thackway	Yeoman	Yeoman	Weatherhead
	V.C.	Yeoman	Yeoman	Yeoman	Weatherhead	Weatherhead	Mendl
Childrens	C	Mrs Walford	Mrs Walford	Mrs Walford	Carver	Carver	Coleridge
	V.C.	Carver	Carver	Carver	Coleridge	Coleridge	Taylor
Welfare	C	Piper	Piper	Piper	Hulme	Hulme	Kenny
	V.C.	Hulme	Hulme	Hulme	Kenny	Kenny	Albert
Social Services*	C						Piper
	V.C.						Sundius-Smith
Finance	C	Crofton	Crofton	Crofton			
	V.C.	Anslow-Wilson	Sandon	Sandon			
General Purposes	C	Villiers	Villiers	Villiers			
	V.C.	Orme	Orme	Orme			
Finance and General Purposes†	C				Orme	Orme	Collenette
	V.C.				Collenette	Collenette	Craig-Cooper
Co-ordinating and Policy†	C				Crofton	Crofton	Crofton
	V.C.				Thackway	Cocks	Cocks
Establishments	C	Marshall	Marshall	Marshall	Gullick	Gullick	Stevenson
	V.C.	Stockwell	Stockwell	Stockwell	Stevenson	Stevenson	Gresty
Health	C	Petrie	Petrie	Petrie	Brooks	Brooks	Christmas
	V.C.	Brooks	Brooks	Christmas	Christmas	Weatherhead	Sundius-Smith
Housing	C	Baldwin	Baldwin	Baldwin	Roberts	Roberts	Muller
	V.C.	Roberts	Roberts	Roberts	Thom	Thom	Cocks
Town Planning	C	Paul	Paul	Paul	Paul	Baldwin	Baldwin
	V.C.	Thom	Thom	Thom	Baldwin	Mendl	Campion
Works	C	Brew	Brew	Brew	Brew	Corbet-Singleton	Corbet-Singleton
	V.C.	Corbet-Singleton	Corbet Singleton	Corbet-Singleton	Corbet-Singleton	Walford	Walford
Voluntary Services Liaison	C				Mrs Walford	Mrs Walford	Mrs Walford
	V.C.				Kenny	Kenny	Tomlin

* Created in December 1970 by merging the Childrens and Welfare Committees.

† The Co-ordinating and Policy Committee took over the major responsibilities of the Finance Committee, and remaining functions were

starts he inherits the chairmen', and has no choice as to who shall assume those positions.

Morris-Jones makes the point that 'some political roles are filled from among those who already fill other lesser political roles so that one selection follows "on top" of another. . . . In these cases the choice for selection at the higher level is limited by what has come through to the level immediately below' (Morris-Jones, 1969, p. 115). This is the case with the selection of people for the positions of both chairmen and vice-chairmen. A chairman: 'Some people are groomed for chairmanships, it's like a tree, and some people are put onto a committee and watched with a view to their becoming vice-chairman after a couple of years and chairman after another couple.' What, then are the positions that a chairman will occupy before he becomes a chairman?

First, all chairmen and vice-chairmen are selected from the ranks of sitting councillors, and not from persons who might have been co-opted onto the committees (in fact very little use is made of co-option as it is regarded with extreme disfavour by the more senior and influential councillors). Second, all the chairmen and the vice-chairmen come from the majority group on the council. Third, before a Conservative councillor is appointed to a chairmanship, he has to pass through an apprenticeship as a vice-chairman of the committee: chairmanships follow 'on-top' of vice-chairmanships. Fourth, certain committees (such as Housing, Town Planning, and Works) are regarded as particularly important and have an especially high status in the eyes of majority group councillors, and this being the case it is considered desirable that before a councillor becomes even a vice-chairman of one of these committees he should have passed through both a vice-chairmanship *and* a chairmanship of one of the more minor committees. For example, the first chairman of the Housing Committee on the combined Borough of Kensington and Chelsea had been chairman and vice-chairman of the Housing and Town Planning Committee on the Kensington Council, and before that he had been chairman and vice-chairman of the Public Health Committee. The second chairman of the Housing Committee had been vice-chairman of that committee for four years, and before that she had been chairman and vice-chairman of the Libraries Committee on the Kensington Council as well as a party whip.

Let us see how far committee chairmanships follow on-top of committee vice-chairmanships. The creation of the new London Borough of Kensington and Chelsea increased the range of functions which the borough authorities enjoyed and new committees had to be created which did not have counterparts on the previous Metropolitan Borough Councils and so in these cases it was not possible to follow any apprenticeship rule. In fact in the case of both the Childrens, and the Welfare Committees, the chairmenships were given to councillors who had previously been chairmen of other committees. For those committees which did exist on the old councils of Kensington, and Chelsea, however, we find that in almost every case either the vice-chairman became a chairman of the committee (as in the case of Finance, and Works, Committees) or the chairmen stayed on (as in the case of Health, and Housing, Committees). On the first council of the new combined borough, no chairman (with the exception of the chairman of the Finance Committee) had less than six years service on the council of either Kensington or Chelsea, and the average length of past service was thirteen years. The picture is much the same in the case of the chairmen appointed in 1968: the apprenticeship rule was followed, or else the existing chairmen stayed on.[14] The average length of past service was again over thirteen years. In the changeover of chairmanships in 1970, we find that in all but two cases[15] the chairmen either stayed on, or else the apprenticeship rule was followed. The average length of past service was over thirteen years.

Since it is really automatic that the vice-chairmen go on to become chairmen, it is important to specify the recruitment rules which are used to fill committee vice-chairmanships.

The chairmen and the vice-chairmen are expected to 'know the facts', and have an 'adequate technical background', so that they (and this really applies to the chairmen) can 'guide the committee' and be 'able to answer questions about the work of the committee on the spot'. Of course, it is difficult to devise any precise measure of a councillor's knowledge, and in Kensington and Chelsea, as in many other places, 'length of service' or past 'experience' on the council are used as guides. Knowledge and experience are said to go together, chairmen 'have the experience, otherwise they wouldn't be chairmen; they have the expert knowledge', and any chairman will be expected 'to know his stuff, because he's experienced'. A chairman pointed out that, 'people are chosen after long experience in politics, and unless you've been on the council at least two terms then you haven't a hope of becoming a vice-chairman. I think this is right as you get experienced chairmen and the role demands experience', and another chairman noted how, 'it's necessary for the chairmen to have a background of service on the council and especially on the appropriate committee.'

14. The chairmen of Works, and Town Planning, Committees, stayed on. There were three new committees; the Co-ordinating and Policy Committee represented an enlargement of the Finance Committee, and the Finance and General Purposes Committee represented an extension of the responsibilities of the General Purposes Committee (in both cases the apprenticeship rule was followed); the Voluntary Services Liaison Committee (first called the Social Services Liaison Committee) was entirely new, but was chaired by a councillor elected in 1937. The apprenticeship rule was not broken with the appointment of Alderman Mrs Gullick to the chairmanship of the Establishments Committee, as prior to her marriage she was Alderman Miss Stockwell.
15. In the case of the Housing Committee: Cllr Thom was made Mayor and was, therefore, unable to become chairman: Cllr Muller had been chairman of that committee on the Kensington council. In the case of the Health Committee, Cllr Miss Weatherhead was unable to become chairman as she was made chairman of the Libraries Committee: a past vice-chairman was made chairman of the committee

In fact if we look at the length of service of the vice-chairmen, we do indeed find that they do have a background of service on the council, for the vice-chairmen on the first council had an average of nine years past service, and those appointed in 1968 had a slightly longer period of past service.

One further point needs to be made with respect to the attributes that are seen as qualifying a person for a chairmanship or a vice-chairmanship of a committee on the Royal Borough, since there is sometimes a distinction made between those persons who are suitable for the 'political' committees and those who are suitable for what are regarded as the 'non-political' committees: 'There are two sorts of committees, the political ones – Housing, Town Planning, and Works in a way; and the non-political ones, Health, and Welfare, Childrens and Libraries – though Health and Libraries can sometimes be a bit political. ... Now take Miss Roberts, she's a very good chairman of a political committee, expert, well-briefed, and good at putting her point of view. The chairman of a non-political committee doesn't have to have quite this emphasis on the political side of things – Mrs Walford is a case in point whose interests are not quite so party political.' As I mentioned earlier, it is often the case that a councillor moves into positions of authority on a political committee after he, or she, has been through similar positions in the non-political committees, but, in addition, there are councillors whose chairmanships are restricted to the non-political committees.

The recruitment rule for the selection of committee chairmen which requires an initial apprenticeship as vice-chairman, represents a continuation of the practice of both the previous local authorities which combined to form the Royal Borough of Kensington and Chelsea.[16] However, limiting the length of time which any councillor can hold a chairmanship to two years (as it is written into Standing Orders) represents a continuation of the practice of the Kensington council. A chairman from Kensington: 'In Kensington there's been a tradition of two year terms for chairmen, whereas in Chelsea they went in for four years. The Standing Orders of Kensington and Chelsea now have two years written in, and there's a very good reason for this as it is just possible that one might be stuck with a not so good chairman and it would be invidious to have to give someone the sack – it's just not done. In two years someone can make a contribution, but if someone is less suitable then there is less danger of him being there over-long. Also if someone is there too long he might well become too much of an expert vis-a-vis the ordinary elected member.' Not surprisingly in view of the fact that the tradition of Kensington was followed, there was not total agreement as to the suitability of the two year rule. A Chelsea

16. In fact, in both Kensington, and Chelsea, we find that the apprenticeship rule was usually followed in the appointment of chairmen, but in Kensington there were far fewer deviations from the pattern.

chairman: 'The length of committee chairmanship is now two years, and that is too short. Four years as we had in Chelsea was too long and it frustrated the young chaps to be held back, but two years is too short because you can't find out enough in that time.'

How far has the two year retirement rule been followed? In fact all the chairmen on the first council served three years, and two served a period of four years. Breaking the rule in this way was justified because in the first place the local elections (which were originally scheduled to take place in 1967) were delayed by the central government till 1968, so interfering with the council's planned cycle of office-holding; and in the case of the two chairmen who went on beyond the 1968 elections this was justified either because their vice-chairmen were unable to devote enough time to their council responsibilities to become chairmen, or because the committee was engaged in a piece of work where continuity of leadership was considered to be of prime importance. In 1970 the two year retirement rule was followed in the case of all but two of the standing committees,[17] and in 1971 the two committees whose original chairmen did not retire till 1969 had their chairmen replaced, this time in accord with the requirements of standing orders.

At the start of this section on the recruitment rules, I mentioned that a full consideration of the recruitment process demanded that we take cognisance of the factors affecting the supply of potential candidates for any particular office. When we consider the position of chairman, there is a restriction on the supply of candidates, as some councillors, who are keen to become chairmen and who satisfy the recruitment rules, are unable to do so as they have to answer the question 'Can I do it?' negatively, because the time demands of that position mean that they cannot combine it with the necessity of earning their living. A comparatively senior Chelsea councillor: 'On Housing, Works and Planning, it's pretty much a full-time job. I could never contemplate doing that, interesting though it might be.' This restriction in the supply of councillors available to become chairmen means that it is difficult to avoid a situation where the chairmen will be drawn disproportionately from the ranks of the retired members of the council; from those councillors who own their own businesses, are senior in their profession, or else are in occupations where they can get time off work; and from those councillors who happen to be married women are not themselves engaged in full-time work. In other words, the recruitment rules which tend to exclude the younger councillor from chairmanships are reinforced by factors which make it difficult for persons at the start of their careers to be available to become chairmen, and more easy for senior and retired people to assume those responsibilities.

17. The leader of the council continued to serve as chairman of the Co-ordinating and Policy Committee, and Alderman Mrs Walford continued to serve as chairman of the Voluntary Services Liaison Committee.

The Leader

The Leader of the council is elected by the councillors of the majority party on the council. There have been two leaders of the council. Alderman Anslow-Wilson was elected after a tight contest in 1964, and following his retirement in 1968, Councillor Sir Malby Crofton was elected to the leadership.

The first councillors of the Royal Borough of Kensington and Chelsea were elected in May 1964, and at the first meeting of the council the chairman of the council[18] and the aldermen were elected. The party balance after these elections was fifty-three Conservatives and seventeen Labour representatives. The leader of the Kensington Borough Council and the leader of the Chelsea Borough Council were both Conservative aldermen on the new borough, and both put themselves forward as prospective leaders. Of the Conservative councillors and aldermen, sixteen had their roots in Chelsea, and thirty-seven had their roots in Kensington.[19] The leader of the new council was to be elected at a party meeting in May 1964, and if all Conservative councillors and aldermen attended, and if all were loyal to the leader of their own old borough, then the Kensington leader, Alderman Anslow-Wilson would have been elected with a clear majority. In fact this was not the case, for the Chelsea leader, Alderman Sims was elected. Within a month, however, he had resigned the position, and at another party meeting Alderman Anslow-Wilson was elected: Alderman Sims was made vice-chairman of the interim council, and was elected first mayor of the new borough in 1965.

The initial election of Sims is explained by the rather 'loose alliance between Chelsea and North Kensington Conservatives', by the absence of a number of South Kensington Conservatives from the initial party meeting, and by the undeniable fact that at least a couple of South Kensington councillors actually supported the Chelsea leader. Alderman Sims was aware that it would be difficult for him to operate as a leader in a situation where it was likely that over fifty per cent were opposed to him, and so he resigned, and called another meeting, where 'four line whips' ensured the election of Alderman Anslow-Wilson.

At the party meeting on Monday, 29 January 1968, Alderman Anslow-Wilson announced that he would be retiring from the council in May of that year, when the next council would be elected. There was uncertainty among the Conservative councillors as to the procedure which they should adopt to select their new leader (a whip pointed out that 'there were no rules of selection'), but it appears that at the January

18. There was no Mayor of the Royal Borough of Kensington and Chelsea until the two Metropolitan Boroughs of Kensington, and Chelsea, ceased to exist in 1965.
19. In footnote 9, I referred to the rather strange situation of Brompton. In my assessment of the allegiances of councillors, I considered two Brompton councillors as attached to Chelsea, and two as attached to Kensington.

meeting the retiring leader 'asked for nominations . . . and he said that they should be nominated by two councillors and be prepared to stand'. If more than one candidate was put forward then the new leader was to be chosen by a secret ballot among all the Conservative councillors and aldermen on the council.

Two councillors were nominated for the position; Councillor John Baldwin and Councillor Sir Malby Crofton, both of whom represented South Kensington wards. The existing leader asked one of the candidates to stand down, and when this failed there was an attempt to find a compromise candidate, but this too failed, and so a vote was taken at the party meeting on 18 March. The result of the vote was a dead-heat. On the next day, before the council meeting, there was another ballot, and Councillor Sir Malby Crofton was elected leader of the council. It is unlikely that any councillor or alderman from Chelsea voted for Baldwin, and although the losing candidate anticipated solid South Kensington support it is apparent that he did not get this.

Following his election, the new leader made Alderman Thackway, a senior figure in the party, a past leader of the Kensington council and a Baldwin supporter, deputy leader; and Councillor Baldwin was made vice-chairman of the important Planning Committee and was, therefore, guaranteed the chairmanship of that committee in two years time.

Where there are a large number of people involved in the selection process, and where the selectors are a group lacking in much homogeneity, then there is a greater likelihood that there will be conflict around the attributes that are seen as properly fitting a person for a particular position than is the case if there are a small number of selectors who have much in common. Moreover, in the sort of situation where there is a large selecting structure the probable lack of clarity in the recruitment rules means that people who might wish to assume incumbency of a particular position can feel that they have a chance and so may be prepared to stand for the office. If there is only one position which needs filling, then there will be a contest if only two people put themselves forward. The leadership position is a position around which there was almost certain to be conflict as to the suitable candidate.

In the case of the contest for the first leader, the fact that both the leaders of the Kensington, and the Chelsea, councils were elected onto the council of the combined borough meant that there were two 'natural' candidates, and at the same time, Conservative councillors who made up the new borough lacked any strong sense of identity with each other. Chelsea had never wanted to join Kensington to form a London Borough, and Conservative councillors from North Kensington had always been disillusioned about the way they were isolated from key positions on the old Kensington council which was totally dominated by councillors from South

Kensington. In other words, the contest can be interpreted as a simple clash of group loyalties and frustrations where there was a virtual absence of any cool assessment of the qualities of the candidates and consideration of what attributes should ideally be possessed by a leader.

The second contest is more interesting, as there were not two natural leaders, and at the same time, the fact that the new borough had been established for three years could lead us to expect that old loyalties were of less importance. Although it would be difficult to interpret the first contest as a clash of different recruitment rules, it is sensible to interpret the second contest in this light, for the two candidates had a different background of council and political service which was not apparent with respect to the first two candidates.

All the leaders in Kensington since the war had been long-serving councillors with a background of chairmanships behind them, and although this was less the case in Chelsea,[20] both the contestants for the first leadership of the new borough were experienced long-serving councillors:

THE LEADER OF THE COUNCIL: THE 'EXPERIENCE' OF THE FIRST CONTESTANTS

Alderman E. Anslow-Wilson

First elected to the Kensington Borough Council in 1949
1953–4:   Vice-chairman, Civil Defence Committee
1954–6:   Chairman, Civil Defence Committee
1957–60: Vice-chairman, Civil Defence Committee
1958–9:   Vice-chairman, Works Committee
1959–61: Chairman, Works Committee
1962–3:   Vice-chairman, Public Health Committee
1962–5:   Leader of the council

Alderman A. J. Sims

First elected to the Chelsea Borough Council in 1949
1953–4:   Vice-chairman of Works and Highways Committee
1954–5:   Vice-chairman, Housing Committee
1957–61: Vice-chairman, Finance Committee
1961–5:   Chairman, Finance Committee
1955–6:   Mayor
1959–65: Leader of the council

This was not the situation with respect to the second leadership contest, where there was – as one councillor put it – 'the problem of whether to choose someone who'd been on the council a long time, or someone who'd be keen on new ideas.'

20. The four leaders of the Kensington council since the war had an average of eleven years past service on the council, and in Chelsea, the six leaders of the council had an average of six years past service.

THE LEADER OF THE COUNCIL: THE 'EXPERIENCE' OF THE SECOND
CONTESTANTS

Councillor Sir Malby Crofton

First elected to the Kensington Borough Council in 1962
1964–5: Vice-chairman, Finance Committee
1965–8: Chairman, Finance Committee

Councillor J. E. Baldwin

First elected to the Kensington Borough Council in 1953
1957–9: Vice-chairman, Public Health Committee
1959–61: Chairman, Public Health Committee
1961–3: Vice-chairman, Housing and Town Planning Committee
1963–5: Chairman, Housing and Town Planning Committee
1965–8: Chairman, Housing Committee

A chairman pointed out: 'By all the usual signs Baldwin should have had it: he had length of service, whereas Crofton was only a new boy, and this was the primary one. He was well-known to all the councillors and had been chairman of one or two major committees: he certainly shone there, whereas Malby Crofton had only held a Finance vice-chairmanship or something. Also, to a certain extent, the fact that he was chairman of the local [Conservative] association was important, whereas Malby Crofton held no post there at all.' In other words the established and traditional recruitment rules for the leader of the council clearly recognised that a councillor should only become leader on 'top-of', or after, he had moved up through the committee structure; from vice-chairman to chairman, from minor to major committee, and the fact that some chairmen considered also that the chief whip is the 'natural successor', meant that they also took the view that the position of leader should be filled on top of experience within the party hierarchy as well. The leadership position is the pinnacle of the council leadership, and it was seen as fitting that the position should be filled by someone of considerable council background whose attachment to Conservative principles could be assured because of his activity within the local Conservative association. The election of Councillor Sir Malby Crofton represented an innovation, and a break in the established recruitment rules.

With the advantage of hindsight and many interviews, political scientists may be able to give an order to events which was lacking to those involved. In the way I have outlined the leadership contest in 1968 I have perhaps created the impression that the contest was between progressive Conservatives who wanted change and innovation in council policy, and the more traditional Conservatives who were concerned to maintain the existing pattern of public policy and so voted for the 'Old Guard' candidate, John

Baldwin. Such a picture would be mistaken, however, for the reality of the contest was the uncertainty and ambiguity which surrounded it. Many of those who had to choose the leader did so on the basis of information which bore little relevance to the question about the likely future performance of their candidate, and several councillors who were sympathetic to change and innovation voted against Crofton, only to support him later.

In spite of this, however, it is clear that within the majority group on the council there was uncertainty as to the attributes which were seen as fitting a person for the office of leader, but at the same time it is also clear that the established and traditional rules were broken with the election of a comparative newcomer to council affairs. From this we should expect, first, that there will be a similar uncertainty as to the role which he is expected to play and, second, we can expect that a leader who does not 'move up through the usual channels' will see the role in very different terms to someone who is 'properly' fitted to be leader. These questions will be considered in the next two sections of this chapter.

II. BEHAVIOUR RULES

> If he [the councillor] is wise he will take counsel from his fellow-members to bide awhile before making his presence felt.
> R. S. B. Knowles, *Modern Management in Local Government*
> (London, Butterworths, 1971), p. 47.

In Chapter 6, I argued that behaviour rules are set and upheld by the authorities within a group, and I argued that the chairman of the standing committees constituted the core group of authoritative councillors in the Royal Borough of Kensington and Chelsea. Fifteen of the councillors I interviewed in the summer of 1968 were chairmen at some time during the period 1965–70. Their responses to my questions asking them to state what constituted proper and improper behaviour for certain council positions provide us with information on the behaviour rules. I will outline these rules in this section, but in addition, I will also outline the behavioural expectations that were held by the other councillors, as this will give an indication of the extent of group consensus on these matters.

The New Councillor

The 'councillor' is the basic or common role from which all the other positions on the council are recruited, and for this reason the 'ordinary councillor' is not really seen by councillors as a distinct position within council politics. However, councillors did not only think of the formal positions within the council and party hierarchy, since they saw the 'new' councillor (councillors in their first term on the council), as a distinct and recognisable position.

To obtain their views regarding the appropriate behaviour for a new councillor, I asked 'old' councillors (those who were serving at least their second term on the council) the following question which I felt, raised the idea of proper behaviour in a way which was likely to be especially meaningful to them:

> 'What advice would you give to a new councillor as to how to do his job properly once he has been elected?'

In addition, I asked twelve new councillors:

> 'What advice, if any, were you given by the other councillors when you were first elected onto the council?'

For the moment I will outline the views of the fourteen chairmen who were asked the question.

'Silence'. All chairmen[21] stressed the importance of the new councillor assuming a passive, silent, role in discussions in open council, in committee meetings, and party meetings. A number of respondents mentioned that this was the advice which was given to them and they were agreed that it was good advice which should be followed: 'When I first came onto the council I was told to be quiet in committee for six months, and to be quiet in council meetings for at least a year, otherwise you'd open your mouth and make a fool of yourself. The youngsters these days think they know it all. It's too soon to assess these new councillors, but if they do start talking out of turn then they'll become unpopular and contribute nothing.' 'Do not speak in council meetings for the first twelve months was the advice that I was given, and it's good advice. If a councillor puts an incomplete case it will disappoint people and they won't give him so much attention next time.' There is, then, 'a tradition that the new man rather takes a back-seat.'

Although there was basic agreement that new councillors should 'sit down and shut up', the chairmen differed in their views as to how long this rule should be followed, and some were prepared to admit that in certain circumstances exceptions could be made. For example, some chairmen considered that new councillors should be quiet for one year or even two, whereas other chairmen considered that silence was only necessary for the first three months. Moreover, although all the chairmen considered that new councillors should be quiet in council meetings for a longish period, some were prepared to admit that the new councillor could participate rather sooner in committee meetings and sooner still in party meetings:

21. The responses of one chairman stood out from those of other chairmen in reply to many of my questions. 'I think if you are a young man you should stand up as soon as possible and make a contribution. One shouldn't be overawed. It's very important that the young blood chivvy their chairmen as I don't see how they'll learn otherwise. After elections they've been hammering on people's doors and they should have a whole host of impressions and ideas about what needs doing. It's sad to sit on new councillors – not that anyone does – as if you don't encourage these people they could well be fed-up in no time.'

'I always say keep quiet for a while and don't talk in council meetings; although they should be freer to do so in committees and party meetings.' 'In party meetings ... one can feel free to let off steam with less fear of embarrassment.'

Although the chairmen referred to other advice which they would give to the new councillors, no other rule was noted so frequently by this group of respondents.

Attendance and 'homework'. Chairmen expect new councillors to attend party meetings, council meetings, and the committee meetings of which they are members, and although (as we have just seen) they are expected to assume a passive role in the deliberations, they are nevertheless expected to prepare themselves for these meetings by reading the *council* documents which will be sent to them: 'Attend all meetings and make them your number one priority.' 'Keep up a good attendance at committee meetings and also at party meetings and council meetings as well for that matter. If you're elected it's unfair to the ratepayers if you're not conscientious about your duties.' 'I hope they'd hear from someone that they should do their homework. It makes a big difference to committee effectiveness and stops those long discussions which are off the point.' 'Study his agendas, that's what he should do, then he can know what's going on, especially on the committees.'

Specialisation. Local government services within the responsibility of the Royal Borough are extensive, and no councillor is in a position when he can cover all aspects. For this reason the new councillor is 'more or less compelled to specialise. You'll be on one or two committees and on those you tend to stay and if you're ambitious then you'll have your eye on the vice-chairmanship in a few years time.' Even though the advice was as much a pragmatic necessity as a normative rule, several chairmen did nevertheless consider that the new councillor really *should* behave in this way: 'I'd tell him not to overdo the number of committees he's on as if you're going to make a go of the council then it's best to think in terms of sitting on just a couple of committees.' The advice that councillors should specialise in a subject which interests them and then get onto the appropriate committee is often advice which the new councillor finds difficult to put into practice, as 'sometimes all councillors want to go on one particular committee', and additionally the council is especially careful as to just who they appoint to the 'political' committees.

Party loyalty. In many ways the importance of party loyalty will have been stressed to many of the new councillors before they are even elected to that position, but even so, throughout their early career on the council, they will be reminded of the necessity for loyalty. Although they may abstain on matters of conscience they are not allowed to make a lengthy speech on this in the council meeting, and voting against any committee or party decision in the open council is forbidden and does not occur. Even in committee meetings new councillors are expected to follow the lead which will be given them by the chairman, and one reason why they are discouraged from speaking in these open, all-party, arenas is because their contributions 'may give fuel to the opposition'. Not surprisingly new councillors are not expected to form themselves into unofficial and informal groupings, but are supposed to raise such ideas as they may have in the official party meeting where their behaviour can be controlled and their ideas countered by the authoritative councillors without fear of any embarrassment. A past leader commented: 'I always called a meeting of new members and asked them not to lobby each other, but to raise points with me or in the party meeting.'

Involvement with outside interests. Councillor activity in the local Conservative association is largely taken for granted. All councillors are ex-officio members of their ward committee, and there is a clear expectation that they should take an active interest in the affairs of the party outside the council – indeed but for their activity in the local association they would not have been elected to the council, and in the case of South Kensington councillors, if they fail to maintain their activity in the association then they may be asked to stand down at the next election.

Other contact with outside groups is not welcomed, however, and some of the authoritative councillors actually discourage contacts of this kind being made by their new councillors, or at least advise them to treat what they might hear with caution: 'Young councillors have to take care not to be lobbied by pressure groups.' 'Don't take anything for granted and be wary of external groups.' 'If they receive a complaint from a ratepayer then they shouldn't jump to conclusions about this until they have heard both sides of the story. I learnt this myself the hard way. I went storming up to the town hall on the basis of a complaint I received (I always try to go personally to the town hall, rather than writing, or phoning) and I found that I'd been told a story in a terribly exaggerated and incomplete way. . . . When you're young and inexperienced you do fall into traps like this so easily.'

In spite of the fact that new councillors are expected by their authoritative colleagues to limit their contact with pressure groups, and be wary of the information which they might receive from individuals, they are nevertheless expected to 'encourage good relations with the public' and 'go round their area'. 'Councillors and aldermen, but especially councillors as they are elected by the public, should encourage a good relationship between the public and the council. . . . The public really want educating and this is very important with the rates being what they are. The public are dissatisfied when the rates go up and in nearly every case it's not our fault.'

In other words, new councillors should be active in presenting the council to the public, but they should be less active and more wary of presenting the public and their ideas to the council.

Taken together, these behaviour rules for the new councillor stress that he should learn his standards of correct behaviour within the context of the meetings organised by the council and party group. New councillors should 'ask the officer if there are things which they don't understand', and it is recognised as 'important to get to know the chief officers right away'. Moreover, not only did the chairmen stress the importance of the new councillors approaching the officers for advice and guidance, but they also stressed that if new councillors were to look to their colleagues on the council for advice and guidance then they should look to the senior or experienced councillors. An alderman: 'One doesn't officially give advice to new councillors, but naturally one does guide them and they'll often approach you, and they're encouraged to do so.'

The behaviour rules for the new councillor tend to dwell rather more on what he should *not* do than on what he should do, for he is allowed only limited scope for activity and participation within the internal deliberations of the council, and (with the exception of activity within the local Conservative associations) within the wider context of the local area.

In this section I will not discuss the extent to which the rules are known and accepted by the new councillors, but I will give some indication of the extent to which the rules are communicated to the new councillors and reinforced by rewards and sanctions. In addition, I will also outline the expectations which the non-chairmen have for the behaviour of the new councillors in order to see whether their advice conflicts with the advice which the chairman might give.

First, the communication of the behaviour rules to the new councillors. At the first party meeting after the 1968 elections, the new councillors were given a talk by the leader of the council in which he stressed the importance of their making their views known through the 'proper channels'; of working as part of a team; of attending meetings regularly; and of obeying the whip. Prior to their being elected to the council, all Conservative candidates were encouraged to attend council meetings and were invited to attend party meetings so they could gain some familiarity and 'feel' of what would be involved once they were elected. In addition to this, the sitting councillors from each constituency held meetings for the new recruits when they pointed out the work of the council and its committees and were available to answer the questions of the prospective councillors. From this, it does appear as if the new councillor is given a comprehensive picture of just what he should and should not do to be considered a good councillor by those who are in a position to advance his council career.

In fact, however, the new councillor may well find himself in a position when he is rather unclear as to just what is expected of him by his senior colleagues, as it is not possible for the chairmen to communicate all the relevant behaviour rules. In particular it is clear that many of the senior councillors are somewhat reluctant to state that new councillors should 'sit down and shut up', even though they consider that this is the most important rule which the new councillor should follow: 'I wouldn't presume to tell a new councillor, it's a very difficult question. One way of answering is to say sit tight for a few months, but it wouldn't be easy to tell anyone that.'

The new councillor's uncertainty as to what he should do is affected not only by the possible communication blocks that exist within the council, but in addition, the fact that he is likely to have his own ideas about what he should do and may be prepared to respond favourably to environmental cues, means that his position could be one of conflict and ambiguity. A full consideration of the extent of this can only be appreciated if close attention is paid to the new councillors themselves, and this will be discussed in Section III.

When chairmen were asked what advice they would give to a new councillor, many spontaneously mentioned sanctions which could be applied to those councillors who defied the rules, and they pointed out that if they broke the 'silence' rule then they would just not be listened to. The existence of this orientation on the part of the chairman means that even if the silence rule is not communicated, and even if the new councillor does not conform, such contributions as he does make will be unlikely to affect the development of council policy. New councillors are not in positions of formal authority on the council and they have no access to resources which give the possibility of having any independent impact on the decisions being made by the council. The only impact which they can have upon the form of council policy is if their ideas are taken seriously and listened to with sympathy by the chairmen. In other words the new councillors are as important and influential within the group as they are allowed to be. Should they break the silence rule (albeit unaware of its existence) then they will not be listened to, and worse still, they will prejudice their chances of getting a favourable hearing in the future as they become 'branded' and regarded as a 'bore' who 'cannot be trusted to put a fair case'. 'You have to be careful not to speak up and make a fool of yourself as it can hang over your head for years. A case in point happened when a young chap kept getting on his feet when he knew nothing, and even when he was a mature councillor he was still regarded as something of a buffoon.' Refusing to listen sympathetically to a person's ideas is, of course, a major sanction on certain behaviour, but more important perhaps, a councillor who does flout the behaviour rules is unlikely to be singled out for the rewards of formal office-holding in a few years time.

· · · · · ·

The expectations held for the behaviour of the new councillors by the non-chairmen do not conflict with the behaviour rules, and so in most cases, the advice which new councillors may receive from the more junior councillors will reinforce what is expected of them by the authorities within the group. Even though the North Kensington councillors elected in 1964, or in the by-election of 1967, were not always sympathetic to the silence rule and did not consider it a legitimate or proper guide for behaviour, their own experience had made them aware that it had to be followed if a new councillor was to gain any voice in council affairs. In other words, although they may advise a new colleague to keep quiet for pragmatic reasons, the effect of their advice would be the same. A North Kensington councillor: 'The major advice I would give is don't try to shoot your mouth off too soon before you know what you're talking about. Let me give an example, [names councillor] and I were both on at the same time . . . he was more talkative than I and raised a whole mass of points in party meetings and committees and sometimes even in council itself. The reaction of the councillors was "Who the hell is he to tell us these things", and their automatic reaction is that you should be quiet for the first six months to listen and learn. This is what I've tried to do. I still haven't spoken in council meetings, but I do get a reasonable hearing at the party meeting. You have to be careful not to get caught up in all this, but you have to remember that you can achieve nothing on your own.' The councillor referred to in this statement would, on the basis of his experience, now give new councillors the 'silence' advice: 'Don't stick your neck out too far at the start – I did when I didn't know the facts and the possibilities. One really can't go tearing in like this, it just doesn't make sense. I went in feet first and cheesed-off the rest of the party. I don't do it this way now; I write more quietly to the right people. In any club you wouldn't go in and buy everyone a drink right away; one would move in more quietly. You won't get things done by shouting, you'll only make a name for yourself.' One councillor who was put in a position of some importance after the 1968 elections while still comparatively junior stated how the silence rule was 'a policy I followed and a number of older councillors say it's the right one'. Clearly his conformity was rewarded.

Although the more 'senior' North Kensington Conservative councillors were not sympathetic to the crucial silence rule, they would nevertheless advise their new colleagues to observe it. Other councillors who were not chairmen would similarly advise a new councillor to remain silent and learn by quietly asking questions of the more senior councillors, but like the chairmen they considered that this behaviour was right and proper and was not just a pragmatic necessity. A Chelsea councillor: 'Before you stand up, see the chairman and ask his advice and why a particular thing has happened, you learn a lot more that way. I wouldn't criticise anyone for not speaking.' A South Kensington councillor: 'Consult the chairman before you raise any point, even in committee, but better still sit quietly and take things in.'

The Chairman[22]

At the start of this chapter I stated that after outlining the recruitment rules, I would outline the behaviour rules for the various positions on the council, and I have just dealt with the behaviour rules for the new councillor. We are, however, in a rather peculiar position when we come to consider the behaviour rules for the chairman, as the authoritative councillors and the chairmen are one and the same group of councillors, and so if we attempt to identify the behaviour rules for that position, we are in effect studying the chairmen's *self-definition* of role. In other words, although I suggested that the behaviour of the new councillors was rigorously controlled by restraining behaviour rules, I am now suggesting that the chairmen are in the very different position of having the freedom to behave in the way which they themselves think right and proper. For the moment this view is simply an assertion, and before it can be considered cogent and before I can go on to outline the behaviour rules for the chairmen, it is important that I do two things. First, I must identify the other councillors' behavioural expectations for the chairmen, and second, I must identify the resources which are under the independent control of the chairmen. If the non-chairmen hold few restraining expectations, or if the chairmen have resources which enable them to emancipate themselves effectively from such restraints and expectations as may be held out for them by their colleagues, then it will indeed be the case that the chairmen are in a position to define their own role.

First, then, the behavioural expectations of the ordinary councillor. It is important to remember that they recognise the chairmen as the authorities within the group, and in most cases they also consider that the attributes of the chairmen are such as to justify this situation. 'You must remember that the chairmen in this borough have considerable experience of council work and this really does mean that they have the right to be able to give us the benefit of their advice.' The few councillors who do not always recognise the legitimacy of the chairman's leadership are still nevertheless aware that they *are* the leading councillors. In other words, the non-chairmen are aware that the resources which the chairmen possess are such as to build inequality into the relationship between chairmen and non-chairmen,

22. The information for this section is largely based on the responses of thirty-eight councillors (twelve of who were chairmen in the period 1965–70) to the following question:

'You'll remember I asked you a question about some of the other positions here on the council. What about the committee chairmen; how would you describe the responsibilities of that office, what are the sorts of things which you feel they should and should not do?'

so that the ordinary councillor is dependent on the chairmen's ideas for the direction of council policy: 'One has to go along with the chairmen and the experienced councillors on a lot of things, as you can't possibly be informed of everything. It's hard to know what's going on and you have to rely on other people, and that often means the chairmen.'

In recognising the legitimacy of the chairmen's leadership, many councillors are prepared to allow them considerable scope to decide things in their own way, and as such these non-chairmen hold few constraining behavioural expectations for the chairmen. A new councillor: 'It's hard to say what a chairman should do, it's up to them.' Two South Kensington councillors: 'I've never been a chairman and never would be; I'm too busy at——. You should ask the chairman about that.' 'As chairman of a group you have to chair in the way that you can do it. Some chairmen talk a lot, but some don't, it's really up to them.' Moreover, in recognising the legitimacy of the chairman's leadership, such expectations as the non-chairmen did have for the chairmen were often ones which recognised that they should assume a dominant, leading role: 'Yes, they [the chairmen] should guide us, they have that experience, otherwise they wouldn't be chairmen.' Where the non-chairmen did hold restraining expectations for behaviour of the chairmen, then they often recognised that they did not have the resources to reinforce those expectations, and they were invariably reticent to 'tell a chairman what to do'.

When we look more directly at the behavioural expectations of the non-chairmen then we find not only that they hold few expectations, but also that such expectations as they do hold are general and ambiguous, may conflict one with another, and at any event relate only to the chairmen's behaviour in committee and party meetings, largely ignoring other relationships that are involved in the execution of their responsibilities. Of course, the difference between expectations for behaviour that are unclear and ambiguous and those which actually conflict one with another is often a slight one. What is apparent, however, is that the non-chairmen were often unclear as to whether the chairmen should assume an active leading role in committee or the more passive role of allowing all to have a say without the attempt to provide suggestions or impose solutions. However, it does seem that there was more of a preference for a leading role among the senior councillors and those from South Kensington, than was the case with respect to the expectations of Chelsea councillors, North Kensington councillors, and the new councillors, who were more likely to hold the conflicting expectation requiring the chairmen to assume the more passive role. An alderman: 'He should assume very much a leading role. He has a terrific amount of hard work and needs to know all the ins and outs and meet lots of officers. It's not just afternoons and evenings, but really the whole day. They should say "This is the way we'll tackle the thing", and they do make all the leading remarks.' Two new councillors: 'I would like chairmen to allow discussions to range freely, after all its a committee and one should want the twelve or fifteen views, but it's not always like that.' 'They should know how to delegate properly; it's like being a branch or association chairman. One is dealing with volunteers and one has to ask them to do things and has to enthuse them. I'd like to see the chairmen getting hold of people, and if I were a chairman I'd really use people. ... If I were chairman I'd like to bring things up and say what I'm doing and say what I'm not happy about and ask people to think about it. The chairmen are in a position to look at things and say what we've been doing and what we're not happy about. But this doesn't happen – it's a pity. I wish we could take a fresh look at things. ... One appreciates that chairmen have to justify things in council meetings, but this doesn't mean that they have to justify all things in all places. In fact, at present committee meetings seem to involve an explanation of past history, and the question "Are we happy?", and after a bit of badgering things usually go through.'

In spite of the fact that most councillors allowed considerable social space to the chairmen, and held few expectations for their behaviour (contenting themselves with a fairly passive support role) the last statement which I have just cited does clearly show that this was not the case for all councillors. But even though non-chairmen may hold strong views as to the proper behaviour for a chairman, they are not really in a position where they have sanctions or rewards at their disposal to give weight to their expectations. In hard reality they lack the capacity to appoint or dismiss the chairman, and it is difficult for them to defy the chairman's lead in committee or party meeting, or to refuse to endorse the decisions which the chairman makes in the name of the council between meetings.

A number of councillors pointed out that the chairmen's lead is invariably followed: A South Kensington councillor: 'Yes, the chairmen's actions do invariably get acted on. They are not dictated and there is discussion, but the chairmen really are more in the know.' Two chairmen: 'Invariably the chairman's lead wins.' 'I've never had a recommendation of mine, as chairman, turned down.' In many ways, committees and committee meetings are more involved in the detailed administration of established policies and commitments, and it is in the party meeting that matters of policy will be discussed and where policy decisions involving innovation or change will be taken. A chairman: 'basically the chairman has to administer the year-to-year activities of the committee, and he may administer new things, although all major decisions are cleared by party policy first, or else the whips would never be able to work. Unless people have had some chance to say how they felt before it was applied there could be a terrible blow-up.' In other words, policy matters are 'cleared' in the party meeting before they are dealt with in more detail in committee, but even so it is doubtful if this arena is any more restrictive of the chairmen. A chairman: 'Maybe the party will tell him [the chairman] what to do, but usually the chairman has to bring a suggestion before the party for approval. I was never turned down by the party in seven years as chairman.'

Of course, the fact that this particular chairman has never had his suggestions rejected may be taken by some as an indication that he had a particularly keen regard for party and committee preferences so that he had internalised the normative framework within which he had to operate in order to retain support. I would suggest, however, that such a view would exaggerate the extent to which the committees and the party meeting hold a tight rein for the chairmen who in reality have to pay only a limited regard to the sensibilities of their supporters, and are rarely in a position where they have to hold back an idea because they feel it would not be carried by their colleagues. In both party and committee meetings, the chairman will have his friends and allies, and those councillors who do wish to challenge his authority and restrain his behaviour are invariably in the minority.

The council of the Royal Borough meets every six weeks, and there is a summer recess of approximately fourteen weeks. Standing Orders provide that: 'The Mayor, Deputy Mayor, and the Chairman and Vice-Chairman of the respective committees or any one of them may, whenever the council is in recess, or between meetings or committees give such instructions as may be reasonable with respect to any matters that will not admit of delay. Provided that all such instructions shall be reported to the Council or to the Committee concerned at their next meeting.' One chairman pointed out that 'an awful lot of chairman's action is done; there is a huge pile between meetings, and we can't wait five or six weeks for every decision that needs to be made.' Although chairmen are 'sensitive' to the fact that they are making decisions for the council, 'if the chairman is clever, he can get away with anything he wants.' One chairman pointed out that decisions made by one particular chairman under this 'urgent matters' Standing Order were passed by his committee in spite of the fact that there was considerable dissatisfaction with the decisions: '——knew his mind, but he often made decisions which people didn't agree with and this caused a certain amount of friction.... ——made certain decisions for a committee that were not always accepted by the committee even though they were allowed to go through. ... No, I can't remember a specific example off-hand, but I know it's cropped up in Housing in the past.'

The fact is (and this deals with the second point which I raised at the outset of this section on the behaviour rules of the chairmen), the chairmen possess resources denied to their fellow councillors which enable them to emancipate themselves from the control of their colleagues. Most important they enjoy the recognition that they are the leaders within the council, but this recognition is based on an acute awareness of the advantages which are associated with the particular position. Chairmen (and to a lesser extent the vice-chairmen) have more information of a certain type than is possessed by the ordinary councillor which is gained as a result of their closer involvement with the work of the council and its committees. A North Kensington councillor: 'The chairmen of the committees get a lot more [information] sent to them, and the ordinary councillor sees neither Greater London Council, nor London Boroughs Association, documents.' A vice-chairman: 'You certainly are told very much more by the officers than when you're just an ordinary councillor. There's lots of facts and figures you just couldn't know unless you're a chairman or a vice-chairman, and you'll get to know a lot more if you're taken into the chairman's confidence.' What is especially noticeable is the closeness of the relationship which chairmen enjoy with the relevant chief officer, and which in no sense is replicated by the ordinary councillor who will have virtually no personalised contact with the officers unless it is to take up a constituent's problem. Two chairmen: 'Every day you're in touch with the relevant chief officer. . . . There has to be complete confidence between the chairman and the chief officer.' 'Every committee chairman has a very close relationship with his chief officer. With me its the——; I know what he thinks, and he knows what I think.'

Standing Orders give the chairman a particular decisive role in committee meetings: 'The Chairman of a meeting of a Committee shall decide all questions of order and his ruling on all questions of order or upon matters arising in debate shall be final and shall not be open to discussion. He shall be entitled to vote on any question in the first instance, and in case of an equality of votes shall have a second or casting vote.' Admittedly votes are rare (and are not welcomed by the chairman) but this Standing Order does give him a secure position within the committee, a security which is heightened because he will have an especial involvement in the drawing-up of the committee agenda; he will have had a brief meeting with the chief officer before the committee meets to run through the agenda; and once in the committee meeting he controls the contribution which both the councillors and the officers can make, with all comments going through the chair. Moreover, there are a number of additional strategies which he can employ to increase his strength in committee; he can involve the vice-chairman to get his support (and it would be unthinkable for a vice-chairman to speak out 'publicly' against the chairman); he 'can get the key people in the committee round to his way of thinking before the committee starts'; he has 'the right to stop a chief officer's report being brought forward right away'; and he is generally in a position when he can manipulate the amount of information which is brought to the committee's attention. In addition to these resources and strategies which he has at his disposal, and in addition to his capacity to decide between meetings, he also has a special and exclusive relationship with the press. Committee meetings are confidential, and the press and public are not admitted, but Standing Orders allow that: 'Proceedings of Committee may be communicated to the Press by the Chairman after each meeting unless the Committee otherwise determines.' In fact little use is made of this provision, but that this is so is a testament to the style which the chairmen have themselves chosen to adopt.

The above information enables me to suggest, not only that non-chairmen hold few restraining expectations for the behaviour of the chairmen, but also that the resources under the control of the chairmen are such that even in the face of a certain amount of opposition from within the majority group, they are still able to define and execute their responsibilities in the way which they themselves think proper. How, then, do they define their role? What behaviour rules do they set for themselves?

When I outlined the expectations which the non-chairmen held for the behaviour of the chairmen, I mentioned that there was a certain ambiguity and conflict as to whether the chairmen should assume a 'leading' or a 'passive' role in relation to party colleagues. This is much less the case with respect to the views of the chairmen themselves, who are much more inclined to consider that they should assume a leading role: 'On our council, though of course I can't speak for others, the chairman is certainly not expected to take a purely passive role. Of course, while the committee is in session he must ensure that all that want to, can speak, but his job is to give a lead.' 'The chairman is really the person who keeps very busy and he probably does nine-tenths of the work both in and out of committee. I think the chairman has to lead the committee and have close contact with the officers and know what's going on.' 'It's very important for him to give a strong lead in committee.'

Of course, there was not total consensus among the chairmen that this was the particular role which they should all assume, and the chairmen of the 'non-political' committees were more inclined to assert that the chairmen should assume the more passive role: 'They are responsible for seeing that the wishes of the committee are carried out. . . . I don't believe the chairmen should lead. They have an agenda before the committee and the chairman should draw forth the members' views. You'd waste people's time and experience if you just rushed through the agenda and said "Good-night".'

Understandably, the non-chairmen when outlining their expectations for the behaviour of the chairmen tended to dwell on the way in which the chairmen should conduct relations with the ordinary councillor in both party and committee meetings. For the chairmen, however, relationships of this kind were not seen as of particular importance; they were more mindful of other relationships, and they mentioned the proper behaviour of the chairmen with respect to both the leader of the council and the permanent officers of the authority.

Although the leader could expect to be kept informed by the chairmen there was not generally the view that the chairmen should in any way be dominated by the leader: 'The relationship between the leader and the chairmen does depend on personalities; both Alderman Anslow-Wilson and Councillor Sir Malby Crofton, having appointed their chairmen, were content to let them get on with the job, and this is really the way it should be. . . . The leader must obviously have confidence in the chairmen, or else he wouldn't have appointed them.'

Chairmen considered that they should be in close and regular contact with the officers of the authority: 'You've got to be very closely in touch with the chief officers. When I was chairman of——, I was in touch with one of the officers practically every day. . . . The relevant chief officer keeps you informed.' 'Every day you're in touch with the relevant chief officer.' 'I think the chairman has to have close contact with the chief officers.' Chairmen rarely articulated the belief that they should be 'policy-makers' whereas the officers should content themselves with the role of 'administrator', since in most cases questions of control and dominance of this kind did not arise in the relationship; both are usually involved in the common enterprise of managing the services of the local authority, and it is only on the comparatively infrequent occasions when decisions involving change or innovation come to be taken that friction can arise.

When I discussed the behaviour rules for the new councillor, it was easy to outline a number of rules which served to guide and control their behaviour. When we consider the chairmen, however, this is less possible. It is not just that the non-chairmen hold few behavioural expectations for the chairmen, since the chairmen themselves had difficulty in articulating clear rules which they considered should define their role. In a very real sense, the individual chairmen are free to behave in the way which they consider appropriate: 'There's no real drill on what the chairmen should do; it's what you make it.' This freedom does not, however, mean that the chairmen will behave in totally unpredictable and idiosyncratic manner – quite the reverse, for there is an absence of specific behaviour rules precisely because they are not needed to ensure that behaviour is held within certain limits. What these limits are likely to be, and how their behaviour can be predicted I will discuss in Section III of this chapter.

The Leader[23]

Earlier in this chapter, when I discussed the election of the leader in 1968, I suggested that the uncertainty and conflict which existed as to the attributes which were seen as properly fitting a councillor for that position should alert us to the fact that we may find a corresponding uncertainty and conflict when we moved on to consider the expectations which councillors

23. The information for this Section is largely based on the responses of thirty councillors (eleven of whom were chairmen in the period 1965–70) to the following question:

'You'll remember I asked you a question about the position of the councillor and the chairman, well I'd like to ask you a question about the leader. How would you define the responsibilities of that office, what are the sorts of things which you feel he should and should not do?'

held for the behaviour of the leader. I will consider this now, when I outline the behaviour rules for the position, and also the behavioural expectations that are held by the non-authoritative councillors. First, however, I will outline views which suggest that (as with the chairmen) there are no unequivocal restraining rules or expectations for the leader, and I will also note the resources and strategies available to the leader which may enable him to define his own role unrestrained by the rules and expectations of his colleagues on the council.

One chairman pointed out that: 'There are various types of leader and no rules or precedents have been laid down, but it's a very difficult job with no thanks', and another suggested that 'he has considerable room for manoeuvre'. Other councillors within the majority group who were not chairmen expressed similar views, arguing that 'the position is quite a lot what he cares to make it', for 'he has a fair amount of latitude' and 'he's left to interpret the position as he thinks fit'; one councillor expressed the view that 'it's open to much personal influence how he actually carries out his responsibilities. He really is in a position to make the role for himself.'

When I considered the chairmen I pointed out that they had considerable resources under their control: the same is true for the leader, who has a number of resources at his disposal and 'is in a wonderful position to influence'.

The leader is chairman of the party meetings. On the first council the leader was unofficially the 'chairman of the chairmen', and on the second council this position was regularised by the creation of the Co-ordinating and Policy Committee where the leader was chairman. 'He gets all the papers and reports of all the committees and if he goes through these he can know what is happening in every committee and he can attend any of them'. 'If an important issue comes up, then he can get up in council meetings and put his weight behind it, to show the importance of the issue.' In other words, he is in a strong position in all the arenas associated with the execution and making of council policy, and in addition he is 'the main public relations man' linking the council to the wider environment. Although the recruitment rules for the chairman allow the leader to exercise little choice in the appointment of councillors to these positions in the short-run, he is in a position to appoint the vice-chairmen and so in the longer-run, and 'as the years go by', he is able to determine the composition of the leadership group on the council. In addition to these resources, there are a number of strategies which the leader can adopt to make the most of the resources at his disposal. A chairman: 'There are a lot of pressures that a leader can bring to bear. He can commit people in the holiday period, especially if the chairman of the particular committee concerned is not too enthusiastic. . . . If the chairman was dead anti-something which the leader was keen about, then the leader could approach the chairman, have a chat and often that would be enough. But if this failed he could ring up people on the committee and express his views and the average committee member would accept his views so that when it came to the committee decision, and especially the vote (and a good chairman should not need to have votes, but if it did come to that) the chairman would find the majority of the committee against him and he would have to accept that. A good and effective leader works like that; he doesn't need to shout out his views and he doesn't need to work in an underhand way, he is quite at liberty to tell the chairman he proposes to talk to the committee members directly. Leaders can often have their own way, even if it's wrong; there is no rule or reason to it, but it's accepted as parliamentary democracy.'

In spite of the fact that a leader has a number of resources and strategies which he can adopt, and although he can, on occasions, by-pass the chairmen of the committees he has really to work through, and with, his colleagues on the council, and in particular it is difficult for him to undertake activities and commitments which challenge the views and assessments of the chairmen since they are in a position of institutionalised power on the council where they may be able to block a leader's ideas and aspirations. Any leader is only in that position because he has followers, and gaining and securing this support may have certain restraining costs which limit the freedom he enjoys. In the case of local government in the Royal Borough, it would be extremely difficult for any leader to function effectively in that position if he did not have the fairly active support of the chairmen, and for this reason it is particularly important to understand the behaviour rules which these authoritative councillors hold out as guides for the leader. Even though I have already suggested that at least two chairmen considered that there were 'no rules or precedents', it is nevertheless clear that a considerable number of the chairmen did consider that there were certain things which the leader should, but mainly should not, do. If the leader chooses to transgress these standards then, in spite of the resources he possesses, 'things can be made difficult for him' so that he could lose the support (and perhaps gain the opposition) of the most influential group on the council.

When I outlined the chairmen's conception of their own role, I pointed out that the chairmen generally considered that they should be left free from the control and supervision of the leader. In arguing that they should be allowed considerable autonomy to manage the affairs of their committees, they were, at the same time, expressing a view about the proper behaviour of the leader, and they were giving him a comparatively 'small' role limited to the co-ordination of committee activity; 'The leader is certainly not like the prime minister, giving a lot of direction from the centre; it's really much more a matter of co-ordination as the new committee's name [Co-ordinating and Policy] would suggest. He may well exhort and encourage the chairmen on certain lines but I don't think he should really come into direct affairs.' 'He's chairman of the chairmen. He is chairman of the party meeting, but committees should be, and usually are, left to get on with the job themselves.' Chairmen did not only express a view which sought to confine the activity of the leader within the internal affairs of the council, but they also considered he should limit the extent of his contact with the press and outside interests, and although 'he should make statements to the press from time-to-time, he should not be granting interviews to all and sundry.'

But what are the sanctions and rewards which the chairmen can bring to bear to reinforce the views they might have as to the proper role which the leader should assume, and what can they do if he seeks to extend his activity beyond the limits which they consider desirable? A chairman pointed out: 'The only way one can stop the leader marching too far ahead, short of a friendly chat and raising it in one or two party meetings is to raise a censure motion' but there was no case of that in the period from 1965 to the election of 1971. It is possible to go beyond this, however. A chairman: 'If the leader is going against the feel of the party, he will be pulled up short. It's not happened, but suppose the leader was hard-headed and insensitive (and he would have to be to act in this way) sooner or later an issue would come up where a small group of articulate councillors felt strongly. The leader might try to force his point of view, but speech after speech was against this line. The sensitive leader would take notice and back down, but if he continued in his point of view (and it would be incredible if this did happen) then one of the articulate members could well ask the leader for a vote (and the person who requested this could well fancy himself as leader). Now if the vote was adverse, and the leader was an honourable man, then he would resign, but if he did persist, then, in theory, a motion could be introduced saying the party had "no confidence" in Councillor so-and-so, and if that vote was adverse then the leader really should bow out . . . morally he should resign, but he would not have to do so, you have to rely on his sensitivity. If a motion of confidence were passed and he did not resign you would have to make sure that he was not selected for election next time. While we were waiting for this to happen someone might unofficially become leader, and he would have moral standing but no official position. The mayor would have to call on the leader whenever he wanted to speak, but he would not have to call on X or Y.'

Many of the non-chairmen held similar views to the chairmen as to the proper role for the leader, and others were prepared to recognise that the leader should define the role in the way that he felt best. Nevertheless, there were those who expected the leader to behave in a way rather different from the style advocated by the powerful and influential chairmen. These views are of interest, since if the leader's behaviour transgresses their expectations then they may form a factional grouping on the council. Although their expectations are clearly less crucial than those of the chairmen since they lack access to resources which enable them to exercise a powerful controlling role, any leader has to pay regard not only to behaviour rules but also to the pragmatic necessity of maintaining a cohesive and united team. It would be a mistake to exaggerate the difference in view between the chairmen and the non-chairmen on this matter, but even so, new councillors and councillors from North Kensington were more likely to express a view that the leader should assume more of a dominant role: 'He is a sort of super chairman, rather like the prime minister. My own view is that the leader should be slightly less democratic and slightly more autocratic than the average chairman. If there's any conflict then he's the boss.' Councillors of this persuasion were expressing the view that there should be a leader-centred leadership situation where all other councillors were drawn in equally to discussions in committee and party. The chairmen, on the other hand, were advocating the desirability of a group-based leadership structure only loosely co-ordinated by the leader, where they themselves had the role of critical importance.

The situation of the leader is a strange one: not only are there conflicting views as to the attributes which fit a councillor for that office (with the traditional rules breaking down in 1968), but there is also conflict with respect to the proper behaviour which he should display. Moreover, he has considerable resources at his disposal and although the chairmen consider he should assume a small role, if he does seek to extend his responsibilities there are sanctions available which have not been used and whose effect is uncertain. In the last section of this chapter, when I look at the connection between the recruitment rules and the behaviour rules, I hope that some of these uncertainties will be resolved.

III. RECRUITMENT RULES AND BEHAVIOUR RULES

> When the forces 'inside' a man drive him to act in the organizationally approved manner, there is little need to issue preformed decisions and to check his performance for deviation; everything he does can be predicted.
>
> Herbert Kaufman, *The Forest Ranger* (Baltimore, Johns Hopkins Press, 1960), p. 228.

In the first section of this chapter, I identified the recruitment rules used to guide the choice of those who were selecting Conservative councillors, chairmen, and the leader of the council, and in the second section I identified the behaviour rules for these positions and I also noted the behavioural expectations held by the non-authoritative councillors. In this section I want to look at the relationship between these two types of rules. I will argue that they represent alternative methods through which the authorities on the council control behaviour so that it is predictable and does not challenge the maintenance of established council policy – policy which, in fact, is a tangible embodiment of their own ideology or view as to the proper role of government. How far their control of behaviour and defence of established policy is successful will depend on the extent to which the established recruitment rules are maintained, and on the extent to which the position-incumbents subject to restraining behaviour rules are prepared to accept the rules as guides for their own behaviour. These questions will be considered in this section.

In the situation where particular position-incumbents are selected by the authorities with care and according to precise recruitment criteria, then there is no need to develop specific rules for their behaviour because appropriate standards are built into the recruitment rules and have been learnt prior to their assuming the particular office. However, if the authorities cannot control selection then there is no guarantee that those who are selected will behave in a manner which is acceptable to them. In this situation, if the authorities are to defend commitments and maintain the established policy of the organisation, then they need to control and restrain the behaviour of those who have been selected by socialising them into patterns of required behaviour through the communication of specific behaviour rules. Etzioni makes the point that, 'all other things being equal, socialization and selectivity can frequently substitute for each other. . . . An organization may . . . be highly selective in its choice of members; if it selects participants which match its requirements closely, it need invest relatively few resources in socializing them. If it can impose few selective criteria, it may have to divert a large proportion of its resources to the socialization process and will hence tend to be less effective' (Etzioni, 1961, pp. 158 and, 172. See also, Selznick, 1957).

Now if we look at the ratio of recruitment rules to behaviour rules for each of the positions that I have considered in the last two sections, then, generally speaking, where there are many precise and rigid recruitment rules over which the authorities on the council have considerable control, then there are comparatively few behaviour rules. However, for those positions where the recruitment rules are wide and ill-defined and applied by people outside the leadership group on the council, then there are more specific behaviour rules. The office of chairman is a position in the first category. The 'new councillor' is a position in the second category. The position of leader is more interesting and difficult to categorise with respect to the predominance of either recruitment or behaviour rules. The election of Sir Malby Crofton to the leadership in 1968 broke the established recruitment rules and resulted in an attempt by the chairman to assert the existence and importance of restraining behaviour rules. The position was confused because prior to this, it had never been necessary to control leadership behaviour directly through rules of this kind, because the selection of leaders according to the established recruitment rules requiring a long council apprenticeship meant that the authorities could be sure that required standards of behaviour were internalised.[24] in a man who already had a strong identity with established objectives and commitments. In other words, with the leader the balance of recruitment rules to behaviour rules has not been so fixed; on the first council the balance was similar to that for the position of chairman, but on the second council, the balance was similar to that for the position of new councillor.

This relative balance between recruitment and behaviour rules can be seen as a difference in terms of the time and manner in which particular position-incumbents are socialised into the pattern of required behaviour. Where there are clear recruitment rules established by the authorities, then socialisation occurs *before* a person assumes incumbency of the position, and there is an *absence* of any specific teaching, but where there are few recruitment rules and where the process is outside the control of the authorities, then socialisation has to occur *after* a person occupies a particular position, and rather more specific *teaching* and communication of the behaviour rules is necessary. This latter method of controlling behaviour is less effective and may not be successful, as although in the case of the chairmen and the first leader required standards were internalised in position-incumbents and were implicit in the recruitment rules, this was not the case with the second leader or the new councillors where we need to pay specific attention to the extent to which they knew and accepted the behaviour rules.

The New Councillor[25]

It is particularly necessary to study the orientation of new councillors to their position and to the behaviour rules because in many cases new councillors are recruited to the council by structures which have few connections with the council and so may fit-in rather badly with the council group, but at the same time (and indeed because of this) they are subject to a particularly large number of behaviour rules. In order to see how far their behaviour conforms to the required standards it is necessary to appreciate the knowledge which new councillors have of the behaviour rules, and it is also important to assess how far they regard them as appropriate guides for their behaviour, either because they consider them legitimate, or because they are mindful of the rewards and sanctions which may be available to reinforce the rules.

The information which I assembled in Section 1 of this chapter, where I identified the recruitment rules used to select Conservative councillors, makes it possible to predict which councillors will be most (and which least) likely to conform to the behaviour rules. The South Kensington councillors

24. Simon (1957, p. 11) makes the point that there are two methods of influencing the behaviour of someone within an organisation, and one of these involves 'establishing in the operative employee *himself* attitudes, habits, and a state of mind which leads him to reach that decision which is advantageous to the organisation' – original emphasis.

25. In a different context, see Price & Bell, 1970a.

were selected with care and according to criteria which were established by a group which included several senior councillors, but in North Kensington there was a shortage of candidates so that people had to be requested to stand. In Chelsea, recruitment and selection was by a group which was almost totally outside the control of the authorities on the council. In other words, we could expect that the new councillors from South Kensington will be most likely to conform to the behaviour rules, whereas those from North Kensington will be least likely to behave in the required manner. We can assess how far this is the case by looking at the twelve new councillors who were interviewed and asked the question:

'What advice, if any, were you given by the other councillors when you first were elected to the council?'

together with follow-up probing questions.

First, I shall consider the knowledge which the new councillors had of the behaviour rules. In Section II I outlined the extent to which new councillors were given advice by the leaders of the council, and although I suggested that there were certain blocks to the full communication of all the behaviour rules, it was nevertheless the case that there were specific attempts to teach the new recruits how to behave. In spite of this, five of the new councillors I interviewed mentioned that they got no formal advice, and of these two stated that they had gained no 'feel' of what was expected of them by the senior and authoritative councillors: 'For me there was nothing which I detected which said it was O.K. or not O.K. for me to do this or that. The feeling was that one was a new councillor and things might prove strange and complicated and one would need to go and see people.' The majority of councillors (including those who said they had received no formal advice) nevertheless knew many of the behaviour rules and in particular, they were well aware of the silence rule: 'As soon as you stand up at the council meeting or even the party meeting, you are frowned on. The stock answer if you raise something is that people say there's no point in discussing it as it was discussed a couple of years ago.' 'One feels that one's expected to keep quiet.'

Although the great majority of new councillors were aware of the all-important silence rule, they nevertheless differed in their assessment of its legitimacy as a guide for their behaviour, and as expected, councillors from South Kensington were more inclined to see the rule as reasonable and proper and they were also more inclined to look to their senior colleagues for advice and guidance: 'The leader gave some advice; he suggested people, when they're new, shouldn't talk too much, but this seems pretty sensible to me.' 'I get all this information coming in and I very much rely on the older people on the council for advice. For example, when I was invited to a meeting of the Notting Hill Adventure Playground I asked a chairman I knew if the body is valuable and then I go and explore on my own; but one needs to find out before how committed one should be to these various groups.' Although a councillor from North Kensington also considered that the silence rule was proper (though 'irritating') it was the new councillors from this part of the borough who were inclined to consider the rule an inappropriate guide for their behaviour, and if they looked to other councillors for advice then they would choose their colleagues from North Kensington, none of whom occupied any position of authority: 'The impression I have to date is that people on the council seem to think you're damn lucky to be here, and you should enjoy being in the ranks of the high and mighty. This seems to be a silly view, as one can't claim any kudos for being here as one merely had the right label round one's neck. No advice was formally given, but I feel that if you do chip in too much they will sit on you – "You new councillors don't realise our difficulties, we've been through all this before" – one feels slapped down. The leader says he doesn't expect any votes against the agenda in council meetings. They say they want your ideas, but alongside this such a statement seems a bit pale. I'd like to see it so that one is encouraged to raise points and ask questions.' 'The North Kensington councillors meet as a group fairly regularly and if something comes up then we chat among ourselves. . . . I've had no formal advice but before I was on the council I knew people here from North Kensington who I could ring up at any time to ask a question.'

Now it is not uncommon for new councillors elected from North Kensington to refuse to obey the silence rule at the start of their council careers; in the last section I pointed to a councillor elected prior to 1968 who did this, and my interview with councillors elected in 1968 made it clear that some had already flouted this rule, and were considering flouting the rule which forbade them to lobby for their point of view: 'I personally want to change the idea where all decisions are made in advance of the council meeting where there is no genuine discussion. I aim to get the signatures of other councillors who are dissatisfied with the way we run things and then I'll take this to the party meeting with I hope twenty or thirty names on it.' However, as a result of a process of trial and error and through gaining knowledge from trusted friends on the council, new councillors come to recognise the necessity of following the silence rule if they are ever to gain a voice in the council. In other words, they tend to shift away from the 'rebel' role to a ritualistic and pragmatic acceptance of those rules which limit their activity within the internal affairs of the council.[26] But at the same time, their failure to gain any active role within the affairs of the council and its committees, as well as their tendency to think of the responsibilities of the councillor in general terms as a 'representative' mean that they may well turn outwards from the council to take a more active part in the affairs of the local community: 'I don't like the idea of a councillor being in the council chamber too much. I get bored with pompous people who think that they have positions. The council

26. Merton (1938) discusses five types of adjustment to culture patterns; conformer, innovator, ritualist, retreatist, and rebel.

tends to be a place where people protect themselves. It's all been very boring to date – constituency work had proved much more exciting and I thought it would be the other way around.'

When I identified the behaviour rules for the new councillor, I mentioned that a number of the chairmen considered that the new councillor should not be active in courting relationships with local interest groups, precisely because they recognised that groups of this kind (especially in North Kensington) could well be raising ideas which challenged the council's policy commitments. However, if the silence rule was one which they found difficult to communicate (or teach) to the new councillors, then it was even more difficult for them to tell new councillors that they should limit their contact with local interest groups. Of course, the rule that new councillors should do their homework and attend all the meetings associated with their council and committee work inevitably restricted the time which new councillors would have available to spend on constituency activity, but if they were keen, and frustrated with the internal affairs of the council, then they could well be active in 'searching' in their areas. In Chapters 8 and 9 I will indeed suggest that new councillors are more active in searching in their areas for ideas and problems, and in addition they are more sympathetic than are the chairmen to those groups which challenge the pattern of council commitments. For the moment, however, it is important to note that this activity is likely to put the new councillor into a position of extreme role conflict since involvement with local groups and constituents could well result in his receiving acceptable expectations for his behaviour from outside the council which urge him not only to take an active interest in the internal affairs of the council, but urge him actually to work for changes and innovations in the existing pattern of council policy. The new councillor is, however, well aware that his activity within the council is restricted, and he is increasingly likely to recognise that if he does start raising ideas for changes in council policy then he will not be listened to now, nor in the future, as he will be branded by the senior councillors as someone who 'cannot be trusted to put a fair case'.

The position of the new councillor, enthusiastic to fulfil what he sees as the responsibilities of his office, is one which can be intolerable, and in this sort of situation he may well choose to 'retreat' from the conflict and frustration by not standing again for the council.[27] Several of these ex-councillors in fact go on to assume an active role in some of the less radical groups demanding change and innovation in the pattern of established council commitments. Luckily for the authorities on the council, this experience of conflict and frustration affects only a limited number of new councillors. Most new recruits are volunteers; many have had some contact with sitting councillors and have a certain awareness 'of what they are letting themselves in for'; and, of course, some are selected with care (by a group which has a large percentage of senior councillors on it) so that they

27. For example, in 1971, nine new councillors chose not to stand again.

are likely to accept automatically the legitimacy and appropriateness of assuming only a limited role during their period of induction into council politics. There are, however, a significant number of councillors who have found the position of councillor one which they could not adequately and satisfactorily fulfil within the context of local government in Kensington and Chelsea.

The behaviour of the new councillors will conform to the behaviour rules to varying degrees and for different motives; some follow the silent, passive role, some choose not to; and, of those who do follow the rule, some do so because they consider it to be a proper and legitimate guide, whereas others do so because they are mindful of the rewards and sanctions which are available to reinforce it.

So far I have not dealt with the reasons why the authorities on the council consider that the new councillor should assume a comparatively passive role on the council. In fact, they take this view because they are aware that councillors recruited by variable and none too selective recruitment rules lack any proven attachment to the existing pattern of council policy commitments, and in order to compensate for the absence of control which they can exercise through the selection process, the authorities attempt to assert their control by restraining the behaviour of the candidate once he is elected to the council until he has been adequately socialised into his role and into an acceptance of council policy and group purposes so that their overt control is no longer necessary. The tone of the behaviour rules for the new councillor is one which confines his behaviour to learning within the council and its committees – involvement in external organisations (other than the local Conservative association) is neither welcomed nor encouraged precisely because these represent information sources which might provide the new councillor with ideas which challenge the legitimacy of the council's policy commitments. One chairman pointed out that the new councillors have to assume this learning role and content themselves with assuming no voice in council deliberations, because: 'They've got to realise that what they do now is influenced by what their predecessors have done and they too will influence what later generations of councillors will do. . . . Past history is tremendously important. The best description one can give about joining the council is that it is rather like coming in to Act III of a play where much has already been established and must be taken for granted. Everything you do is influenced by things in the past. One learns from experience, one can't learn how to run a council theoretically. Local government here is really like a serial starting at least a hundred years ago. The greater the fund of experience one has to draw on the more likely one is to make good decisions. It's not a question of brilliance, but it is vital to have a fund of experienced people. The new boys and girls are enthusiastic, but this must be tempered by what is practical and what isn't.' Another chairman expressed a similar view as to the primacy of experience and past history as critical guides in the making of policy decisions and therefore, justified the exclusion of new councillors from anything but a learning role: 'It's a mistake for new councillors to jump up and say their piece before they know the form; I'd give it a year. Experience counts for much more than you realise. Knowing how the machine works, the officers and the history of issues is important and no councillor can get this in five minutes.' Another councillor pointed to the necessity of the silence rule because of the complexity of financial matters, but behind this view there was an awareness of the dangers of new councillors raising ideas which challenged or questioned established council commitments: 'Finances in the borough are very complicated and even someone like myself who is intensely interested and who has been on the council for fifteen years can't keep all the facts and figures in his head, and, therefore, the new man is particularly likely to make a serious blunder and get the wrong end of the stick. For instance, we were told that it was very wrong that we should make enormous profits, as she [the new councillor] put it, from lending money for improvements or purchase of houses. Now that, of course, is absolute nonsense, we have to pay money and pay interest and we have overheads, so if anything, on a strict cost basis, we not only don't make money but we lose a bit for this service we provide. This is what can happen, you see, this questioning of our policies almost before they know what they are.' One new councillor who broke the silence rule pointed out that since then he has been treated warmly because he showed that he was prepared to defend council policy in open council: 'I made a speech early on in my council career. Though I didn't say I would at the party meeting I did clear this with the leader first and he was happy about it. They seem to be terrified on the council of Conservatives standing up in the council meeting and criticising a decision. You really have to be careful how you go about it. . . . Since I made my speech in the council, there has been a thawing process as people realise that I'm not a danger.' In other words, the silence rule is not in itself of critical importance, but it is a means of restricting contributions until new councillors have learnt to respect the established pattern of commitments and the ethos of the authoritative councillors; if they are already sympathetic to this, then their contribution is not discouraged.

The *effect* of these new councillor behaviour rules on the actual behaviour of the new councillors is, as I have already suggested, dependent on the knowledge which they have of the rules and on their preparedness to accept them as appropriate guides. However, the *implications* of these rules for the likely development of council policy is *not* dependent on the extent to which new councillors conform to the rules, for even if the new councillor is ignorant of the crucial silence rule, if he does talk and his ideas do challenge existing policy commitments then his ideas are discounted as not worthy of consideration as they came from an inexperienced source who has shown contempt for what the authorities regard as a sensible behaviour rule. In other words, this rule aims to restrict the contribution which new councillors can make to council debate and decision-making processes until such time as they have learnt the 'ethical premises' (Simon, 1957) which underlie the council's activity, but if they do participate then the fact that their participation is improper means that should they raise (as well they might) suggestions which conflict with the council's commitments then the authoritative councillors are able to dismiss the ideas from their attention.

The Chairman

By the standards of most organisations, the majority group on the council of the Royal Borough is able to exercise a considerable amount of control over the selection and recruitment of new members, and in spite of the differences which I have chosen to emphasise between the attributes of the various new councillors and the implications of this for the likely patterns of conformity to the behaviour rules, the fact that all new councillors within the majority group are Conservatives who have usually had some contact with sitting councillors and have probably been active within the local Conservative association carries with it implications for their behaviour which are likely to preclude the consideration of certain public policies and to result in a certain sympathy for established council commitments. However, within the restricted context of the majority group, the chairmen are selected with very much more care than are the new councillors. Not surprisingly, therefore, when compared to the situation of the new councillor specific behaviour rules are much less evident for the chairmen and are less *necessary* to ensure that behaviour is satisfactory and predictable to those who have come to assume the major responsibility for defining and upholding organisational purpose. For the chairmen, the behaviour rules for their activity are *implicit* in the recruitment rules which are used to fill those positions. Control and predictability are built into these recruitment rules, and if they are always followed when councillors are selected for the position of chairman then the behaviour rules are learnt *before* a councillor assumes that office, and they are bound to be *acceptable* to a chairman because they will have become internalised within him so that they are almost put beyond his conscious questioning. (See esp. Kaufman, 1960.)

What then are these behaviour rules that are implicit within the recruitment rules? In other words, just what are the behavioural implications of the recruitment rules? In Section I of this chapter I noted that committee chairmen were appointed to that position only after they had served an apprenticeship as vice-chairmen of the particular committee in question; a vice-chairmanship which was unlikely to be gained unless a councillor had served within the majority group for four or five years. Moreover, before any councillor becomes chairman or even vice-chairman of one of the major political committees, he will have probably been through these positions on a more minor committee. In other words, chairmen are long-serving councillors who have worked their way up to those positions by showing themselves to be 'good' new councillors who can be rewarded with an apprenticeship of a minor committee vice-chairmanship which will serve as a training ground before they can be trusted with more important responsibilities. Nor surprisingly there are few behavioural rules for the chairmen, and those which do exist do not relate to the important responsibilities of the office. Slow assimilation, training on minor committees, apprenticeship as a vice-chairman, and anticipatory socialisation,[28] result in the internalisation of organisational objectives and purpose and the automatic knowledge and unthinking acceptance of behaviour patterns which have as their first object the maintenance of existing policy commitments in which these chairmen have invested a considerable measure of their own energy and with which they have come to be closely identified.[29] Moreover, the maintenance of established commitments involves, at the same time, the warding-off of challenges for change or innovation whether they come from within the council chamber or from outside. Indeed, the behaviour rule which restricts the new councillor's activity to the passive learning and acceptance of council policy and values represents a specific attempt to eliminate one potential source of dissonant ideas from impinging upon the council's policy-maintaining activity: their ideas with respect to interest groups and information sources (which will be discussed in the next two chapters) represents the way in which, almost unconsciously, they avoid and resist ideas for change and innovation from outside.

Although the chairmen are free to behave in a manner which they consider to be appropriate, this is unlikely to result in patterns of unpredictable and idiosyncratic behaviour as their recruitment and training results in their wanting to do only that which does not challenge the policy commitments established by their predecessors. If it does somehow happen that a chairman 'goes off the rails' then the rule which limits chairmanships to only two years means that his contribution is restrained at least by a time limit, and at the same time the rotation and change of chairmanships prevents the build-up of personalised power which could challenge the group-based character of council leadership, which almost inevitably reinforces established commitments and makes change rather difficult.

The Leader

Just as the authorities on the council cannot dominate and control the selection of all the new councillors, so they are unable to dominate the selection of the leader of the council since he is elected at a secret ballot by *all* the members of the majority group. Moreover, the problem of control is

28. 'The identification of an individual with a group to which he does not yet belong but which he proposes to join' (Caplow, 1964, p. 176).
29. Simon (1957, p. 218) defines identification as 'the process whereby the individual substitutes organizational objectives . . . for his own aims as the value-indices which determine his organizational decisions.'

further exacerbated because although the new councillor does not possess resources which enable him to have any independent impact upon the direction of council activity (and if he does break the rules he is not listened to) the leader does have resources which makes it very much more difficult for the authorities within the council to establish behaviour rules which they can enforce upon the leader to restrain his activity. In other words, a particular leader may (like a new councillor) possess attributes which the chairman regards as inadequately fitting a person for that office, but at the same time (unlike the situation of a new councillor) the chairmen are probably less able to compensate for this by the successful use of specific and overt restraining behaviour rules.

In many ways, both the contestants for the first leadership of the council of the Royal Borough of Kensington and Chelsea possessed attributes which conformed to the basic recruitment rules used by the chairmen, since both were senior councillors who had served an apprenticeship which included the leadership of their own councils. The final election of Alderman Anslow-Wilson, however, undoubtedly met with the approval of the majority of the chairmen (all but two of whom were, like Anslow-Wilson, Kensington councillors). In this situation, predictability and control were built into the recruitment rules, and, as with the chairmen, required and proper behaviour was learnt prior to position-incumbency. The chairmen did not *need* to attempt to control and restrain the behaviour of the leader by the imposition and assertion of behaviour rules: Alderman Anslow-Wilson already knew what he should and should not do; proper role behaviour was internalised, and there is no doubt that the majority of the chairmen were satisfied with the way in which he interpreted his responsibilities: 'Alderman Anslow-Wilson was leader in the strict and proper sense of the word, he used to chair the informal meeting of the chairmen, but he was easy-going and prepared to let them get on with the job.' 'Anslow-Wilson was the nicest of all the leaders I have known. . . . Chairmen were left to their own devices for he rarely had any firm convictions. He was a very patient man.' In other words, Anslow-Wilson defined his role in 'small' terms as involving the loose co-ordination of the group of committee chairmen. He 'tried to make sure the council stayed together and united' and his activity was confined to the maintenance of the group as an effective unit which meant that his own activity was directed on the council itself and not to questioning and challenging the effectiveness of council policy in terms of its implications for public need.

The election of Councillor Sir Malby Crofton to the leadership in 1968, represented a break in the established recruitment rules, and certainly the other candidate for the leadership had the attributes which the chairmen saw as properly fitting a councillor for that office, since he was senior in the council, well-liked by the other chairmen, had been chairman of a number of major committees (including the prestigious Housing Committee), and was active in the South Kensington Conservative Association, where he had been Chairman. I suggested at the outset of this section that the authorities' success in controlling and restraining behaviour was partly dependent on the maintenance of established recruitment rules. If their rules are broken then they need to compensate for this by the assertion of restraining behaviour rules. This is, however, a less effective method of control. In order to establish the success which the authorities enjoy in controlling behaviour in this sort of situation it is necessary to appreciate how far a particular position-incumbent is receptive and responsive to the rules which are held out as guides for his behaviour, either because he regards them as legitimate or as reinforced by sanctions which make deviance difficult. In addition we also need to know the resources which he possesses (and I identified the resources of the leader in the last section) as they may enable him to by-pass some of the rules and restraints.

The 'irregularity' of Councillor Sir Malby Crofton's election to the leadership meant that it might be necessary for the chairmen to attempt to control his behaviour positively and directly, because the attributes which he possessed meant that he could well not have internalised the rules of what they saw as proper leadership behaviour. Most important, the fact that he was regarded as a 'new boy' and was not active in the local Conservative association, meant that there was a fear, not only that he might change established policies, but that he might innovate in a way which challenged what the chairmen saw as the proper scope of government. Any control attempt was bound to be fraught with difficulty, however, as there was no tradition of any restraining behaviour rules for the leader, and the fact that the leader possessed resources which were denied to the new councillor meant that if he was not responsive to the hastily constructed behaviour rules then it would be no easy task to force his behaviour into line.

I have already suggested that the majority of the chairmen considered that the leader should assume a small role, limited to the loose co-ordination of the committee chairmen's activity. Moreover, I have also suggested that an implication of the established recruitment rules was that his behaviour should be confined to the maintenance of established policies, but where change or innovation was recognised by the group of chairmen as necessary then it should be in accord with what they saw as 'Conservative principles'. In fact a chairman pointed out that: 'We expect the leader to carry on what's gone on in the past and be consistent. We consider what we've done to be satisfactory or else we wouldn't have done it before. Where necessary he should accept innovations but in such a way that the party will accept them.' Moreover, the Leader 'mustn't overstep the mark', and he must remember that 'a large amount of council decision-making is determined by financial considerations and he must work within the limits of this and Conservatism.'

Councillor Sir Malby Crofton was well aware that his election to the leadership represented a 'departure from standard practice', and one of his first acts as leader was to appoint a deputy leader: 'He had to appoint a deputy leader to appease and assuage those who said he was not of enough experience. He chose Frank [Thackway] because he had served longer than most and had been leader himself as well as chairman of a number of committees. In addition to this Crofton tries to consult people of experience to keep them in the picture.' In other words, Crofton lacked 'idiosyncracy credit' (Hollander, 1964) which meant that he had to move particularly carefully in order to establish himself as a credible leader with those senior and authoritative councillors who opposed his election to the leadership; but even so: 'The position has changed enormously with the new leader. ... Malby Crofton is coming out with new ideas and leading and bringing the council along with him.' A chairman expressed a similar view: 'Crofton, so far, has delved more deeply and exercised more detailed control than any of the others [other leaders] but whether he'll keep it up or not, I don't know.'

There is little doubt then, that Crofton saw the leadership as involving more than the co-ordination of committee effort and the maintenance of established policies, and although this view challenged the chairmen's conception of the role, Crofton was able to establish something of a power base for himself in the newly created Co-ordinating and Policy Committee, and his style and objectives gained the support of many of the large number of new councillors elected in 1968 as well as the support of councillors from North Kensington and Chelsea. A new councillor: 'There's a lot of things that need changing here; our secure majority has made us complacent so that we rarely give any thought to whether things are O.K. I think this is where the leader can come in, as he should stand back and say what we need to do to improve things.' A Chelsea councillor: 'In the present circumstances there is a lot to be done, and this is the way Crofton sees it, and I think he's right.' In other words, Crofton attempted to by-pass the chairmen he had inherited under the apprenticeship rule, but his capacity to do this effectively was restricted by the fact that the chairmen enjoyed positions of institutionalised control and this meant that it was difficult for him to challenge their views as to the proper scope of government, or the established rules regarding the qualities which councillors needed to possess if they were to become vice-chairmen: the councillors he appointed in 1968 had an average of over ten years' experience on the council.

In 1971, although a number of the senior and authoritative councillors retired, this was more than matched by the Labour defeat of many of the new councillors who had supported Crofton. This loss undoubtedly further strengthened the position of the senior councillors and those from South Kensington who were opposed to innovations and changes in council policy. The strengthening of this group's position is evidenced by the censure motion which they brought against the leader in the autumn of 1971 when he attempted to co-opt back on to the committees many of those councillors who were defeated in the 1971 elections; by the rise to prominence of a South Kensington councillor who commanded the unofficial support of a number of the councillors opposed to change and innovation and who was seen as a potential leader should Councillor Sir Malby Crofton choose to retire; and also by the refusal of the party to allow Councillor Sir Malby Crofton to appoint a new deputy leader of his choice following the death of Alderman Thackway. Councillor Sir Malby Crofton may have wished to extend the responsibilities of the leadership and he may have wished to consider extensive change and innovation in council policy, but his capacity to do so was restricted by the weight of support and authority behind the restraining behaviour rules which were held out for him and which represented a conscious articulation of the standards implicit in the established recruitment rules for the position which were broken when he was elected to the leadership.

IV. IMPLICATIONS AND CONCLUDING REMARKS

In this chapter I have outlined the recruitment and behaviour rules for three positions on the council, and I have argued that they represent alternative methods of controlling behaviour. If position-incumbents are selected with care according to the recruitment rules of the authorities on the council, then appropriate behaviours are built-in and there is no need for restraining behaviour rules, but where recruitment is outside of the control of the authorities then they will attempt to control the behaviour of those who are recruited by the use of more overt restraining behaviour rules. So far, however, I have emphasised the importance of these rules for the behaviour of the individual position-incumbents, but what are the implications of these rules for the collective activity of the council? What part can the different positions play in the deliberations with respect to the development of council policy? First, the behaviour rules attempt to exclude those who have been recruited by criteria which suggest that they might not be sympathetic to the maintenance of established council policy commitments from taking a major part in council decision-making. There is no doubt that the new councillor is effectively excluded, and although it was more difficult to exclude the second leader of the council his capacity to change and innovate was restricted. Second, the chairmen assume the major role in directing the activities of the council, and although they are subject to no behaviour rules, the manner of their recruitment means that they will have been socialised into an acceptance of the existing pattern of policy commitments and they will see it as their prime responsibility to defend those commitments in the face of challenges both from within, and outside, the council. The way in which they handle external relations will be discussed in Section B.

Section B
The external relations of the council

The two chapters which comprise this section come to terms with the critique which I directed earlier against that work which assessed the impact of environmental forces upon public policy by concentrating on surrounding structures and inputs, while ignoring the orientations and perceptions of those in government and the way in which they selectively import aspects of their environment into their decisional activity. In Chapter 8 I outline the model which councillors have developed, and use, to assess interest groups and their claims; and in Chapter 9, I deal with the more general question of the councillor and his information, noting the sources on which councillors rely as well as those which they avoid and resist.

8 The councillor and interest groups

For most of us participation in politics takes the form of protest.
>A. J. Ayer, *Philosophy and Politics*, Eleanor Rathbone
>Memorial Lecture (Liverpool, Liverpool University Press,
>1967), pp. 22–3.

If you can dismiss the criticism of American policy as coming from a
beatnik, a bearded slob, then you don't have to deal with the argument
he raises.
>Alfred Hassler, of the Fellowship of Reconciliation, cited in
>George Thayer, *The Farther Shores of Politics* (London,
>Allen Lane, 1968), p. 464.

In Chapter 3, I pointed out that the majority of studies which have assessed
the influence of interest groups on public policy have done so by paying only
scant attention to those in government who have to deal with any influence
attempts. I suggested then, and in Chapter 5, that if we wished to understand what part groups played in the process of policy formation it was
necessary to appreciate the manner in which the governmental decision-
makers categorised interest groups and their claims, and developed rules
which provided criteria for granting access to some but not to others.

In this chapter I want to outline the framework and the categories used
by councillors to deal with interest groups. After I have outlined the various
categories that make up the framework, I will discuss the inter-relation-
ships among them and provide a less static picture of the rules of access and
the scope for interest group activity within the councillor's normative
framework.

I. THE RESEARCH: COUNCILLOR CATEGORIES

I became aware of councillors' views about interest groups and their
demands in several stages. At first I relied on regular attendance of council
meetings, paid close attention to local issues, and conducted unstructured

interviews with councillors and interest group leaders. As a result, I formed the impression that councillors made consistent distinctions between certain types of interest groups and certain types of demands.

First, councillors made very different evaluations of the worthiness, reliability and helpfulness of the differing *groups* with which they came into contact. For example, at council meetings favourable references were made to the Kensington Housing Trust, the District Nursing Association, the North Kensington Playspace Group, and the Women's Royal Voluntary Service; more guarded references were made to the Notting Hill Social Council's 'Blenheim Project' to provide assistance for young drifters; and at the council meeting in January 1967, there was an outburst from the leader of the council against the Kensington and Chelsea Council Tenants Association when he pointed out that the council were 'not bad landlords [and] when we've had bad relations it's because the tenants are Communist-led and egged-on by one of their councillors'.

Second, it was also clear from debate at council meetings that councillors had distinct preferences as to the *policies* which they felt the council should, or should not, be pursuing. The ideology of councillors frequently served to justify their not acting on particular suggestions which were directed to them by either interest groups or the minority party. For example, a petition requesting the council to consider acquiring a block of flats in North Kensington was not acted upon: councillors were not sympathetic to compulsory purchase, or to 'attacks on private landlords'. One Labour councillor was well aware of the importance of councillor ideology in affecting councillors' responses to particular problems, as he stated in open debate on this problem: 'I'm not putting forward compulsory purchase as a sensible option to the Conservatives as I know that their ideological bias stops them from taking such action.' The importance of councillor ideology was not confined to housing matters: when the council introduced its scheme for parking control in the southern part of the Borough, there were waves of public protest (to which, for the most part, the councillors were sympathetic) but the demand that on-street parking should be free for residents was turned down. As the chairman of the Works Committee stated at a council meeting: 'I believe that the person who owns the car should pay for the cost of the scheme. We've split it [the cost] two-thirds to short-term parkers and one-third to residents, and the balance of available places is the opposite. I think this is a fair balance. I don't think that the residents should get it scot-free, and it should never become a burden on the rates.'

Third, and finally, occasional reference was made to the *style* in which groups expressed their demands for council action. For example, in the report of the Housing Committee to the council at the council meeting in May 1967, alarm was expressed at the sending of a petition by the Notting Hill People's Association as it was considered that the issue had previously been resolved in a private meeting between members of the

Association and a few councillors: 'We regret . . . that the Association felt the need to present a petition which reiterates opinions and suggestions already made.' In the period up to January 1969, there were four occasions in the history of the council when 'disorder' led to the mayor clearing the public gallery. The sanction of clearance clearly indicates something of the feeling of the majority group councillors to those instances of fairly anomic interest articulation, but statements by the mayor on those occasions suggest quite clearly the role which the public should assume at council meetings: 'Members of the public can attend and watch deliberations of their councillors – that is their right – but they may not participate or take part – that is for their elected representatives' (The mayor, council meeting, October 1967).

Observation of council activity in the year prior to the summer of 1968, suggested that councillors thought about interest group inputs in terms of three distinct categories, examples of which have been given above.

1. The source of the demand: *the group*.
2. The policy content of the group demand and its implications for council activity and resource commitment: the *demand* itself.
3. The method of articulation adopted by the demanding group: the *communication method*.

At a later stage in my research, I was able to pursue the subject further. Interviews with councillors in the summer of 1968 included questions on these three categories, which on the basis of previous observation, seemed to influence councillors in their reception of demands. Although I covered categories one and three by direct questioning and I have clear information on what the councillors regard as the 'good' and 'bad' groups, and the 'proper' and 'improper' methods of group communication, it was not so easy to see how I could collect systematic information on category two, so that I could build up a full picture of councillor ideology. In fact I conducted general discussions with councillors on a number of issues in the area, and this did provide something of a picture of the councillors' views on the proper scope of government.

The 'good' and the 'bad' groups

Given the fact that I was concerned to see how councillors assessed the value of specific groups, I had to direct their attention to a limited range of groups from within their area. A list of twenty groups was drawn up,[1]

1. Some indication of the number of associational interest groups in Kensington and Chelsea is provided by the following information. In the Council's estimates of 'grants to voluntary associations' for the year 1968–9, provision was made for grants to some fifty or more organisations. The council provides representatives on over 80 outside bodies'. The list of organisations' and clubs and societies' drawn up by borough officials includes almost 200 groups. One organisation active in North Kensington has calculated that there are some 150 groups and voluntary bodies active in that part of the Borough alone.

which, on the basis of my past year's work in Kensington and Chelsea, did seem to be a reasonable cross-section of groups that had been fairly active and involved in the political process at some point in the last three years, either in assisting the council in the maintenance of existing policy or in urging change or innovation in the pattern of the council's resource commitments.[2] The typed list was handed to councillors and they were asked the following question:

> 'Here is a list of groups which I hope is a reasonable cross-section of those in the Borough. I wonder if you could advise me as to how helpful[3] you feel they are in making the borough the sort of place you would like to see to live and work in – not just for their own members but for other people as well?'

Forty-four Conservative councillors were asked the question, and thirty-eight were prepared to make specific assessments of the groups.[4] No councillor made assessments about all the groups on the list: on average respondents made evaluative statements with respect to eight or nine of the groups. In categorising responses to this question, it was apparent that it was necessary to have two categories of helpful response (Helpful and Very Helpful) as several councillors wanted to make distinctions of degree among the groups which they considered as helpful. By and large councillors were more sparing in referring to groups as not helpful (though they were less sparing in these judgements in interview than they were in speeches at council meetings). Finally, some respondents were unsure as to how to categorise particular groups, pointing out, for example, that although some things about the group meant that it could be considered as helpful in other ways this was not the case.

2. Two councillors did specifically say that the list was a good cross-section. One councillor felt that I had drawn attention only to those groups which 'hit the headlines'. Some councillors said that I should have included additional groups on the list, but only three other groups were mentioned; the Red Cross, the Chelsea Society, and the North Kensington Community Centre.

3. The term 'helpful' was chosen because it was seen as a fairly neutral term which would allow councillors to talk about groups which they liked and disliked. In fact I think it is reasonable to suggest that councillors saw the question as a chance to talk about groups which they thought of as good or bad.

4. Two new councillors said that they had been members for too short a time. One councillor said all were helpful and would not discriminate. One very senior councillor said that he did not know enough to answer. One senior councillor just did not want to distinguish. The Mayor would not answer, pointing out that in his years of office he had to avoid controversial opinions. One alderman said all the groups were helpful except the 'political' ones, which he would not identify. One new councillor said it was necessary to give context and he would single no group out. In fact of the above eight, two did go on to offer specific assessments of groups, so Table 4 is a summary of the responses of 40 Conservative councillors and aldermen.

TABLE 4. *Statements as to the helpfulness of the groups*

	Very Helpful	Helpful	Unsure	Not Helpful
Kensington Housing Trust	23	11	0	0
Notting Hill Community Workshop	0	3	4	4
Kensington and Chelsea Arts Council	3	10	2	4
Kensington and Chelsea Inter-Racial Council	0	4	5	17
Ratepayers Association	1	4	0	2
K & C Council Tenants Association	1	1	0	15
Kensington High Street Association	1	9	0	0
Neighbourhood Service Unit	0	7	4	2
K & C Chamber of Commerce	5	12	1	0
Family Service Unit	13	6	0	0
Kensington Council of Social Service	3	3	1	0
Kensington Architectural Group	0	9	2	4
Campden Charities	16	7	0	0
District Nursing Association	11	10	0	0
North Kensington Playspace Group	5	11	1	1
Kensington Society	4	17	0	1
Task Force	4	8	1	0
Notting Hill Social Council	0	8	4	2
Women's Royal Voluntary Service	12	12	1	0
North Kensington Family Study	0	1	0	1

TABLE 5. *The 'Helpful' and 'Unhelpful' groups*

Kensington Housing Trust	57
Campden Charities	39
Women's Royal Voluntary Service	36
Family Service Unit	32
District Nursing Association	32
Kensington Society	24
Kensington and Chelsea Chamber of Commerce	22
North Kensington Playspace Group	20
Task Force	16
Kensington and Chelsea Arts Council	12
Kensington High Street Association	11
Kensington Council of Social Service	9
Notting Hill Social Council	6
Kensington Architectural Group	5
Neighbourhood Service Unit	5
Ratepayers Association	4
North Kensington Family Study	0
Notting Hill Community Workshop	−1
K & C Council Tenants Association	−12
Kensington and Chelsea Inter-Racial Council	−13

2 points for 'very helpful';
1 point for 'helpful';
0 points for 'unsure';
−1 point for 'not helpful'.

What the policy of the Council 'should' and 'should not' be

So far I have outlined councillor assessments of a range of specific groups that were active in their area – the assumption being that councillors will be more ready to allow effective access to groups which they consider as helpful than they will to the groups which they consider as unhelpful. It is also important to realise that councillors are not indifferent as to the policies which they feel the council should and should not be pursuing. Political scientists have often been at pains to point out that they do not regard political decision-makers as neutral pinballs devoid of policy preferences, but nevertheless, there have been very few attempts to see what part the 'values' of those in government do play in the policy process. In this section I take the view that just as the source of the demand will affect the chances of a demand gaining effective access, so the ideology and policy preferences of the councillors will also act as a critically important screen which will affect their response to demands. The assumption in this case is that councillors will be likely to allow effective access to a demand that does not run counter to their own policy preferences but they will probably deal unsympathetically with demands which run counter to their own views about what should be the scope of council activity.[5]

The ideology of the councillors (their position regarding the proper scope of government) is discussed in Chapter 10, and here I will just briefly lay out certain themes which were articulated by the chairmen, and which are germane to the topic under discussion.

Their dominant conception as to the proper scope of government was one which saw governmental activity confined to the provision of 'traditional services' (see Williams & Adrian, 1963, esp. chap. 1). They argued that the general services used by all residents should be good, and refuse collection, street cleansing and street lighting were thought of as particularly important spheres of government activity, and in these cases there was a concern to offer a high standard of service. There was a specific recognition of the needs and problems of a particular type of resident – the car owner, the ratepayers, and those who were worried about traffic or aircraft noise, or were concerned to preserve the 'residential' nature of the Borough. The overall orientation of the chairmen was, however, one which gave the council a fairly small role and which saw its activity as limited to the provision of statutory services. Concern with the level of council expenditure and the 'needs of the ratepayers' was invariably uppermost in the minds of the chairmen, and running alongside this they stressed the value of 'self-help, 'self-reliance', and 'voluntary collective' effort (as opposed to government activity) in the solution of 'public' problems (see chap. 10), together with views which asserted the value of 'private enterprise' and the need to have a certain regard for the 'commercial' life of the Borough.

5. See the comment by Zeigler (1964, p. 276): 'those groups whose goals do not conflict with the legislators' perceptions of the public interest will be more effective than those groups whose goals do conflict with such perceptions.'

The 'proper' and 'improper' methods of group communication to the Council

The following question was asked of forty-six Conservative councillors, after there had been a discussion of a number of issues in the area:

> 'If a group of constituents, or an organised grouping, has a particular idea which they want to put before the Council in one of the sorts of areas we have been discussing, what is the proper or correct way for that idea to be presented to the Council?'

The assumption behind this question was that councillors would be more prepared to assess sympathetically a suggestion that was sent to them through a proper channel than they would where the style adopted was seen as improper or illegitimate.

The most notable feature of the collated responses (see Table 6) is that

TABLE 6. *The assessments made by Councillors as to the 'Proper'[6] and 'Improper' methods of group communication to the Council*

	Proper method	Other possible methods	Unsure	Improper methods
Going through the ward representative	32	2	0	0
Contacting the chairman of the relevant committee	8	2	0	3
Petition	4	11	7	7
Contacting an officer	2	9	1	2
Raising the issue in the local Press	0	1	2	6
Demonstrations	0	1	1	18
	46			

the majority of councillors considered it was better for groups to communicate through the ward representative or the chairmen, than to deal directly with the officers or to use the press or some form of demonstration.

The answers about the use of petitions suggest uncertainty about the legitimacy of this means of presenting demands: although fifteen councillors thought the petition *could* be used, only four councillors saw it as the

6. Frequently councillors in replying to this question referred to the possibility of more than one method of communication being acceptable. Where councillors did reply in this way then they either volunteered or were prompted to suggest which was the 'best' way. Not all councillors did refer to more than one method as being appropriate, and these responses are added to those methods that were identified as 'best' by those councillors who referred to more than one method, to provide column one – the 'proper method' to contact the council. The number of items in this column is, of course, equal to the number of councillors who were asked the question – forty-six.

best way of communicating a policy preference to the council, and of these only one referred to this as the only way that could be used. Most councillors who pointed out that a petition could be used usually went on to suggest that other ways were better. As a chairman put it: 'The way to do it by the book is to petition the Council, but the correct way to do it is through the local councillor especially if he belongs to the Majority Party'. Although in 'theory' councillors saw petitions as an acceptable means of communication to the council, and although they felt that there were occasions on which there could be (as an alderman put it) 'genuine' petitions, their experience with petitions led respondents to consider them as a form of pressure (Bonilla, 1956), and as an attempt to force the council to move publicly in a direction that was unacceptable to them. Petitions were acceptable where they represented diffuse bodies of opinion around one issue, like pedestrian crossings or traffic management schemes, but they were unacceptable when they came from organised groupings that were attacking the council and trying to urge it to change existing commitments.

II. THE RESEARCH: THE INTER-RELATIONSHIPS AMONG THE COUNCILLOR CATEGORIES

So far I have described certain critical dimensions of the councillors attitudes towards interest groups and group demands. I have not tried to *explain* the pattern of responses that have been revealed. In this section I want to account for the councillors' differential assessments of the helpfulness of the various groups. This necessitates a consideration of the other two categories which I identified, for councillor views on the proper scope of governmental activity and the proper methods of group communication affect the judgements they make of the groups in the area.

After councillors had identified *specific* groups as helpful or unhelpful, a number were asked a follow-up question which invited them to say in *general* terms, what led them to place a group in one of these categories:

> 'In general terms what do you have in mind, what do you look for, when you identify a group as helpful or unhelpful?'

Responses to this question can be divided into two kinds. First, there were statements which suggested that groups were helpful because they provided information, represented ideas, and brought problems to the attention of the council. Second, there were statements which pointed out that groups were helpful where they were either working entirely independently of the council in providing some form of service, or else were offering some exchange to the council by providing a service but with council assistance. The first set of statements referred to the value of groups as 'input' structures, and the second to the value of groups as 'output' structures – as groups that were working alongside the council in some form of service provision. A new North Kensington councillor stressed the value of groups as input structures: '. . . groups exist as there is a need for them, but I don't know what I'd look for if I had to define a helpful group. If it comes up with ideas, or if it has information about the area or the people which we may not have, then it will be of great help.' Although new councillors and those representing North Kensington were generally more inclined to stress the helpfulness of groups in terms of their being involved in the process of interest articulation, this view was not confined to those councillors, as senior and influential councillors also pointed to the value of groups as representative of opinion, but when they did then they were invariably more selective in specifying exactly which groups were 'responsible' and 'reliable' in providing sound information and ideas. A senior South Kensington councillor: 'One is very sympathetic to their suggestions and we look into them very carefully. Bodies like the Red Cross and the Women's Royal Voluntary Service are responsible bodies and they won't put anything up without due consideration. The Kensington Society, the Chelsea Society, and the West London Architects are not fools, and when they put something up it merits attention and consideration. . . . They're responsible and live in the area.'

Of course, it was not the case that respondents answered by referring only to the input *or* the value of groups as most did in fact mention both aspects of group activity when considering their helpfulness. A North Kensington councillor: '[a helpful group as one in which] people are not only prepared to throw out ideas of what needs to be done, but also, instead of just shouting, get down to doing something.' A senior South Kensington councillor: 'They're helpful when they are prepared to give useful advice and guidance. Of course, the Women's Royal Voluntary Service and the District Nursing Association are different, as they're actually doing a job of work.'

Information derived from a general open-ended question is inevitably difficult to code, but there is the strong suggestion that newer and less senior councillors not occupying positions of formal authority on the council were more inclined to suggest that helpful groups were those which were fulfilling an input role, and these councillors were fairly catholic in considering a whole range of groups as helpful in this way. Senior councillors and those who were chairmen, tended to stress far more the value of groups as output structures, which helped the council in the administration and organisation of council services. As a senior South Kensington councillor put the matter: 'It is our policy to co-operate with groups. . . . Where voluntary bodies are willing to do things, and can do things as well as a local authority, the only difference being that the ratepayers are saved money, then I'm all for it.' A chairman: 'The important thing to bear in mind is that a lot of these groups are doing things which, if they were not done by these groups, would have to be done by us. A lot more would fall on the ratepayers if these bodies weren't there.' Where the chairmen and the senior councillors did refer to the input value of groups, then they tended to consider a more restricted range of groups to be legitimate representatives of opinion. This interpretation from the general question is reinforced in the difference between the responses of chairmen and non-chairmen on the question asking them to categorise specific groups. Table 7 (which is a breakdown of Table 5 into chairmen and non-chairmen columns) does reveal that the chairmen are more inclined than non-chairmen to rate the 'demanding' groups[7] as unhelpful.

'Demanding' groups will be less liked by the chairmen than by the non-chairmen, because the acceptance of those groups would involve not only the imposition of an additional burden on the council, but could also involve the possible reversal of existing commitments. Those councillors who have been on the council for a considerable length of time and have been (and still are) centrally involved in the making of decisions and the running of council services can be expected to be both attached to the existing pattern of council resource commitments and also particularly aware of the implications of policy changes and innovations, so that they do not regard the demanding groups as helpful. Table 8 sets out the relevant replies for a detailed comparison. The ratio of helpful to not-helpful assessments made by the chairmen and the non-chairmen with respect to the demanding groups does indeed suggest that the chairmen were more critical of groups which challenged the existing pattern of council resource commitments. The chairmen have more reason to be aware of the financial and policy implications of the demands being made, given their close involvement with policy-making and maintenance, and it is not surprising, therefore, that they regard as 'helpful' those groups whose demands reinforce and conform to existing council policies.

The position within the council occupied by respondents does, then, affect their assessment of groups, but it is clear that this does not account for the general pattern of councillor assessments as there is, in fact, a reasonable level of consensus between the chairmen and the non-chairmen. The search for more inclusive explanations for the pattern of assessments suggests the importance of councillor ideology: there is something of a match between their categorisation of groups as helpful and unhelpful and their views as to what should, and should not, be the proper scope of council activity. If we look at the chairmen's rating of groups alongside their views as to the proper scope of council activity, then we find that the groups which they regard as helpful tend to be those whose activity and demands do not conflict with their own views about what the council should be doing.

7. By 'demanding' groups I refer to those groups which raised demands which, if met, would necessitate the council either taking on new commitments, or else reversing existing commitments.

TABLE 7. *The Helpful and the Unhelpful groups, the differing assessments made by Chairmen and Non-Chairmen*

Chairmen (14)		Non-Chairmen (26)	
Kensington Housing Trust	22	Kensington Housing Trust	35
Campden Charities	17	Women's Royal Voluntary Service	25
Family Service Unit	16	Campden Charities	22
District Nursing Association	12	District Nursing Association	20
Women's Royal Voluntary Service	11	North Kensington Playspace Group	18
Kensington Society	8	Family Service Unit	16
K & C Chamber of Commerce	7	Kensington Society	16
Kensington High Street Association	6	K & C Chamber of Commerce	15
Kensington Council of Social Service	6	Task Force	11
Task Force	5	K & C Arts Council	10
North Kensington Playspace Group	2	Neighbourhood Service Unit	6
K & C Arts Council	2	Kensington High St Association	5
North Kensington Family Study	1	Notting Hill Social Council	5
Kensington Architectural Group	1	Kensington Architectural Group	4
Notting Hill Social Council	1	Ratepayers Association	4
Ratepayers Association	0	Kensington Council of Social Service	3
Neighbourhood Service Unit	−1	Notting Hill Community Workshop	1
Notting Hill Community Workshop	−2	North Kensington Family Study	−1
K & C Inter-Racial Council	−6	K & C Council Tenants Assoc.	−5
K & C Council Tenants Assoc.	−7	K & C Inter-Racial Council	−7

Points allocated as for Table 5.

TABLE 8. *The differing assessments of the helpfulness of the Demanding groups made by Chairmen and Non-Chairmen*[8]

	Chairmen		Non-Chairmen	
	Helpful	Not helpful	Helpful	Not helpful
Notting Hill Community Workshop	0	2	3	2
K & C Council Tenants Association	0	7	2	8
K & C Inter-Racial Council	0	6	4	11
Kensington Architectural Group	3	2	6	2
Notting Hill Social Council	3	2	5	0
Neighbourhood Service Unit	0	1	7	1
K & C Arts Council	3	2	10	2
North Kensington Playspace Group	3	1	13	0
	12	23	50	26

8. There is no weighting of the helpful statements. 'Very helpful' and 'helpful' assessments are both counted as one. 'Unsure' statements, of course, are not included.

It is possible to divide the groups on the list which I handed to councillors into two categories,[9] as in some cases groups are in a co-operative and favourable relationship to the council, whereas in other cases groups are regarded with disfavour and the relationship between the council and these groups is one of conflict.

Co-operative group/council relationships

A number of the groups on the list are not so much involved in making demands on the council, but are rather working alongside the council in the provision of council services. A good example of this type of group is the housing trust, since even though they make considerable demands on the council for financial assistance, the council benefits not only from interest payments on the loans, but also from the fact that the provision of rented accommodation for working-class families in the borough reduces the pressure on the council to provide council housing, and many councillors consider that it is quite improper for the council to spend vast sums of money on the development of municipal housing. There are five groups on the list which are in this category and they are regarded favourably by chairmen and non-chairmen alike: the groups are, the Kensington Housing Trust, the Family Service Unit, Campden Charities, the Women's Royal Voluntary Service, and the District Nursing Association.

Councillors view these groups with favour as they consider that government should assume a restricted role in the provision of special services for those in need, and should confine its energy to the provision of general services used by all, so making only small demands on the population for rate income. This being the case they consider that there is much room for private collective effort and the voluntary principle in the solution of social problems. (For a similar comment, see, Committee on the Management of Local Government, 1967, vol. 2, Table 6.7, p. 192.)

In fact some input groups are regarded with favour by the councillors as their demands do not challenge the councillors' own preferences as to the proper scope of government activity. A degree of co-operation exists between the council and these groups which make demands that square with the council leadership's preference for private enterprise, the prosperity of the commercial part of the borough, and the needs of the middle-class resident. Hence the legitimacy attached to representations from

9. Not all the groups are included, as there are a number which it is more difficult to categorise in this way. *Task Force*, for example, is a group which is assisting the council in the provision of a service but it is regarded with rather less favour than other groups of this kind because it is a comparatively new body and was more aggressive in promoting itself. Similarly, the *North Kensington Playspace Group* is rather difficult to typify. It is a demanding group which has gained a considerable measure of acceptability (especially among the non-chairmen) and there is little doubt that one factor which accounts for this is not just the changing views of councillors as to the role which the council should assume in the field of play provision, but also the extreme care which the group took in approaching the council through the proper channels.

interest groups such as the Kensington Society, the Kensington High Street Association, and the Kensington Chamber of Commerce. Non-chairmen are less exclusive than the chairmen, and, for example, tend to be sympathetic to the demands of the North Kensington Playspace Group as well, since they are more prepared to recognise that government can itself assume some responsibility to provide play and amenity facilities whereas the chairmen tend to see this as more of a 'private' responsibility.

An example of the co-operation which exists between the council and these sorts of groups is provided with the retirement of Mr Waring-Sainsbury from his position of Town Clerk of the Royal Borough of Kensington and Chelsea. The local Chamber of Commerce held a lunch in his honour and congratulated him for 'his unfailing efforts to help the Chamber promote its aims and objectives', and made him a vice-president of the chamber. For his part, Mr Waring-Sainsbury 'emphasised that it had been a pleasure to co-operate as much as he could with the Chamber and he had, during the past three years, been most impressed with the work it had done for both members and the Royal Borough, with its growth, stature and status, and with its influence on commercial life. It had proved itself to be an important factor in its help, and indeed advice to the Royal Borough of Kensington and Chelsea' (K & C Chamber of Commerce, *Newsletter*, 21 December, 1968).

Unfavourable group/council relationships

Chairman look unfavourably on those demanding groups which press for new services or for changes in the provision of existing services since this would not only involve a reversal of established commitments but would also involve the council in moving into new areas which the chairmen consider should lie outside the scope of governmental activity. Hence their lack of sympathy for such groups as the Notting Hill Social Council, the Notting Hill Community Workshop, the Ratepayers Association (which was active in lobbying for free residents' parking), the Neighbourhood Service Unit, the Kensington and Chelsea Inter-Racial Council, and the Kensington and Chelsea Council Tenants Association. The Notting Hill Housing Service (*Housing Survey*, 1968) noted that it was 'difficult to get any kind of official help for projects which seemed controversial and equally difficult to get help from charitable foundations' which often followed the lead given by the council.

To observe, as I have done, that the chairmen's assessment of groups tend to be consistent with their policy preferences is not to suggest that there is necessarily a causal connection between the two. Older pressure group theorists tended to argue (as I suggested in Chapter 3) that pressure groups 'caused' public policy. It would be difficult to argue that this was the case in Kensington and Chelsea, where there is a strong suggestion that the relationship is the other way around so that councillor attitudes to interest groups are based on their views as to the proper scope of government. The councillors' assessment of groups sits within the framework of their policy preferences and these cannot simply be regarded as the residue of different group demands, but are a reflection of a more complex process, and in the case of the chairmen and senior councillors are partly based upon and reflect their acceptance of the existing commitments of the council.

In this section I have suggested that a particular relationship exists between the councillors' assessment of groups and their views as to the proper role of government. I have argued that the groups which they consider as helpful either do not make claims on the council, or else make claims that do not conflict with the councillors' own views as to the proper scope of council activity. On the other hand, the groups which they consider are not helpful are all making demands which either challenge established council commitments, or else urge the council to extend the range of their activity beyond the limit they consider to be proper. Moreover, although the helpful groups used proper methods of communication to the council, the groups which the council regarded as not helpful had all resorted to some form of public articulation of interest outside what the councillors considered to be the proper channels.

III. OVERVIEW

In Section I, I suggested that councillors thought about interest groups and demands in terms of their assessments of groups, policies and communication styles. In Section II, I suggested that there was a tendency for a certain pattern of assessments to go together. The helpful groups had acceptable demands (or none at all) and went about the process of demand presentation (if they were involved in this) in the proper way. By way of contrast, the unhelpful groups had demands that were unacceptable, and they invariably had a style of demand presentation that was regarded as improper.

This picture is a static one, and only applies in situations where no new groups are forming, and where the groups that do exist continue to pursue the same activities and use the same styles of communication to the council. In fact, over time, councillors may change the assessments which they make of specific groups, and they may also change their views as to the proper role for government and the acceptable styles for interest articulation. An assessment of a group represents a councillor's appreciation of the past history of group–council relations, and their particular categorisation may change if the nature of the interaction between the group and the council changes. For example, I will show below how groups which at one time were regarded with disfavour by the authorities may be viewed differently if they change the nature of their activities and the way in which they present themselves to the council.

So far I have argued that there are two usual combinations between the three assessment categories: there are helpful groups with acceptable demands (or no demands at all) and a proper communication style; and there are unhelpful groups with unacceptable demands and an improper communication style. What about the six other possible combinations between the assessment categories? I will suggest that these other combinations are not really likely; I will argue that there is a dynamic tendency for the unhelpful groups to change; and finally, I will suggest that there are factors which inhibit the likelihood that demands for policy change and innovation will be given sympathetic consideration by the councillors.

The unhelpful groups

The combination unhelpful group with unacceptable demand and a proper communication style is unlikely. Groups which lack the sympathy of the council and which urge the council to reverse commitments or innovate, invariably make a first attempt to gain access for their demands by the quiet, more acceptable methods, but the fact that they invariably fail to gain effective access by these methods forces them into a more aggressive style of demand presentation. This situation was recognised by a North Kensington councillor: 'You should get in touch with your councillor first, but if it's not council policy then a petition is necessary. Write to the press, march on the town hall, and so on, but the initial thing to do is to actually make sure that the council do reject a thing before making it unpleasant. Most of the things that come up in petitions have usually been raised by quieter means but without much success.'

The impetus for these groups to adopt an aggressive style of demand presentation does not only come from the problems which they are likely to experience in gaining access to the council by the proper methods, but is also prompted by the nature of their support base and the particular ideology of the group leaders. These groups are usually deficient in resources and are quite unable to attain their objectives without major council assistance, and this means that they are dependent on the council to satisfy the aspirations of their members. At the same time, however, there is a strong suspicion of the council, particularly on the part of the rank and file support (and potential support) which means that the group members are wary of any attempt on the part of their leaders to go in for quiet methods of demand presentation. Not only is there a certain pressure or expectation from the rank and file that there should be aggressive demand presentation, but additionally, the leaders' concern to demonstrate to their followers that they are active in the pursuit of group demands, as well as their desire to recruit wider support for their cause, means that they may consider that it is necessary for them to provide a focal point of political activity, such as a demonstration or petition, which not only demonstrates their activity, but also serves to draw the attention of a wider public to the group and the demand and so may serve to mobilise people and increase their consciousness of the reality of local political power relations. The

G

attainment of heightened public consciousness is often regarded as an end of as great importance as the attainment of any particular demand.

On the one hand then, the leaders may not be allowed much social space by their followers in the patterning of group activity in relation to the council, and on the other hand, the leaders may desire participatory politics and a widened support base: both of these factors may lead a group away from a quiet style of demand presentation. Even though a 'noisy' style may not in any sense cause the council to reject the demand, it does predispose them to treat it unsympathetically. In the absence of success, groups which are at any event resting on a rather shaky and transactional support base, and are starved of adequate financial resources, may tend to fold.

There may be change to the combination, unhelpful group with acceptable demands and a proper communication style. Although I have just argued that there are factors which prevent unhelpful groups with unacceptable demands from adopting proper communication styles, so that they tend to be forced back into the usual and typical combination, this is not the only possible development that may occur. Unhelpful groups which fail with their unacceptable demands may scale down their demands and move away from touchy 'political' issues to ones where they feel they have a greater chance of success because the councillors' policy preferences are less firm. In the context of Kensington and Chelsea, housing demands may be dropped and demands for playspace provision may be raised in their stead.

There is no necessity for an unhelpful group with acceptable demands adopting an improper communication style. I have already suggested that all groups usually make a first approach to the council though a proper and acceptable communication channel, and it is really only *after* their demand has been refused that they feel a need to consider alternative means which must inevitably involve them in a more public style. In a situation where a group has changed its demands away from those that are unacceptable, then, unless the group itself is regarded with total suspicion, it is likely to meet with success at the first approach through the quiet method and there is no need for the group to contemplate aggressive styles of demand presentation.

These represent the three possible combinations of assessment categories that might go with the unhelpful group. However, at another extreme it is possible that an unhelpful group might not just turn to become an acceptable demanding group, but may come to develop its activity in such a way that it turns away from making any demands on the council. Groups which start out seeking to urge the council to change or innovate in council policies may themselves provide solutions to the problems which originally they saw as the responsibility of the council. The group's involvement with the task, the leader's sense of responsibility to the followers and clientele, and the possible build-up of organisational resources, may mean that group energy is channelled into service provision, or output activity and away from demand and input activity. In the context of Kensington and Chelsea, two groups which urged the council to be more active in providing public housing formed themselves into housing trusts, and a group which sought to get the council to assume a wider responsibility in the field of play provision finished up providing these facilities itself with only a limited amount of council assistance.

Unsuccessful 'pressure' groups can only sustain themselves for a limited amount of time, and unless they change their activities in some way then there is a good chance that they will be forced to disband. This is not the only pattern, however, as unhelpful groups, by associating themselves with different demands and articulation styles may transform themselves into groups that are likely to be regarded more favourably by the councillors, the more so if they turn away from directing demands to the council to providing services themselves. The councillors' assessment of groups represents their view at any one point in time of their assessment of council/group interaction, and if group activity does change then after a period, councillors too may change the way in which they categorise the helpfulness of any specific group.

The Helpful Groups

The situation with respect to the helpful groups is almost the reverse of that of the unhelpful groups. Unhelpful groups are often forced to adopt improper communication styles, and, if they are to survive, there are factors which encourage them to change the nature of their demands and the pattern of their activity. In contrast to this, the helpful groups do not need to adopt improper communication styles and there are factors which discourage them from changing the pattern of their activity.

A helpful group with acceptable demands does not need to rely on improper communication styles. Groups that are well-regarded by the council and are raising acceptable demands have no need to resort to pressure tactics. Groups of this kind are likely to be in close, and constant, communication with the council, and are assured of effective access through restrained, private methods. The point was recognised by a senior Chelsea councillor: 'It would be quite inappropriate and unnecessary for the Kensington Society, or the Chelsea Society to send in a petition; it's a once and for all thing and doesn't help establish an on-going relationship.'

Helpful groups will be reluctant to take up unacceptable demands, even though they may be able to gain effective access for those demands by proper communication styles. Groups that are well-regarded by the council are usually aware that this is the case and that they have the sort of relationship in which they can expect that such demands as they do raise will have a sympathetic hearing. These groups are conscious of their good credit-rating with the council and they are usually concerned not to jeopardise that by either associating themselves with unacceptable demands, or unhelpful groups. The secretary of one of the leading housing trusts in the area (and a group exceptionally well-regarded by the council) pointed to the importance of this when explaining the reluctance of the trust to involve itself with the Notting Hill Summer Project:[10] 'We tried to help the Notting Hill Summer Project, but we realised we were in deep water and so we got out. We could have given a veneer of respectability to the organisation, but it would not have helped us or the people in the area.' The Notting Hill Adventure Playground (and especially the warden of that playground) is another body which enjoys a certain amount of goodwill with a number of the councillors, and although at first this body was closely associated with the Summer Project, there was always a certain wariness of the project, and eventually the warden drew away. The housing trusts displayed a similar reluctance to involve themselves with the Notting Hill Peoples Association[11] when it was urging the council to acquire property that was owned by the failed Davies Investments Limited, in spite of the fact that they had considerable private sympathy with the aims of that group.

The pattern of helpful group with unacceptable demands and an improper style of communication is unlikely. The considerations which I have just outlined apply equally to this pattern. If a helpful group does take up an unacceptable demand, however, then its credit-rating with the council might mean that it could gain effective access for that demand without even the necessity of using pressure tactics. It might, of course, be the case that the demand was so unacceptable, or that the group's credit-rating was only moderately good, that when the demand was presented by the quiet method it was not acted on by the council in any positive way. Now if the group were sufficiently committed to the claim then it might be prepared to adopt a more aggressive style of demand presentation, although in doing so it would be aware that it would be jeopardising future relations with the council. I know of no cases of this in the recent history of interest group activity in Kensington and Chelsea.

In terms of the changing patterns of relationship between the differing assessment categories, there is a twofold tendency which is important in

10. The project was organised by the Notting Hill Community Workshop and the Notting Hill Social Council and was centrally concerned with housing conditions and play facilities in North Kensington. The Project was regarded with extreme suspicion by many of the leading councillors.

11. A group closely associated in the councillors' eyes with the Notting Hill Community Workshop and the whole network of 'do-gooders' in the northern part of the Borough.

limiting the possibilities of policy innovation and change being introduced to the council by way of interest group activity. First, there is a possible tendency for unhelpful groups urging unacceptable demands to transform themselves, either into groups which are raising acceptable demands, or into groups which are fulfilling more of an output role. Failure to alter themselves in this way may mean that they may cease to be able to survive. No one with a knowledge of areas such as Notting Hill can fail to be struck by the extent to which groups in these areas rise and fall with amazing rapidity. Second, the reluctance of the helpful groups to take up unacceptable demands or to form alliances with unhelpful groups is important because this activity might provide an effective means of gaining council approval for what were at first considered to be unacceptable demands. However, the fact that helpful groups are not prepared to take up such 'unacceptable' demands means that demands for change or innovation in council policy have to come either from new groups or from groups that are regarded by the council as unhelpful, and it is precisely these groups that lack the sympathy of the council and the capacity to gain access by proper methods. The fact that demands for change and innovation come from unhelpful groups and through improper channels may not cause the final rejection of those demands, but it does mean that the councillors are provided with information which deflects them from having to consider the demand itself seriously: they can instead focus attention on the 'unreliable' and 'unrepresentative' source of the demand, and on the improper way in which it was communicated, and so justify their not acting on the demand without ever having really to give it any direct or public consideration.

IV. CONCLUDING REMARKS

No government can give detailed consideration to all the demands they receive, still less are they able to respond favourably to all demands. They need to develop, and cannot avoid developing, rules-of-thumb which they can use to categorise demands. In this chapter I have outlined the rules-of-thumb which councillors use to assess interest groups and group claims in Kensington and Chelsea.

The councillors' categorisation of groups, and in particular their lack of sympathy for demanding groups urging change or innovation in council policy, does not only affect the likely development of council policy and the extent to which group views are taken into account, but because the councillors' categorisation of groups is known to many of the groups themselves, this has an effect on group life within the borough. Unhelpful groups are put in a position when they have to change or else go out of existence; helpful groups are put in a position when they know that it is dangerous for them if they adapt to changing circumstances; and the group-world forms in the mould of two dominant patterns with all the certainty of a self-fulfilling prophecy.[12]

12. This is a study of just one local authority, and there is no reason to suppose that the sorts of rules which I have identified are the same in other governmental contexts – but see, O'Malley, 1970; Bornfriend, 1969; and, Weiner, 1962, where similar themes are developed.

9 The councillor and his information

It is generally assumed that in a democratic system representatives act on more or less direct knowledge of the needs and attitudes of their public.

Committee on the Management of Local Government, vol. 2,
The Local Government Councillor (London, H.M.S.O., 1967),
p. 223.

the real trouble with local government is that it is far too close to the electorate.

Committee on the Management of Local Government, vol. 5,
Local Government Administration in England and Wales
(London, H.M.S.O., 1967), p. 40.

The information which decision-makers have at their disposal is the basis on which they respond to the world about them: it is the link between them and their environment, and is also critical in affecting the decisions which they will make, for 'all officials arrive at decisions on the basis of what they perceive and not on the basis of what is objectively true or real' (Milbrath, 1963, pp. 184–5). It is important to see what sources of information decision-makers rely upon, precisely because it can be assumed from the start that no person is able to cover all aspects of any situation with which they are involved. Selectivity in the use of information is unavoidable, and although people vary in the extent to which they try to explore 'all sides' of a problem (Bruner, 1966; and, Cherry, 1966), the human organism has a limited capacity to take in information and more importantly the occupancy of particular positions in society serves to restrict and define still further what information sources will be looked to in the solution and exploration of particular problems.

Politicians are in a position where they must inevitably be especially selective. They are not only advocates of public issues, which means that they will be likely 'to ignore or suppress information which may undermine the force of their case' (Barker & Rush, 1970, p. 18. See

175

also, Bauer, Pool & Dexter, 1964, pp. 415–21), but they are also likely to be faced with a range of demands which necessitate their action in the absence of any 'first-hand' knowledge of the relevant situations. The magnitude of their problems and the span which they cover ensure that they place heavy reliance on their 'advisers' who in many ways serve as links to the 'real' world, filtering in what they feel their political masters need to, or at least want to, know. (Barker & Rush, 1970; Clapp, 1963; Lindblom, 1968, pp. 12–20; Sharkansky, 1970c, pp. 40–2; and, Simon, 1957, p. 163.)

The degree of selectivity displayed by any politician will be partly affected by his professional status. If he makes his living in politics, and if he has special information services at his disposal, then he can overcome some of the difficulties and limitations of information shortage and faulty or partial evaluation. If, on the other hand, he is a part-time politician, fulfilling a political role while keeping up a non-political occupation, then he is inevitably thrust into an objective position in which he must exercise greater selectivity. This is the case with councillors in British local government, and it is a group of councillors in a London borough which is my special concern.

In Britain, local councillors receive no payment for their services, and the majority are in alternative full-time employment (Committee on the Management of Local Government, 1967, vol. 2, p. 19). Councillors are part-time amateurs facing complex tasks in a wide range of problem areas. They are unlikely to have adequate skills to cope with many of the problems themselves, and, because of the necessity of earning a living, they have only limited time to spend on their public work (Committee on the Management of Local Government, 1967, vol. 2, p. 92). The 'skill problem' and the 'time problem' have both been recognised in the institutional devices that surround the councillor. There are professional officers to give advice, and a committee system to enable a degree of specialisation.

The increasing scope and complexity of local government meant that it 'became increasingly difficult for the work of Local Government to be carried out with any efficiency by a group of amateurs who for the greater part had their ordinary occupations to pursue during the greater part of the day' (Hasluck, 1936, p. 60), and so the professional side of local government developed, not only to 'administer' council decisions, but also to provide advice on which those decisions could be based, for a 'councillor, or even councillors collectively, could not be expected to have all the relevant facts in his or their hands, to think out the various alternatives, or to supply information on past performances or predicted results' (Headrick, 1962, p. 75). The 'committee system' is seen by some commentators as the 'characteristic mark of local government' (Hart, 1968, p. 128), and a Central Office of Information pamphlet makes clear why it was necessary for this method of undertaking council work to develop: 'No councillor is able to devote all his attention to council work; usually he is a man (or woman) with his living to earn, and only a limited amount of time to place at the disposal of the public. Moreover local government services are today so numerous that few could pretend to detailed knowledge of the workings of the full range' (Central Office of Information, 1966, p. 13). The committee system is a means of coping with this limited time, and the specialisation ensures that councillors can really come to grips with some aspect of their council's work, but only at the expense of denying attention to other areas.

In virtually all the urban local authorities in Britain, councils are organised along party lines and candidates are often elected to the council after they have served a length of time in a local party organisation. It is difficult to exaggerate the importance of this fact of the councillor's situation when considering their openness to potentially available information sources. First, their involvement with a party means that they will be likely to have a particular ideology and, as I have just shown in the last chapter, this will affect their responsiveness and receptiveness to demands that are directed to them. Moreover, a councillor's involvement with a political party will mean that although he is going to have links with his ward, they will be links with a very particular section which will in no sense constitute a broad range of opinion.

Political leadership in most societies tends to be enjoyed by those of higher status and income and this is certainly the case with local councillors, who 'on the whole have higher incomes than their electors' (Committee on the Management of Local Government, 1967, vol. 2, p. 25), and tend to be disproportionately drawn from the ranks of employers and managers of smaller businesses. Skilled, semi-skilled, and unskilled manual workers are proportionately under-represented on councils, a feature which is particularly marked in Kensington and Chelsea where there are no councillors from the majority group who belong to these occupational categories. In a situation where councillors do not have first-hand knowledge of all sections of the community; where the representative does not share the values of the people who elected him and is not in touch with their realities, then, if we are to have truly representative government, it is particularly vital that the representative should communicate directly with those sections of the community that are not represented within the council. At the same time, however, because men tend to have most contact with those who are in a similar socio-economic position to themselves, we can expect that this is unlikely to be the case, with the result that a whole dimension of social experience is unlikely to play much part in council decision-making. Does the business of standing for election counteract this and make a councillor aware of the variety of social situations and needs in his locality? It is true that in order to become a councillor it is necessary to contest and win periodic elections, but in Kensington and Chelsea, the electoral situation is one in which the bulk of the majority group councillors have no need to maintain close relationships with electors because the seats are safe for their party irrespective of their own activity.

There is, then, the likelihood that the situation of councillors (particularly in Kensington and Chelsea) will be one which will mean that they are going to be especially selective in their use of information. The rest of this chapter will outline and discuss the responses of the councillors and aldermen who were interviewed and were asked a set of questions on this problem.[1] Four of the interview questions were most important in this context, but I shall also refer to the material obtained by other questions, such as those dealing with interest groups, a subject which was more fully discussed in the previous chapter.

I. THE RESEARCH: DATA

Question 1: Information sources used by councillors in decision-making

After a general discussion about a number of issues with which the council was involved at the time of interview,[2] I invited the councillor being interviewed to assess the importance he attributed to a variety of information sources which could possibly have helped him in coming to a decision:

> 'Obviously when you come to decide on issues before you – like the ones we've been discussing – you assess the information relevant to the problem. Here are some possible sources of information.[3] I wonder if you could advise me as to how important they are for you personally in helping you to make up your mind on an issue?'

Table 9 shows the responses of the forty-one Conservative councillors and aldermen who were asked the question. In answering this question, councillors invariably referred to more than one source as being of importance, and if this was the case, then they were encouraged to suggest the main source on which they relied (column one). Additional references to sources that were seen as important are tabulated in column two, and the totals of these two columns represent all the positively evaluative statements referring to the various information sources. Certain respondents as well as mentioning sources that could or should be relied on, also referred

1. There are problems of relying on interviews, as decision-makers may not refer to some sources, either because they take them for granted, or are not aware of them, or may be wary of discussing them with the interviewer. It is, however, difficult to see what other method could be used to get into this question as a lack of research access invariably prevents participant observation and a detailed analysis of cases.
2. The issues on which discussion centred were, on-street car-parking; underground car-parking; the new town hall; rehousing policy; and the provision of play facilities. Of course not all issues were discussed with all councillors.
3. A card was handed to councillors on which was typed the sources that make up the list on Table 9.

TABLE 9. *Information sources used in decision-making*

Particular source	(1) The main source per cent of councillors		(2) Other important sources	(3) Unimportant sources
Officers	44	18	12	1
Agendas	10	4	2	0
Other councillors	15	6	13	1
Local organisations		0	6	8
Local press		0	1	9
Party officials		0	1	3
GLC/Central Government/ London Boroughs Assoc.	2	1	3	12
Constituents and residents		0	7	4
Particular sources not relevant	29	12	—	—
	100	41		

to sources which they saw as unimportant or as positively dangerous and unreliable. These responses are tabulated in column three.

The major feature of the collated responses is the heavy reliance that is placed on sources that are 'internal' to the council. The officers, other councillors, and the agenda constitute the main sources of information for over two-thirds of the respondents (69 per cent) and of the six councillors who refer to the importance of other councillors, five of these single out the chairmen or 'senior' councillors as of especial importance. Two councillors: 'You can't chew over everything, and the officers are there to digest information and give you a balanced picture – to make a precis for the chairmen and other members.' 'In Kensington we are lucky, we have a lot of experienced councillors, people who are in a position to talk wisely on many matters because of their years of chairmanship of a variety of committees. Say we had a library matter before us and it was a question of costings and paperbacks, well, the officers would give you their advice, but you might well ring up Frank Thackway [an alderman who had been leader of the Kensington council, and chairman of many committees including Libraries] as you know him and know he will have views.'

The other major feature of the collated responses is the large number of councillors (29 per cent) who referred to the irrelevance of particular information sources. The reasons they gave for this differed. On the one hand, there were those who said that particular information sources were not relevant to them because they were not in any position to make a decision, or were so dependent on others that they were in no sense able to exercise what they saw as any independent judgement. On the other hand, some councillors suggested that particular information sources were not relevant because they could rely on their 'judgement' and 'experience' and this was adequate for those decisional situations where a precedent had been established, and where there was a need for innovation then they could rely on their 'philosophy'. Examples of these differing viewpoints are given in the interview statements cited below. Two councillors from North Kensington: 'I haven't really been faced with a decision as to which way to vote, and so the issue hasn't cropped up yet.' 'It's difficult to generalise, but one has a lack of knowledge on many points and subjects, and one has to give weight to the combined views of the Chairmen and chief officers, and these views must in many instances carry the day. They know more about things. One doesn't necessarily bow to them all the time, but the problem is unless one is a chairman oneself, then it's hard to know enough ever to trump them.' Two chairmen: 'It's difficult to say, especially after a long period on the council. On day-to-day decisions, one wouldn't need to consult anybody as it would just be a matter of interpreting existing policy . . .' 'Unquestionably the main thing that I rely on is precedent.'

Turning to councillors' views as to the 'unimportant' information sources, the factor which best serves to unify the various responses is to note their suspicion of sources that were 'external' to, or outside of the control of, the council and its officers. Local organisations, the local press, other governmental structures, constituents and residents, and even party officials from the local associations were regarded with suspicion by some councillors.

Question 2: The search behaviour of councillors

This section is based on councillor responses to the following question:

> 'Speaking for yourself, how do you get to know about the needs and attitudes of people living in the borough?'

The question was designed to explore the councillors' 'search' behaviour with respect to the area within which they were governors, to see how they 'imported' the local environment into the council chamber. After councillors had spent some time in reply, they were encouraged to suggest the main method they used. The responses of the forty-seven respondents are tabulated in Table 10 in the same manner as the previous question. Table 11 shows the responses to the question from a number of different surveys of local councillors.

There are two things which stand out in the comparison. First, in Kensington and Chelsea there is not much reliance on informal personal contacts and friends, and second, considerable importance is attached to election canvassing as a means of ascertaining the needs and attitudes of constituents. The fact that councillors in the Metropolitan Boroughs relied upon informal personal contacts less than councillors in all other types of authority (39 per cent as against 67 per cent) makes the importance attributed to this method by Tower Hamlets councillors all the more remarkable. Connelly explains this by pointing to the close links which exist

TABLE 10. *Methods of ascertaining the needs and attitudes of people living in the Borough of Kensington and Chelsea*

Methods	(1) The main method	(2) Other important methods	(3) Unimportant methods
Informal personal contacts and friends	4	13	0
Voluntary associations	3	13	4
Political parties	6	12	2
Local press	0	6	6
'Surgery'	0	4	7
Officers' reports	2	3	3
Formal approaches and letters	6	3	1
Election canvassing	13	3	2
Party canvassing	3	5	3
Other councillors	1	5	0
Through living in, working in, or walking round the Borough	6	5	0
No methods cited; because:			
Hard to know	1		
Not important to know	2		
	47		

between the councillor and the community based upon the work and family situation, and he notes also that councillors regard the taking up of constituents' problems as a particularly important aspect of their public responsibilities, and they rely on a whole network of 'problem collectors'. This finding is in marked contrast to the situation in Kensington and Chelsea, and Sheffield, as even though this method is of considerable importance to Sheffield councillors, in both authorities there is less reliance on it than is displayed by councillors from other authorities of the same type (Kensington and Chelsea 9 per cent, Metropolitan Boroughs 39 per cent, Sheffield 30 per cent, County Boroughs 60 per cent). In Sheffield 'there is a greater reliance upon more formal channels of communication, including the political party organization, the local press, and letters or visits received from the general public' (Hampton, 1970, p. 205). In Kensington and Chelsea there is heavy reliance on election canvassing,[5] and to a lesser extent the local party, formal approaches and letters, and the 'feel' gained as a result of living or working in the borough, are all regarded as important. Unlike councillors in Sheffield, councillors in Kensington and Chelsea did not see the press as a particularly important source of information, and it was regarded by many as particularly unimportant because of

4. Elections occurred in the spring of 1968, and I was interviewing in the summer of that year. It may be that the elections were fresh in the councillors' minds, and if I had interviewed a year later they may have been seen as of less importance.

TABLE 11. *The main methods of ascertaining the needs and attitudes of people in their areas used by councillors in Kensington and Chelsea, Tower Hamlets, the Metropolitan Boroughs and Sheffield*[4]

| | Percentage of councillors | | | |
The main method	K & C 47	T H 10	M.B.s 46	S 108
Election canvassing	28	—	7	2
Political parties	13	10	15	13
Formal approahces and letters	13	—	9	17
Through living in, working in, or walking round the Borough	13	0	—	—
Informal personal contacts and friends	9	90	39	30
Voluntary associations	6	—	11	4
Party canvassing	6	—	—	—
Officers' reports	4	—	4	4
Other councillors	2	—	—	—
Local press	—	—	—	19
'Surgery'	—	—	11	3
Other answers	—	—	2	7
Not answered	—	—	2	2
No methods cited; because:				
Not important to know	4	—	—	—
Hard to know	2	—	—	—
	100	100	100	101

its alleged 'socialist bias' and general 'anti-council' attitude. Whereas in the Metropolitan Boroughs 'surgeries' were regarded as an important method of ascertaining public needs and attitudes, in Kensington and Chelsea, these were regarded as 'unnecessary', especially by councillors who came from South Kensington or Chelsea where it was felt that people could take up problems on their own. After the 1968 elections (amid a certain amount of opposition) a councillor-run advice service was begun in North Kensington.

Question 3: The extent to which members of the public contact their councillor

This section is based on the responses of forty-seven councillors to the following question:

'In the average month, roughly how many people in this area have been in touch with you personally as a member of the council?'

This question was designed to see how often councillors were contacted by the public, and it identified one source of 'inputs' that were directed, or

5. The table is based on information from, Hampton, 1970, Table 8·11, p. 204; Committee on the Management of Local Government, 1967, vol. 2, Table 8·9, p. 224; and, Connelly, 1970. See also, Rees & Smith, 1964.

'sent' to them from their area of authority. As a follow-up to this question councillors were asked if they had a busy period,[6] and were encouraged to outline the issues on which they were contacted, and the methods by which they received this contact. Table 12 shows the number of times

TABLE 12. *The number of times councillors are contacted by members of the public in an average month*[7]

| Number of times contacted in average month | Percentage of councillors | | |
	Kensington and Chelsea 47	Metropolitan Boroughs 46	Sheffield 107
None	11	13	6
1–4	62	17	5
5–8	4	9	7
9–12	6	15	15
13–19	4	44 (=13 or more)	10
20–49	4	—	23
50 and over	9	—	34
varies too much to answer	9	—	—
not answered	—	2	—
	100	100	100

councillors in differing authorities are contacted by members of the public and the comparison reveals just how few people contact their councillor in Kensington and Chelsea when compared to the situation elsewhere. Over 70 per cent of the Kensington and Chelsea councillors saw less than four constituents in the average month, whereas in the Metropolitan Boroughs as a whole, less than a third were in this position, with 44 per cent claiming to have seen 13 or more. In Kensington and Chelsea under 10 per cent of respondents received as many contacts as this, although in Sheffield two-thirds of the councillors received 13 or more contacts in the monthly period. Connelly's finding with respect to the Tower Hamlets councillors was staggering, for the 'average number of contacts with constituents each councillor in the sample had in a week was 38 – taking informal information and advice giving, this number could be trebled' (Connelly, 1970. But see, Rees & Smith, 1964, pp. 46–9).

6. No councillor said that he had a regular busy period, but that contacts 'came in bursts' depending on 'what issues catches the public eye'.
7. The table is based on information from Hampton, 1970, Table 8.8, p. 199; and Committee on the Management of Local Government, 1967, vol. 2, Table 8.11, p. 227. The survey of councillors undertaken for the Committee on the Management of Local Government points out that some respondents may have included not just meetings with individual electors but meetings with groups of people and maybe even public meetings and meetings of voluntary associations. Even allowing for this it is still suggested that councillors see over 12 people a month in a personal capacity, and this is still very much larger than is the average in Kensington and Chelsea.

Councillors in Kensington and Chelsea were generally aware of how little they were contacted by the public, and were a little embarrassed by the fact, although they explained this by pointing to the generally declining interest of the community in local affairs (especially in the London area) over which they felt they had no control. Councillors often stated that they were appalled by the low level of interest in local government, but then in the next breath some stated how they did not welcome public contact anyway. A chairman: 'People ought to be more interested in local government, and shouldn't just contact you when things go wrong. But in fact one seldom sees very much of the public – there certainly isn't a stream of people coming to this flat, thank God, as one wants some private life.'

Barker and Rush, when discussing the Member of Parliament's relationship to constituents argue that 'a Member is himself the main probable determinant of how many constituents approach him for assistance' (Barker & Rush, 1970, p. 387), because he is in a position to manipulate his visibility to those who might contact him.[8] In Kensington and Chelsea, councillors do not put themselves into a position when they are particularly visible to their constituents. The Town Hall as 'a matter of policy' does not give an enquiring member of the public the phone numbers of councillors (and several are ex-directory); the addresses of councillors are not pinned conspicuously to notice boards; few councillors attend any 'surgery' or advice centre; and they display limited activity in the local grass-roots organisations. In Sheffield, the telephone was 'the most frequently used method of communication between councillors and members of the electorate' (Hampton, 1970, p. 199), and in Tower Hamlets visits to the home were the most common method. In Kensington and Chelsea, however, as Table 13 shows, neither of these methods are as important as the contacts made through letters, which is hardly surprising in view of most councillor's lack of sympathy for either phone calls or personal visits.

Although the councillors from the majority group in Kensington and Chelsea do not encourage informal contacts from their constituents, there

TABLE 13. *How councillors are contacted by members of the public in Kensington and Chelsea*

Method of possible contact	Number of councillors stating that they have received contact by a particular method
Letter	29
Phone calls	18
Through party or advice centre	7
Informal contacts in street or pub	5
Home visits	4

8. Bauer *et al* (1964, p. 420) point out that members of the public tend to write to those representatives who share their views, for 'anticipatory feedback discourages messages that may not be favourably received from even getting sent.'

are several factors which may help account for this pattern of limited public contact. The Maud survey showed that the manual workers on the council had the greatest contact with electors, and Hampton's study of Sheffield councillors showed that longer-serving councillors and 'Labour councillors were in contact with their electors far more frequently than the Conservative councillors,' who were 'far less ready . . . to visit or receive constituents at their homes' (Hampton, 1970, pp. 198, and 201). Now those who are the subject of this enquiry are neither Labour councillors, nor in the manual worker category, and also a large percentage were new councillors,[9] so that the pattern in Kensington and Chelsea conforms to some extent to the pattern one would expect from other evidence. In addition, the social character of Kensington and Chelsea has a bearing on this question. In the richer southern part of the borough, the elector has little need to contact the council. The stress on the private provision of amenities means that there will be a reduced interest in public activity. The fact that council policy is made by councillors who are in a position similar to that of many of the residents in the southern part of the borough means that there is a keen awareness of the needs of that sort of resident. Moreover, if the middle-class resident does have a problem then he is more likely to take it direct to the officers of the authority. In the northern part of the borough, although the council is vitally important in affecting (or failing to affect) quite basic areas of people's lives, the failure of many to perceive that this is the case, the lack of time, social skills and confidence, as well as knowledge of just who is the local councillor, all serve to prevent persons in need from contacting their councillor.

Question 4: The importance attached to constituents' views

In the previous sections, I have touched on the part which councillors feel constituents should play in the governing process. I asked a few councillors a question which was designed to indicate the extent to which they took constituents' views into account in their deliberations. The following question was asked of twenty-eight councillors:

> 'On the whole are the views of constituents important to you in helping you to make up your mind on issues before the council?'

Twelve councillors replied that constituents' views were important, fourteen said that they were unimportant, and two stated that they were unsure

9. Four Labour councillors were interviewed, and although the two working-class councillors had an average of 10–12 contacts a month, the two Labour councillors who were professionally employed only had one or two contacts in the same period. Of the chairmen on the council – who are all long-serving councillors – almost a third claimed to have been in contact with over 13 people in the average month. Just over a quarter of those interviewed were non councillors who were elected only a few months prior to interview, but in fact nearly all of them had been contacted by members of the public and their responses do not differ markedly from those of the longer-serving councillors who were not chairmen.

as it depended on a variety of circumstances. Some councillors mentioned that constituents' views were important in theory, but not in practice, and where this sort of view was expressed then respondents were categorised as answering 'no' to the question. A chairman: 'Yes, they are important in theory, but in practice one just doesn't hear from the ordinary member of the public but only the cranky element with bees in their bonnets.' Not surprisingly, councillors who felt that constituents' views were unimportant tended to see themselves not so much as delegates, but more as representatives of a party, or as representatives in the Burkean manner. A chairman: 'No, they are not important. One is elected, and elected as a representative of a party. It's up to you to make up your own mind. This is the way I see it.' A new South Kensington councillor: 'You're an elected representative and you should use your loaf. You shouldn't go outside the council for opinion . . . you can't swamp the council with co-opted people who are not elected as it's not fair to the people who elected you.'

The councillor and interest groups

Answers to the questions that were asked of councillors regarding their assessment of a variety of dimensions relevant to interest group behaviour, are clearly important in any discussion of councillors and their information sources. This question has already been discussed in the previous chapter, but some points relate to the present subject. First, councillors were not generally sympathetic to groups which were providing information, ideas, or demands for their attention, favouring instead those groups that were working alongside, or with, the council in some form of service provision which eased their own burden. Second, in so far as they did admit that groups could provide them with information, then they were prepared to allow that only a small number of groups could fulfil this role, and they were generally unsympathetic to public styles of presentation where there was any attempt to 'pressure' the council into a line of action which they regarded with disfavour.

II. THE RESEARCH: ANALYSIS AND INTERPRETATION: AVOIDANCE AND RESISTANCE

> In all governments all over the world, a standard routine for reaching a policy decision is to gather and analyse facts, doing so with at least *implicit theory*.
>
> C. E. Lindblom, *The Policy-Making Process* (Englewood Cliffs, N.J., Prentice-Hall, 1968), p. 6 – my emphasis.

In the preceding section I outlined interview data about how councillors in Kensington and Chelsea regard different means of obtaining information, and what relations they have with their public. The answers represent the councillors' 'rules of priority' regarding possible information sources and styles of presentation, and show that they are ranking the value which they ascribe to information coming from certain sources or through certain channels. The way councillors relate to information sources does not give them just an unbiased precis, and it is important to identify the grounds for their selection.

We cannot assert dogmatically that in all situations 'people seek out information that supports or reinforces their beliefs, and avoid information which challenges their opinions'. The 'experimental evidence does not demonstrate that there is a general psychological tendency to avoid non-supportive and seek out supportive information'. Nevertheless there does seem 'to be ample evidence, both systematic and anecdotal, for the existence of *de facto* selectivity' (Freedman & Sears, 1965, pp. 59, 69, and 89. See also, Brehm & Cohen, 1962, pp. 50–60; and, Berelson, Lazarsfeld & McPhee, 1954, esp. pp. 251, 233, and 87), and 'in general, communicators likely to transmit messages consonant with group attitudes and values are assigned high credibility, and those with dissonant communications are assigned low credibility' (Secord & Backman, 1964, p. 202). In other words, once opinions are formed then there is a resistance to changing them (Lane & Sears, 1964, pp. 53–4; and, Klapper, 1960), and it is easier if we avoid sources of infomation and particular message channels which we expect (or know on the basis of past experience) are likely to throw up 'dissonant' ideas, and choose instead to rely on safer, more trusted and known sources which we feel more confident will provide us with information which is 'consonant' with our existing beliefs and convictions.

I suggest that the councillors' use of information will reveal that certain sources are *avoided* whereas others are specifically looked to: I will suggest that their pattern of exposure to information will be such as to reinforce their existing beliefs. Second, although politicians are in a position in which they can partly control what is sent to them, there will be occasions when councillors in Kensington and Chelsea have ideas sent to them which they cannot avoid but which clash with their own views. I suggest that councillors may *resist* those ideas by relying on a range of what I will call 'exclusion devices', which justify their ignoring and responding negatively to any claims which may be embodied in that information (Davison, 1959).

The data which were laid out in the last section will be discussed in the light of the above ideas, and then in Section III, I will look at the differential selectivity of councillors, which will help us to suggest some of the variables which we can expect to affect the extent of selectivity.

Selective search and the avoidance of certain information sources

The evidence of councillor avoidance of particular information sources is gained from a consideration of their responses to questions one and two which asked them to identify the information sources they used in decision-making, and the means on which they relied to ascertain the needs and attitudes of constituents. We need to see the extent to which councillors are involved in only limited and selective search for 'new' information, and the extent to which they choose, instead, to rely on 'old' information, and that which is sent to them from known and trusted sources on which they have relied in the past, and with which they have established a regular contact.

If we look back to Table 9 we find that councillors show an overwhelming tendency to rely on information for decision from sources internal to the council itself. It is these sources that are regarded as particularly 'credible'[10] (Hovland, Janis & Kelley, 1953; Schweitzer & Ginsburg, 1966; Backman & Secord, 1966, pp. 94–102; and, Hovland & Weiss, 1951). Councillors categorise them as 'reliable' and 'trustworthy' because the people concerned 'know the facts', either because they are 'experts' (the officers) or because they are 'experienced (the senior councillors). If councillors do not rely on internal sources of information then they are likely to state that particular information sources are not relevant, either because they are not in a position where they can make or influence decisions, or because they have enough experience (or old information) not to need new information from any source.

What sources are looked to is only a partial statement of the selectivity displayed by councillors, for it is important also to know what sources they do not look to, as well as those which they positively avoid. The local press, local organisations, party officials from the local associations, other official and governmental structures, and constituents and residents, are all seen as of comparatively minor importance as providers of information for decision. In addition, local organisations, the local press, and other governmental structures are seen as sources of information that should, where possible (and it is admitted that this is difficult with respect to the other structures of government) be positively avoided.

It seems reasonable to suggest that the internal sources, on which the bulk of councillors rely for their information for decision, are not likely to provide information that conflicts with their existing ideas and commitments, and at the same time the avoidance of external information sources means that councillors are choosing not to rely on, or come into contact with, ideas which are more likely than those generated internally to clash with existing commitments and pose new claims of a different and unwanted kind. Senior councillors are likely to pass on information which is partial and consonant with existing policy, and are more likely to question the legitimacy of any new claim which challenges the council's existing policy commitments, than to question the policy itself – policy which they themselves are intimately involved in maintaining and defending. The officers, it might be argued, cannot be regarded as a 'safe' source of information, because they are experts who have the specific responsibility of providing the councillors with 'impartial' and 'objective' advice which takes in all sides of a problem. In fact, however, they too need to be selective in their

10. For a discussion of source credibility in on-going political situations, see, La Palombara, 1964, esp. pp. 285, and, 189; and, Banfield, 1961, esp. p. 282.

use of information and in what advice they choose to give to the councillors, and I suggest that the information which they pass on is unlikely to challenge the existing policy of the council or what they perceive to be the ideology of the senior councillors. The officers have been intimately involved in the development of council policy, and are likely to have personal and professional stakes in its continued maintenance, a stake which is increased because of the administrative convenience and necessity of having a stable and known range of commitments around which to arrange office routines. It is hard for them to look in on themselves, their departments and policies and to criticise dispassionately what 'their' council has done. Officers stand outside the party battle, but they are not untouched by it, or unaware of it. Not only do the officers (as one chairman put it) 'frequently apply for a post in an authority where the dominant political views are in line with their own', but even if this is not the case they are still going to have to work inside what is the ideology of the senior councillors, and over time they will (as an officer put it) 'know what does and does not go' and will tailor their advice accordingly. A chief officer: 'An officer must make it clear that he's not involved with politics, but he does have to pay regard to council policy; if the council do say "no" to something then you have to let it drop and you can't keep raising it.'

Table 10 shows how councillors find out about the needs and attitudes of the public in their area, and enables us to see how far the sources which they look to are likely to result in their gaining a 'biased' view of the 'real' situation, because their search behaviour is such that they come into contact with only a limited section of their constituents, and a section at that which is likely to share their own views. In fact, what stands out is the councillors' reliance on election canvassing as a means of ascertaining public need, and although this is a fairly ritualised activity where the main concern is to identify supporters and get out the vote rather than to convert voters or talk about issues, it is clear that this particular method is highly *unselective* in terms of what ideas the councillor is likely to hear. As a North Kensington councillor put it: 'Canvassing is unpleasant but essential, and I hate it, but how else do you find out about problems you hadn't thought of, and how else do you get at people? It certainly gives you a very vivid picture. It's a means of keeping in touch with problems in the area and it's very good for us.'

The other means on which the councillors rely do, however, reveal a greater detachment from the 'ordinary' citizen, and a greater selectivity, as is most obviously revealed in the importance which is attributed to contacts made in the local Conservative associations. A chairman: 'It's very much the South Kensington Conservative Association for me. There's 5,900 members and that's a very considerable slice of the population.'

The reliance upon the 'feel' gained as a result of walking round, working in, or living in, the Borough, is unlikely to result in the councillors' views being challenged, as the range of potential stimuli available in those situations is so great that councillors must impose their own evaluative framework on to the scene in order to make sense of it, and this is going to lead to things being selected and understood which fit into the cognitive and evaluative map which already exists in the councillor's mind. The contacts gained as a result of formal approaches and letters is likely to result in councillors gaining an awareness of the needs of the middle-class resident (of which they are already well aware) because letterwriting tends to be a middle-class activity, and Barker and Rush found, in connection with M.P.s and their public that 'working class people write only under grave provocation, preferring if possible to visit the Member's surgery' (Barker & Rush, 1970, p. 176). As I have already mentioned, a surgery only exists in one part of the borough and that was an innovation which came in 1968.[11]

With the exception of the heavy stress placed upon election canvassing the councillors tend to rely on information sources and to gain knowledge of constituents' needs and attitudes in ways which are unlikely to result in their receiving ideas which challenge their own beliefs. Now the fact that supportive information is gained and non-supportive information is largely avoided as a result of their patterns of search may be incidental and unintentional and not the result of any deliberate attempt. The officers may be looked to because they are conveniently available, other councillors may be sought out because they are friends, and the local Conservative associations may be relied upon because councillors attend those bodies and it is seen as more convenient and easy to find out things there than to contemplate looking to organisations to which they do not belong. Although, then, there may not be a deliberate search for supportive information and a deliberate avoidance of non-supportive information, and although there may not even be a conscious attachment to existing beliefs and policies, the fact is that the search behaviour of councillors tends to result in their gaining information which *reinforces* rather than challenges their own ideology and the appropriateness of the existing policy of the council.

It may well be that councillor avoidance of particular non-supportive information sources is not intentional or deliberate, but when we turn to the actual resistance to certain sources of information, then it is clear that this resistance is based upon a positive dislike of information and ideas which challenge existing commitments and views, and represents a *deliberate* refusal to act on those ideas. I will now deal with this other aspect of councillor selectivity with respect to information search and use and see what means they adopt to exclude and resist communications and demands which are sent to them and which run counter to their own ideas and views.

11. In fact the issues on which councillors were contacted by members of the public reflect (with the exception of housing) the concerns of the car-owning, permanently and comfortably settled resident: Refuse collection 20; Housing 17; Parking 13; Street cleansing 7; Traffic 7; Noise 4; Dog excrement 3; Health and welfare 4; Rates 2; Street lighting 2.

The resistance to influence attempts : 'exclusion devices'

No government can respond favourably to all the claims that are directed to them and so there is inevitably the necessity of having to resist particular influence attempts. This necessity increases to the extent that those in government are particularly selective in their use of information for decision. Claims that are directed to government will tend to come from sources which are *avoided* by government, and from interests which are not represented *within* government itself. The more governmental decision-makers are selective in their search for information for decision and the more the membership of government does not represent a cross-section of their public, then the greater will be the range of demands that are directed to them which run counter to their existing commitments, and the greater will be their need to resist those claims if they are to sustain their established policies. In Kensington and Chelsea the membership of the council does not represent a cross-section of the constituents, and as I have just shown, councillors do confine their attention to particular information sources, and they are, therefore, likely to receive particularly challenging demands precisely because their policy is based on the experience and needs of only a section of their constituents. If they are to sustain that policy then they need to be particularly effective in resisting demands, especially where they come from sources which they have avoided.

In general, councillors resist particular influence attempts and justify their exclusion of particular messages, not by paying specific attention to the content of all the messages that are directed to them, but by operating on the basis of two general rules which minimise the need for the detailed consideration of all that is sent to them. On the one hand, they are suspicious of particular *sources* of information, and on the other hand, they are suspicious of certain *styles* of communication. In addition they have a number of *general exclusion devices*, which they can use to justify the exclusion of particular messages irrespective of where they came from or how they were sent to the council.

Excluded sources. Column three of Tables 9 and 10 gives an indication of some of the sources that were regarded with disfavour by councillors, and below are cited some statements which were made by councillors and which indicate their suspicion of any ideas which come from certain sources.

(a) The local press. A chairman: 'The best influence would usually be the local press, but it's recognised that the *Post* is hostile to us and so we don't really consider it.' A South Kensington councillor: 'They tend to report after the events and after one knows things oneself. No press is very accurate, and one can't believe it; you really have to check back from it. They misquote council meetings and pick up the wrong things as often as not.'

(b) Local organisations and interest groups. In the previous chapter on

interest groups there is a list of the particular groups that were regarded by councillors as unhelpful and whose ideas were not regarded as worthy of any detailed consideration. The groups that were generally regarded as unhelpful were the Notting Hill Community Workshop, the Kensington and Chelsea Council Tenants Association, and the Kensington and Chelsea Inter-Racial Council. In addition, the chairmen were out of sympathy with the Ratepayers Association and the Neighbourhood Service Unit, and were not enthusiastic about either the Kensington and Chelsea Arts Council, or the Notting Hill Social Council. All these groups were demanding groups; all were in some way providers of dissonant information. Specific comments on some of these groups are cited below: they represent but a fraction of those which were made in the course of interview. A chairman, on the Kensington and Chelsea Council Tenants Association: 'It's not representative, it's just three or four estates in Chelsea, and because it's unrepresentative we're bound to treat with reserve any of their suggestions.' A chairman, on the Kensington and Chelsea Inter-Racial Council: 'It's new and I'm suspicious of the people who are in it who are black power extremists, and if they get control – as looks likely – then it will become a dead duck.' A chairman, on the Notting Hill Community Workshop: 'They're going about it all the wrong way. They seem to think all tenants are always right and all landlords are always wrong, but it isn't like that, there's good and bad in all.'

   (c) Other governmental structures: the Greater London Council, the London Boroughs Association, and the central government. These sources were regarded with suspicion because a number of councillors felt that they were not aware of 'local needs'; or else were 'biased against a Conservative council' (at the time of interview the central government was Labour-controlled, as was the GLC until the 1968 elections); or more generally it was felt that they represented an attack upon the proper 'independence' of an elected local authority to decide its own policy without external interference. On occasions it was admitted that they had no choice but to follow the advice of those organisations, but as I showed in Chapter 1, the council has on a number of occasions stood out against the guidance of the central government.

There are really no other sources of information that are regarded with general suspicion so that their ideas are to be excluded from attention before being given any hearing. Certain councillors are suspicious of the ideas of constituents and residents, others are suspicious of the ideas of local party officials, and, of course, other councillors are suspicious of particular sources for fairly idiosyncratic and personal reasons, such as an objection to and distrust of a particular personality. By and large, however, sources other than those which have been specifically singled out in the above discussion, are not generally excluded on sight, and only if they pose a challenge to the council's policy and the ideas of individual councillors does it become necessary to exclude their ideas from consideration, and this occurs by the application of general exclusion devices rather than by a wholesale categorisation of the source as generally and invariably to be resisted.

Excluded styles. Earlier in this chapter I noted how councillors did not like being contacted by constituents by home visits or by use of the telephone, but instead preferred to be contacted by letter. In the chapter on interest groups, I set out the views of the councillors regarding the ways in which they felt they should be contacted by interest groups, and here again there was a preference for written or private contact and a hostility to more vigorous and public methods of demand presentation involving the use of petitions, demonstrations, or stories in the local press. Important consequences follow from this regarding the likely demands and ideas that will not get through to the council for sympathetic consideration. First, as I mentioned in the previous chapter, interest groups that are advocating innovation and change in council policy are unable to gain access by the quieter methods, and yet if they resort to the more public methods of demand presentation the councillors are provided with information which they feel enables them to justify to themselves, and perhaps to others, the exclusion of the particular demand. By virtually forcing groups to adopt a particular style of demand articulation they can publicly and respectably ignore the demand itself and instead attack the 'undemocratic' and 'irresponsible' methods of the group. Second, and from the individual point of view, letterwriting tends to be a middle-class habit, and as such many of those contacting the council will often be worried only about details of administration and not with the actual policy itself, as council policy is particularly sensitive to the needs of that sort of resident.

In considering that the mail was the most legitimate method of public contact with the council, councillors were excluding a particular type of demand, and a range of contacts from a particular type of constituent, and if those demands or constituents are to gain a hearing from the councillors then they are going to have to filter into the council, if at all, by more devious and less acceptable methods.

General exclusion devices. Table 12 showed how little councillors were contacted by individual constituents when compared to other councillors from different authorities. In fact, as I mentioned then, councillors in Kensington and Chelsea were often aware of how little they were contacted by members of the public, but some chose to explain this by suggesting that it was indicative of a satisfaction with the way council affairs were conducted. A chairman: 'When you consider the population of the borough, the number of letters we receive is quite trivial. It doesn't necessarily reflect that we are a well-run borough, but if we were more inefficient we might get more – but I don't propose to find out.' Given that this was the case, then councillors tended to consider that the people who were contacting them were not 'typical' of the 'ordinary' resident and that they were often 'too ill-informed' to be taken seriously. That persons contacting the council are not seen as typical tells us more about the councillors' conception of the typical resident than it does about the actual nature of the person attempting to make contact. For the councillor the typical constituent does not *by definition* contact the council, and, therefore, councillors are able, should they so choose, to consider *any* person who contacts the council as untypical and, therefore, not to be taken too seriously. Two chairmen: 'They [constituents] are frightfully ill informed. We've tried to combat it and we've talked of having a PR man for years.' 'Once elected we never get the views of the ordinary constituents, but only of the vociferous minority. Once one is elected the individual constituent has very little sway on the administration of the council. You have to get on with the job and you know the full facts.' Even if members of the public were to contact the council with sensible points of view – and it was admitted that this could be the case – then this did not necessarily affect the course of council action because such contact often came 'too late' or else did not show sufficient regard for the 'problems of the council'. The comparative isolation of councillors from public contact itself constituted an obstacle to the constituents' ideas being acted on because councillors were cautious for fear of acting on a minority point of view. A chairman: 'Really one doesn't get an adequate enough post bag to say what the constituents as a body are thinking, and this makes it hard, as well as dangerous, to act on the views which we do get.' Constituents' views were important to one chairman as he frankly admitted, only if he agreed with them, and one suspects that much the same could be said of the other councillors: 'They're not very important unless I'm in agreement with them, and I would have thought that I was in disagreement with the views I hear as much as I'm in agreement with any of them.'

The statements I have cited above represent some of the ways in which councillors assess and exclude the ideas which may be sent to them by individuals. Often similar points were made with respect to the difficulty of acting on the ideas of groups, because they too were seen as 'ill-informed', 'unrepresentative' and 'one-sided'. But because groups are more likely than individuals to raise matters of a policy kind this suggests that councillors will have a particular need to resist group claims, and certainly there seemed to be more generalised adjectives which could be attached to categorise groups in an unfavourable way than existed with respect to individual claims. Groups were regarded with suspicion if they 'did not have the interest of the borough at heart', and councillors were unsympathetic to demands if they felt they came from groups that 'were only there for their own ends', or 'to make capital out of the situation', or because they were 'out to embarrass the council' either for 'political motives' or because they 'had chips on their shoulders', or were 'irresponsible do-gooders' who were not 'genuine'. Councillors had a cynical view of group activity which took a radical form which was sharply critical of the council, pointing out that they 'had seen it all before' or that the people in the groups were 'just five-minute wonders'. This belief gave the councillors something of a siege mentality, for there was the idea that if they could sustain their policy in the face of attack, after a while the attacking group would just disappear (as often happened). At any event councillors were reluctant to contemplate policy change just because a group of 'banner waving hooligans' demanded it, and they were suspicious of groups where there were the 'same old faces' who were assumed to be 'communists', 'troublemakers' or 'professional agitators'. Councillors were critical of ideas which were raised by groups of persons who had no direct interest in the issue, but were 'do-gooders' from 'outside the area', but at the same time they could be equally suspicious of groups that *were* personally involved because then they felt they could have 'an axe to grind' or were 'biased'. Either way, groups wanting change could be frustrated.

Behind these rather *ad hoc* and piecemeal justifications for not acting on particular ideas or suggestions that were directed to them lies a more all-embracing view which justifies their resistance to claims. Councillors frequently had an orientation to their role which stressed that it was proper for them to decide autonomously on the basis of expert advice from the officers, where interests from outside would be taken into account not directly but as a result of the information-gathering of the officers and through the experience of the senior councillors. The belief that they should be 'representatives' and not 'delegates' meant that councillors were potentially sceptical of *all* information and ideas that were directed to them from any source outside the council. They tended, indeed, to be suspicious and critical of any political activity occurring outside the council, especially if that activity was in North Kensington. As far as they were concerned, the discussion of policy matters and the taking of decisions were matters for councillors working in committee and in formal debate, and not matters for public demonstrations. The normative justifications for these attitudes were that the prolonged and detailed work of committees, and the search for consensus, were the best means of establishing the grounds for just and reasoned decisions, whereas emotional and public debates, and hasty decisions were seen as likely to lead to a lack of consistency and a usurping of their rightful authority.

The generality and contradictory nature of these 'exclusion devices' is the source of their strength, for although they may not be used all the time, or by all councillors, they are *available* for use and can be tied to virtually any idea or demand which they regard with disfavour. This easy categorisation enables councillors to avoid justifying more fully just why it is that they will not be acting on the suggestions which may be sent to them, and means that they do not need to expose their own ideology to public attack.

195

III. THE RESEARCH: ANALYSIS AND INTERPRETATION:
DIFFERENTIAL SELECTIVITY

> One of the central assumptions of social-organization theory is that a
> person's informational perspectives are crucially limited by his position
> in the particular large-scale organizations in which he participates.
>
> Morris Janowitz and William Delany, 'The bureaucrat and
> the public: A study of informational perspectives',
> *Administrative Science Quarterly*, 2, 1957, pp. 141–62, p. 142.

In the previous section I discussed, in general terms, the material which I
laid out in Section I. I suggested that councillors displayed a certain
'selectivity' in the way they related to information, usually 'avoiding'
sources and channels which were likely to provide information clashing
with their own views, and 'resisting' ideas which were sent to them (but
which they regarded with disfavour) by relying on what I called 'exclusion
devices'. In this section I will look at the differential selectivity displayed
by councillors, but will confine attention to the distinction between the
chairmen and the non-chairmen. The central part of this section is based
upon a consideration of the breakdown of Tables 9 and 10 into these two
categories. I suggest that there are certain factors which mean that the
chairmen will be, and will need to be, more selective in their use of
information than the 'ordinary' councillors.

First, chairmen are more involved than are non-chairmen in both the
day-to-day running of the affairs of their committees, and in the broader
questions relating to council policy. This means that they have to spend
more time than the non-chairmen on activities internal to the council and
are invariably in closer contact with the officers. Although they are able to
gain access to information which is denied to the ordinary councillor they
are likely to be able to spend less time on activities which involve them in
'outside' contacts except in so far as they arise as a direct result of, and
dovetail neatly into, their committee responsibilities.

Second, chairmen have been on the council for long periods of time,
and in consequence have a history of past exposure to information on the
problems which they are now facing. Because of this previous acquaintance
with council problems and with the 'relevant' information sources, they
will not only know what information sources are 'good' and 'useful', but
will also tend to feel that more information as such is unnecessary as they
have 'enough in their heads'. One chairman, for example, pointed out that
it was not particularly helpful to look to interested groups as suppliers of
information: 'It's a help to them [to contact me]. I don't think it's a help
to me. I'm someone to get at if they want to get something done. It may be
a help if you're a young and inexperienced councillor, but not now when
one has more to give than to receive. It does take a number of years to get
into this position, however, and for the first ten years one is learning all the

time, but after that you should be master of the situation.' In contrast to this, the councillor who has spent only a limited time on the council, and who has had less involvement with council affairs, will not have had this history of exposure to information and will have less relevant knowledge stored as 'experience'. In this situation, the councillor could well feel that more information has a utility which justifies an active search. We can expect that new councillors will be especially likely to display this pattern (Huckshorn, 1965, esp. p. 168).

Third, we can expect that if people are publicly committed to a certain line of action they may well be reluctant to expose themselves to information which could challenge that commitment (Hovland, 1957).

Finally, research evidence enables us to suggest that this reluctance will increase if the people concerned lack confidence in the appropriateness of their commitments (Canon, 1964). In Kensington and Chelsea, chairmen assume that position only after they have been on the council for a number of years and have served an apprenticeship as vice-chairman. They have been socialised into an acceptance of established policy, and have a personal commitment to its maintenance, for to change is to admit, as one chairman put it, that 'we've been wrong for twenty years'. The occupancy of the position of chairman gives incumbents an almost automatic commitment to the existing configuration of public policy, which they have to publicly defend and justify. At the same time, they can hardly be unaware of the extent to which those policies have engendered a certain amount of public hostility. Chairmen tend to be defensive when faced with criticism, but at the same time the criticism makes them uncertain as to the appropriateness of their established policy. On the other hand, ordinary councillors (and especially those who are new to the council) have less of an institutionalised involvement with council policy, and if comparatively new to politics may have less of a firm commitment to particular points of view. In this situation information from a wide range of sources poses less of a threat because new councillors lack the commitments which may be challenged by an extensive search for information from a wide range of sources.

For all these reasons we should not be surprised to learn that the chairmen are especially selective in the way they relate to information sources. How far does the evidence sustain these suggestions about differential selectivity? Table 14 shows the responses of the chairmen and the non-chairmen to the question asking them to identify the information sources they used when making decisions.

On some points the responses are similar. Both suggest that the officers and the other councillors are important sources of information, and both suggest that the press and party officials are comparatively unimportant. However, there are important differences. Chairmen frequently pointed out that information from particular sources was not required because their own personal and council experience was adequate. They stressed that it

TABLE 14. *Information sources used in decision-making*

Particular sources	Chairmen (13)			Non-Chairmen (28)		
	Main source	Other important sources	Unimp. sources	Main source	Other important sources	Unimp. sources
	(%)			(%)		
Officers	5 (39)	5	0	13 (46)	7	1
Agendas	0	0	0	4 (14)	2	0
Other councillors	2 (15)	4	0	4 (14)	9	1
Local organisations	0	0	6	0	6	2
Local press	0	0	3	0	1	6
Party officials	0	0	0	0	1	2
GLC/Central Govt./LBA	1 (8)	2	3	0	1	9
Constituents/residents	0	1	3	0	6	1
Particular sources not relevant because:						
(1) not in a position to influence decisions	0	–	–	6 (21)	–	–
(2) past experience a sufficient guide	5 (39)	3	0	1 (4)	2	0
	13 (101)			28 (99)		

was important to confirm and continue existing policy lines, but where change proved necessary then it should be carried out in terms of the political philosophy of the party and conform to what that philosophy indicated was the proper scope of public activity. In contrast to this, the non-chairmen (and especially those newly elected to the council (suggested that whatever information they might have was not relevant, because their position on the council was one where they could not substantially influence the decisions of the council. As one new councillor put it: 'Officers seem to initiate everything, and if it's not them, it's the chairmen of the people from the last council. I feel I'm just here to rubber stamp things. One doesn't get any open questions, or any series of options and one has the feeling that the major decisions have been worked out long ago and one finds oneself simply looking at the submitted plans for an old people's home and one has little option but to say "yes".' This assessment clearly shows that the restraining behaviour rules do actually affect the role which the new councillors are able to assume in the policy shaping activity of the council.

The differences between chairmen and non-chairmen in their assessment of information sources is not simply based on the different reasons which they give for suggesting that particular sources are not relevant. Chairmen tend to view local organisations, the press and even residents with suspicion, whereas the non-chairmen, although hostile to the press and to the information provided by governmental structures from outside their area, are comparatively receptive to information coming to them from local organisations and from constituents and residents.

Table 15 shows the responses of chairmen and non-chairmen to the

TABLE 15. *Methods of ascertaining the needs and attitude of people living in the Borough of Kensington and Chelsea*

Methods	Chairmen (15) Main method	Other important methods	Unimp. method	Non-Chairmen (32) Main method	Other important methods	Unimp. methods
	(%)			(—)		
Informal personal contacts and friends	1 (7)	4	0	3 (9)	9	0
Voluntary associations	0	3	3	3 (9)	10	1
Political party	3 (20)	5	0	3 (9)	7	2
Local press	0	1	4	0	5	2
'Surgery'	0	0	3	0	4	4
Officers' reports	1 (7)	2	0	1 (3)	1	3
Formal approaches and letters	3 (20)	2	0	3 (9)	1	1
Election canvassing	1 (7)	0	0	12 (38)	3	2
Party canvassing	0	1	1	3 (9)	4	2
Other councillors	1 (7)	1	0	0	4	0
Through living in/ working in/or walking round the Borough	2 (14)	2	0	4 (13)	3	0
No methods cited because:						
hard to know	1 (7)	–	–	–	–	–
not important to know	2 (14)	–	–	–	–	–
	15 (103)			32 (99)		

question asking them to state how they found about public needs and attitudes.

Both chairmen and non-chairmen refer to the importance of living in, working in, or walking round the borough, and to the importance of informal links, and both are sceptical as to the importance of the local press and councillor-run 'surgeries'. However, chairmen stress more the importance of the links with the local Conservative association, the value of formal approaches and letters, and the use of the knowledge of other councillors and the officers. Moreover, only the chairmen stated how it was not important to know the needs and attitudes of the public. In contrast to this the non-chairmen pointed to the crucial importance of election canvassing, and to a lesser extent to the value of party canvassing and the links gained as a result of contacts with voluntary associations. A new councillor: 'One keeps one's ear to the ground and there are a lot of groups operating here set up to help people and you get a lot from there – like the Neighbourhood Council, for example.' A North Kensington councillor: 'It's very difficult in fact [to find out public needs and attitudes]. People tend not to want to come forward, but if you knock on doors people are kind and pleased to see you. We have an Advice Centre run in conjunction with the Parliamentary candidates and we work fairly closely with the Lancaster Road Neighbourhood Centre and the Neighbourhood Service Unit.[12] People tend to come forward more easily to these voluntary bodies and so we should keep in touch with them.'

In fact simply to identify the differing methods used by councillors is not enough, for although, as expected, the chairmen relied more on 'safer', known sources, internal to the council, or at least related to party or friendship networks, some councillors expressed a more general orientation to the whole question of ascertaining public needs and attitudes, and it is clear that this orientation differed as between the chairmen and the non-chairmen on the council.

Some councillors expressed the view that they should actively search in order to find out the needs and attitudes of the public, taking the view that people would not come forward unsolicited even if they were dissatisfied with, or disadvantaged by, council policy. Others felt that they should wait to be contacted by the public, and they considered that the failure of people to come forward was indicative of a general contentment and satisfaction with council policy. This division of councillors into 'searchers' and 'waiters' is not random, as searchers are disporprotionately from those who are new to the council, whereas the waiters tend to be chairmen.[13] Responses which illustrate these differing orientations are cited below.

Chairmen: 'I don't give a damn for them [public needs and attitudes]. One of the assumptions one works on is that if you have a roomful of people talking about local government, no one will agree. Once you bring party politics into local government then you act on the basis of political principles. I'm not a strong party man myself, but there are certain principles

---

12. *Lancaster Road Neighbourhood Centre*, created during the period when the Notting Hill Summer Project was collecting information on housing conditions in North Kensington as a base for this and to draw in people. Later became something of an advice centre for people in the area.

Neighbourhood Service Unit, 'founded in 1966 with the object of creating amenities that were lacking and sorely needed in the multi-racial, overcrowded areas of North Paddington and North Kensington'. It formed playgroups, gave legal advice and helped in housing matters. Not really active in seeking 'political solutions' to problems, more of a case-work body.

13. One chairman can be categorised as a 'searcher', but this respondent expressed a number of views which were at odds with those of the other chairmen.

which I see as important and by and large these are also the principles which are part of the Conservative philosophy.' 'It's not necessary to go canvassing on the streets, If you are known to people and they know they can contact you then they will tell you what worries them, without needing to go and find out.' 'They have to come to me . . .' 'When you consider the population of the borough, the number of letters we receive is quite trivial. It doesn't necessarily reflect that we are a well-run borough, but if we were more inefficient we might get more, but I don't propose to find out.'

New Councillors: 'Election canvassing, go out and meet them, really go round.' 'Go out and meet the people. Very few people will come to you, as a councillor you have to go to them.' 'I have canvassed here personally over a period of eighteen months, and I should think I've been to practically every door in the ward. This is the way it should be.'

The evidence presented in this section gives weight to the supposition that chairmen would be more selective than ordinary councillors in the ways in which they related to possible information sources. Caricaturing the distinction it can be said that if the chairmen tend to rely on 'old' information from sources 'internal' to the council and choose to 'wait' for public contact, then the non-chairmen (and especially the new councillors and those from North Kensington) stress the value of 'new' information and point to the need to look to sources 'external' to the council through an active 'search'.

IV. IMPLICATIONS AND CONCLUDING REMARKS

In this chapter I have brought together material on the information sources used by councillors, and on the way in which they relate to their local 'environment'. I suggested, first, that councillors develop certain rules of priority which involve avoiding and resisting messages from certain sources and channels, and second, that there are important differences in the rules which are used by the chairmen and the non-chairmen. If we are to consider the implications of these findings for the likely development of council policy then we really need to pay specific attention to the rules of the chairmen since they are the key influentials on the council who appear to be largely unrestrained in their policy-making activity by the other councillors. However, the fact that our findings illustrate significant differences between the chairmen and the other councillors, suggests that there may be factionalism on the council which may have quite different implications for the likely development of council policy. Each of these possible alternatives will be considered below.

If we consider only the chairmen's responses then we can expect council policy to continue into the future largely unchanged, because there is a vicious circle of factors which combine to produce this outcome. We can break into this circle by suggesting as a starting point, that chairmen are strongly attached to existing policies which they think deal adequately with the situation as it exists and is likely to develop, for one way of dealing with complexity and change is to largely ignore it by considering that present trends are likely to continue into the future. These beliefs will mean that decision-making is regarded as the routine re-affirmation of the existing policy, and this being the case they will not feel the need to search for new information on problems and solutions, because these are already seen as known, understood and adequately solved. In these circumstances chairmen considered it enough to rely on their experience and on internal sources of information, as there is only need for research when existing decisions are perceived as inadequate. This pattern of information use means, however, that chairmen are going to avoid seeing new problems and hearing new claims and the information which they do use is likely to confirm and reinforce the existing pattern of council commitments. As March and Simon (1958, p. 173) point out: 'persistence comes about primarily because the individual or organization does not search for or consider alternatives to the present course of action unless that present course of action is in some sense "unsatisfactory".'

Starting by suggesting that the chairmen are attached to the existing pattern of council policy is only one way into the circle of factors which result in policy continuation, for we can start the argument by pointing, first, to the actual pattern of information use by the chairmen. It is a fact that chairmen do stress the importance of relying on experience as a base for decisions, and it is a fact that they express a reluctance to search for new information, choosing instead to rely on sources internal to the council. The rest follows: the result is the same; the reinforcement of existing policies, and the failure to consider, or even see, alternatives. We do not then *need* to consider the motives or objectives of the chairmen to argue that their behaviour with respect to potential information sources is such that we can expect it to lead to policy continuation and persistence.

In terms of the material which I have assembled in the last two chapters, what makes the non-chairmen a potentially factional group is that they are less involved with, and committed to, council policy, and at the same time their more active searching for information and their greater sympathy for 'demanding' groups gives them ideas which challenge the appropriateness of existing council policies. In contrast to this, the chairmen are both committed to council policy and are in contact with a more restricted range of information sources which are less likely to raise ideas which challenge the council's commitments.

In fact not all the non-chairmen are likely to serve as the basis of a faction within the council, for the breakdown of councillors into chairmen and non-chairmen hides the fact that many of the non-chairmen displayed a pattern of responses to the questions not dissimilar to those of the chairmen. As I have been careful to point out in this chapter, it is the new councillors and those from North Kensington whose responses diverge most sharply from those of the chairmen, and this suggests that cleavage within the majority party could have its roots in the differences which exist between councillors either in terms of the areas from which they are elected, or in terms of generational differences between councillors based upon the stages they are at within the council career cycle. The marked differences in the responses of councillors to the questions set out in this section suggests that there is a basis for factionalism on the council. However, when I discussed the internal regulation of council activity in Section A of this part of my study I made it clear that the authorities within the council are able to shape and control the behaviour of councillors so that the maintenance of established policy is not threatened. If this control should break down then the material presented in this section suggests that there could be change in council policy.

In this chapter I have pointed out that it is necessary to study the way in which political decision-makers relate to information sources in order to see what interests are being represented within the authority structure; what is the likelihood that there will be continuity or innovation in public policy; and what is one possible basis of factionalism. In spite of the importance of this topic to an understanding of the development of public policy, there has been extremely little work undertaken on the information sources that are used by governmental decision-makers, and 'little systematic data exists on the flow of information to the legislator [or councillor] and the sources on which he depends' (Meller, 1960, p, 143). We have a certain amount of work which has pointed to the information deficiencies of public decision-makers, but in many of these studies structural reforms are suggested (Crick, 1964; and, Coombes, 1966), and there has been a general failure to recognise that selectivity and *not* just information deficiency lies at the heart of the problem and that this cannot be obviated merely by increasing the flow of information (Bauer, 1969; and, Hyman & Sheatsley, 1947). Where researchers have attempted to deal with the information sources used by decision-makers then they have often been content to identify sources that are used, but have failed to go on to discuss the *implications* of the pattern for public policy-making. (Barker & Rush, 1970. See also, Hattery & Hofheimer, 1954; Froman, 1963; Garceau & Silverman, 1954; Bauer *et al*, 1964; Huckshorn, 1965; Gleeck, 1940; Dechert, 1967; Russett, 1962; and Geiger & Hansen, 1968.) We know far more about the information used by voters and the factors leading up to their decision at the polls than we do about those who are making far more important political decisions, where problems of selective perception and the drive to search out information that is consonant with existing attitudes and policy preferences are matters which have received scarcely any attention. This ommission says much about the values of political scientists, and only makes sense if it is assumed that elected decision-makers are the passive servants of the electorate, and in Part One of this study I rejected this view as an adequate characterisation of the position of councillors in Kensington and Chelsea.

Section C
The proper role of government

The study of the political ideology of governmental decision-makers has been a neglected aspect of modern political analysis. However, no study of public policy should ignore the fact that those in government are likely to have preferences as to the proper role of government which they will support and justify by their perception and definition of 'public' problems. In the single chapter of this section I will outline the political ideology of the chairmen of the Royal Borough of Kensington and Chelsea.

10 Councillor ideology

> We all have said, at one time or another, that a city or organization has a 'climate' or 'style' in public matters and that people – even those who may wish it were different – have come to expect things to be done that way.
>
> J. Q. Wilson, 'Introduction: City politics and public policy',
> in J. Q. Wilson (ed.), *City Politics and Public Policy* (New
> York, Wiley, 1968), p. 12.

In this chapter I want to outline the ideology of the Conservative councillors from the Royal Borough of Kensington and Chelsea, even though many writers would argue that such an exercise is impossible, having suggested that ideology denotes a style of politics which is associated with bias, extremism, totalitarianism, distortion and irrationality (Sutton, Harris, Kaysen & Tobin, 1956; Meehan, 1960; and, Shils, 1958), so that although it assumes a role of critical importance in the politics of the Communist bloc, it is of no importance in the politics of the West, where we have witnessed the 'end of ideology'[1] (Bell, 1962; Aron, 1957; Kirchheimer, 1957; Abrams, 1964; Shils, 1965; and, Lipset, 1963, pp. 403 ff, and 1964), except perhaps on the fringes of politics.[2] The term ideology is customarily associated with the great 'isms' of our time, and especially with Marxism and Communism and a dominant usage of the term considers that an ideology embraces a world view which has contained within it a close,

1. What precisely is meant by the 'end of ideology' is not always clear. Sometimes all that is suggested is that Marxism no longer appeals to the intellectuals. On other occasions there is the idea that people in the West no longer think in ideological terms (and in particular attention is paid to the lack of revolutionary sentiment on the part of the working class). Sometimes there is almost the idea that there is a lack of class conflict and a consensus which has rendered old ways of thinking based on arguments of right or left irrelevant and out of date, and instead a new pragmatic approach is seen as the best way to solve the few problems which are said to remain.
2. By this I mean to suggest that some writers argue that ideology is important in minor 'extremist' parties, and other writers suggest that within the established parties ideology is a vestige lingering on among the grass-roots activitists, but passed over by the pragmatic leadership.

coherent, and consistent critique of the existing society, together with a programme of action which will guide the behaviour of believers so that a different society – a utopia – is created. Parties which have ideologies are seen as committed to radical change in accordance with a preconceived plan which generally involves increasing the scope of government in ways that are obviously going to disturb existing social and economic relationships. Writers holding these assumptions would argue that modern Western political parties (and especially those of the moderate right) do not have ideologies. British Conservatives, for example, are said not to have a 'cut and dried body of political doctrine' for they reject the 'shallowness of doctrinaire reasoning' (Goldman, 1961, pp. 13, and 6), and instead they 'plunge straight into the facts, and though they may emerge at the end with a policy, they are generally content to leave the principles for another day' (Howell & Raison, 1961, p. 125. See also, Hailsham, 1957; Coleraine, 1970, esp. p. 19). There is a very established view that the British Conservative party cannot be considered as a party of ideology: it is a view held by Conservatives themselves, by spokesmen of opposition parties, and by disinterested academics. Such a view is sustained by arguments which point out that a party of such diverse support and a party which is above all geared to electoral victory and the pursuit of power must be pragmatic, empirical, and flexible, and cannot afford to be tied to any particular ideology. (Boyle, 1950; Hailsham, 1957; and, Raison, 1961. See also, Harris, 1968; and Rose, 1965, esp. pp. 42, 49, and, 143.)

Moreover, within the more restricted field of local politics, we are often told that British local government allows no scope for the expression of political values for it is simply 'administration', and because there is no real choice at the local level there is no place where ideology can creep in. Where writers do admit that there is scope for political decision-making then they may still suggest that the values of councillors are not a subject of study as councillors are regarded as neutral servants of the people, responsive only to their wishes as they are expressed through the medium of regular elections. Even when councillors are seen as occupying a fairly autonomous role, unrestrained by local elections or the central government, then writers may still assert that ideology should not, and usually does not, play any part in influencing the deliberations of councillors, and where it does then this is seen as an aberration which should be avoided by all clear-thinking men who have the best interests of a locality at heart. Local government is seen as a matter of 'common-sense'; 'there is no Conservative or Socialist way to lay a sewer'; there is indeed no scope for conflict or party politics. What are problems and what the council should (or should not) do to solve them are matters on which complete agreement is possible, and where ideology or party politics do thrust themselves into local government then this is said to result in the undesirable imposition of 'doctrinaire' solutions which bear little relation to the 'real' problems and needs of a situation.

Now these traditions of writing need to be challenged. Local councils are *not* simply agents of the central government, and they are *not* simply conversion mechanisms passively responding to external influence attempts whether from constituents, or from interest groups. Local councils are *not* inert cash registers, and they are *not* just 'little black boxes', for they are themselves reservoirs of power and initiative capable of shaping decisions with only limited reference to external influences. A study of inputs and environments is not enough to account for the form of public policy. But neither is it adequate to concentrate all attention on relationships and processes internal to any authority structure while ignoring the values and preferences which the decision-makers bring to any decisional situation. Indeed, Boaden and Alford (1969) in their study of decision-making in English county boroughs point out that genuine differences about the desirable scope of local government exist and they argue that these differences in 'disposition' can be measured by noting the political complexion of local councils. Their 'expectation that Labour dominated councils will be more ready to be active' was confirmed by them in the case of the provision of both housing and education services in the county boroughs. Their findings led them to suggest that 'the actual dispositions of the major parties would ... merit attention' (Boaden & Alford, 1969, pp. 206, and 223). In fact in earlier chapters in this study I have pointed to the importance of the 'dispositions' (or ideology) of the councillors in Kensington and Chelsea in accounting for aspects of their behaviour. In Section B, for example, I pointed out that their preferences as to the scope of government played an important part in affecting the way in which they related to interest groups and information sources. I argued that interest groups were listened to and gained favourable council response if they raised demands that fell within the framework of the councillors' own views as to the proper role of government, but that if this was not the case then group demands were resisted and the groups themselves were likely to be regarded as prejudicial to the best interests of the borough. A similar theme was developed in the chapter on the councillors' use of information, where I suggested that councillors avoided sources which challenged their own views as to the proper role of government and the policy commitments of the council, and that if information from these sources did filter through to them then they could resist the suggestions by relying on a range of exclusion devices. In that section I was noting how councillors felt the environment should relate to them, but in this section I am dealing with the way in which they consider the *council* should relate to its environment. In this chapter I aim to set down the norms which the councillors feel should govern the behaviour of the council as a whole. Whereas in Section A I looked at the norms, or behaviour rules, which served to define the proper behaviour of the individual councillors, in this chapter I shall examine the leading councillors' views as to what should be the proper behaviour of the council as a whole. I am studying the councillors' conception of group purpose; I am looking at their preferences about what government should and should not be doing: in a word I am dealing with their views as to the proper role of government; with their political ideology.

The view which I outlined earlier which suggests that there is no ideological politics in the West and in the parties of the moderate right, needs to be countered because such a view confines the use of the term ideology to those bodies of ideas which are held by groups of men who are concerned to justify and implement drastic *change* in society and in the role of government. Now if we are to accept this usage of the term, then our attention is directed away from the beliefs of men in those parties which are more concerned with *maintaining* existing social relations and the existing scope of government,[3] and we fail to study them because our definitions tell us that their ideas as to what government should and should not do are ever-changing and are nothing other than those of common-sense accepted by all except the most bigoted. It must be admitted that a party which does not wish drastically to expand or contract the scope of government may not need self-consciously to formulate a political belief-system in which it justifies its preferences as to government's proper role by referring to the causes and cures of what it sees as social or public problems. Formulation and theorising will most likely occur where a party wishes to change the established scope of government, but since this involves the criticism of the existing order, if the arguments and criticisms gain widespread support, then the leaders and groups defending that order may have to clarify and state their reasons for doing so (Boyson, 1970; Hayek, 1944; and, Viereck, 1950). It is for this reason that parties which are content to manage and maintain the established scope of government invariably condemn any theorising or formulation of political beliefs (Oakeshott, 1962, esp. p. 21), since this calls into question the traditional way of doing things, whereas in the absence of formulation the established order can be taken for granted as beyond dispute, embodying the only practical approach to the solution of certain problems.[4] If political decision-makers

3. There is a similar problem in the study of interest groups, since the accepted definition of that term means that attention is restricted to those groups which are attempting to change (rather than maintain) the existing configuration of public policy, and there is a tendency to miss altogether the 'non-groups' that do not exist because certain categories of the population do not need to form into groups as their interests are already safeguarded.
4. Cecil (1912) makes the point that 'before the reformation, . . . it is not possible to distinguish conservatism in politics, not because there was none, but because there was nothing else' (p. 25). He considered that 'what brought Conservatism into existence was the French Revolution', and he views Conservatism as 'operating against the tendencies that that Revolution set up' (pp. 39, and, 244).

do not formulate theories about what should be the proper scope of government, this does not mean that they do not have a view on this matter, or that they do not have a range of arguments which they can use to sustain their view, it is rather indicative of the absence of any effective challenge to the order which they maintain and it suggests that consensus and agreement surround the established activity of government. Conceptions as to the role of government are shared, conceptions as to what are social problems, their causes and cures are shared. The views hold the middle ground, they are the ruling ideas which dominate the consensus, they are seen as commonsense and are regarded as non-political and leading to solutions which are regarded as both obvious and inevitable. When this occurs it does not signify 'the end of ideology' but only the absence of a sustained challenge to the existing order and the supposed arrival of a new political consensus. Now the existence of consensus around the established scope of government does not mean that this scope can somehow be defended as objectively right and as based on a value-free stance where there are no alternatives that can sensibly be considered. That we accept certain political actions as inevitable, and that we see certain politics as essentially practical and non-ideological means only that we share the views of those upon whom we pass this judgement. Our acceptance of an ideology may make it appear as the obvious practical approach to public problems, but it is not useful to think of some politics as ideological whereas in other cases politics is seen as only a practical activity: one man's ideology is another man's common-sense.

In fact, during the course of my interviews with councillors from Kensington and Chelsea many mentioned the importance of political 'principles' or party 'philosophy'; two chairmen: 'Once you bring party politics into local government, then you act on the basis of political principles and it's these that are important in providing a basis for action. I'm not a strong party man myself, but there are certain principles which I see as being important and by-and-large these are also the principles that are part of the Conservative philosophy.' 'One's political philosophy must have a bearing on the judgements we make, and so it ought to, since people are elected on a party political label.' A Chelsea councillor: 'One comes to a decision on the basis of two things; one's basic political philosophy and the factual background. The great thing is not to make a decision until you have all the facts and then to make a decision in the light of what you believe to be right. If Socialists had the same facts they could well come to a different decision.' A Labour councillor also pointed to the importance of the party philosophy of the majority group and also went some way to suggest the differences that divided the parties on the council: 'They [the Conservative councillors] certainly have a basic political philosophy, and that is where there is to be council intervention in private matters then the case for that intervention must be extremely strongly made with no alternatives available. .... This particularly comes to the fore in housing, but it can come forward on a whole range of things. It's a question of balance between public and private provision, and we'll tend to put it very much on the side of the public (whether this be on issues such as the size of the book fund, the availability of home helps, or records, or what have you). It comes down to money again and again.'

It was not only councillors of both parties who stressed the importance of understanding the philosophy of the councillors within the majority group, as people not on the council were aware of the importance of this affecting the way they responded to local interest groups and shaped the policies of the council. A report of a conference on housing in *People's News* outlines not only what the reporter saw as the Conservative position, but also other views regarding what should be the proper scope of government in dealing with the housing problem: 'It was clear at the housing conference on Saturday organised by the Lancaster Neighbourhood Centre, that there were two separate sides talking with very little common ground between them. On the one side Councillor Michael Cocks defended the council's housing policy in the Golborne and Colville areas of relying on housing trusts and private landlords to bring their properties up to a standard. On the other side most of the delegates saw this as totally inadequate and demanded measures from the extensive use of compulsory purchase orders to nationalisation of all building land. Somewhere in the middle came the housing trusts. But John Coward of the Notting Hill Housing Trust could offer no wholesale solutions. He estimated that the Trust working to full capacity would probably only be able to acquire houses in the council's areas at the rate of 50–70 houses a year, a mere "flea-bite" as he put it' (*People's News*, 1 December 1969).

So far I have not attempted to give any specific definition of the way in which I intend to use the term ideology, although I have made it clear that I reject the view which confines its usage to radical and change-oriented parties and have suggested that political ideologies are beliefs regarding the proper scope of government.[5] But this is not all, for a particular conception as to the proper role of government will be defended and justified partly by attacking alternative conceptions, but also, more positively, by the articulation of a particular view of the nature of society and societal problems together with an assessment of what are the causes of those problems and their proper cures. Governmental, or public action, is a response to (or an attempt to cure) what are seen as public problems. There are no objective criteria as to what constitutes a public problem, and in any community there are likely to be differing views, for a problem will be defined as 'public' to the extent that it is believed that the causes of that problem lie outside of the control of individuals who are, by themselves,

5. I found the following studies useful, and the way in which I use the term ideology has something in common with the usage in these studies: Agger, Goldrich & Swanson, 1964, esp. pp. 1–36; Williams & Adrian, 1963; Eulau & Eyestone, 1968; and, Friedrich, 1965.

seen as incapable of providing a solution. If political decision-makers consider that the causes of many of the problems which they perceive lie in individual deficiencies, then they are going to tend to stress that the cure for those problems lies in individual improvement and they are going to give government only a small role. If, on the other hand, political decision-makers consider that there are many public problems then they will probably advocate solutions which give government a much larger role. Moreover, where many public problems are perceived there is going to be an almost inevitable dissatisfaction with the existing state of society and it is likely that some utopia will be formulated which is seen as the desirable state towards which public authorities should direct social energy. Differing conceptions as to the proper role of government are, then, based upon differing perceptions as to the nature of social reality. Some people see many problems and see those problems as caused by the particular social and economic structure of a society. Others see few problems and see the causes of those problems as lying within individuals, and not as a result of deficiencies inherent in the nature of the existing social order: they will claim that the problems can (and should) be solved by individuals without extending governmental activity. Needless to say, people who consider that there are few problems and that those problems are capable of solution by individual and private effort will have little need to construct any utopia or formulate any plans about the proper role of government, as for them the ideal is broadly the real which needs only to be managed.

In the rest of this chapter I will outline the ideology of the Conservative councillors in Kensington and Chelsea, but I will restrict my attention to those councillors who were chairmen in the period 1965–70. The information for this discussion derives mainly from interviews with the chairmen in which open-ended questions[6] were asked which led to some general discussions as to the proper scope of government, although specific attention was paid to such matters as housing and play-space and amenity provision.

I. 'PUBLIC' PROBLEMS

The action of government represents a response to the problems of those surrounding government. The range of social situations that could be seen as demanding government action is infinite and before a social situation becomes the subject of government response, it is necessary for those in government to see the situation and to define it so that it is regarded, not simply as a problem, but as a 'public' problem which warrants the collective response of government to provide a solution.

6. For examples of, or comments on, approaches to identifying the content of ideologies, see, Harris, 1968; Armbruster, 1944; Barnes, 1966; Mellos, 1970; and, Minar, 1961.

The policy-makers' definition of public problems can be no larger than the sample of situations of which they are aware, and if they have only a limited and selective perception of the world around them, then they only have a small base from which to identify situations as problems even though if their knowledge of social situations were wider they might be prepared to construe more situations as constituting problems. Certainly, Chapter 9 on the councillors' use of information stressed the extent to which councillors (and especially the chairmen) were highly selective in sampling the world around them, trusting mainly 'internal' sources of information which were known and under their control. Moreover, in Chapter 8 I suggested that councillors (and again especially the chairmen) saw interest groups as first and foremost helpmates in the solution of problems and were reluctant to see them as providers of information or as legitimate articulators of demands unless they were groups of a rather special kind. Groups were regarded as helpful where they enabled councillors to manage the existing scope of government, but they were not regarded as helpful if they sought to shift the scope of government.

The point I wish to take from those two chapters is that the chairmen tend only to see those situations which they have seen before, and they do not willingly seek, or see, 'new' situations which might lead them to redefine what they see as problems. Where they are presented with social situations with which they are unfamiliar, then they tend to mistrust the descriptions given and they avoid the difficulty of considering new problems by refusing to credit the source of the information or the style by which it was sent.

Demands and information from groups and individuals surrounding a policy-maker are an important means by which policy-makers gain a sensitivity to situations in their areas which they might come to see as problems. In the case of the chairmen in Kensington and Chelsea, the evidence suggests that they tend to avoid and resist this, choosing instead to rely solely on their own perceptions and definitions of social situations and problems. Denying much of the experience of others and choosing to rely on their own commonsense and on trusted sources of information means that their perception of social situations rests very much on their own first-hand knowledge and experience and yet they are by no means a representative cross-section of those in the borough in terms of age, income, education, occupation or housing situation. Moreover, if the ordinary councillor is better housed, better educated, older, and in a higher class than the 'average' resident of the borough, then this is especially the case with the chairmen who are certainly older than the ordinary councillor, and are higher in the occupational structure. I suggest then that they are very aware of certain social situations, but tend to be in ignorance of others, and although they are very aware of the problems of a certain type of resident they tend to be rather less aware of the problems of others who live in the borough.

In many ways the chairmen's sympathy with a certain type of resident is evidenced by their assessment of the various interest groups in the borough. In Chapter 8, although I noted that the chairmen showed a marked preference for groups which were active in assisting the council in the provision of some service, they did nevertheless favourably assess some input groups. The groups of which they approved were the Kensington Society (or the Chelsea equivalent), the Kensington High Street Association, and the Kensington Chamber of Commerce. These groups are representing the interests of the comfortably housed, settled, middle-class resident concerned with the 'residential' nature of the borough, and the small traders and shopkeepers. This concern for, and awareness of, the problems of a certain type of resident in the borough finds its expression in the care councillors took to ensure that the needs of the car-owning residents were met at the expense of the commuters who might wish to park in the borough; in the concern which they express over traffic management schemes which might involve the diversion of traffic into residential areas; in their concern about aircraft noise; in their concern that street lighting and refuse collection and other 'general' services should be of a high standard; in the concern which they expressed as to the burden of government on the ordinary citizen; and in their concern with the effects of tourism.

Towards the end of the interviews I asked councillors to identify what they saw as 'the issues facing the borough', a question which in some sense enabled them to articulate their views as to the problems or undesirable situations in the borough. Housing, redevelopment and planning, the problems associated with the motor car, and questions of refuse collection and street cleansing were most frequently referred to by the chairmen, but in addition they also mentioned the lack of amenities in North Kensington, the burden of the rates and the problems involved in the daily running of the borough. The responses of the non-chairmen who were asked the question were not very different, though the North Kensington councillors and the new councillors showed more awareness of the housing issue and the lack of amenities and open-space in North Kensington, and they expressed less concern about the problems associated with the motor car.

This information does suggest that the chairmen were aware of the problems of those outside their own class, since the housing problem and the lack of open-space in North Kensington were problems which were most acutely experienced by the poorer residents of the borough. However, the fact that they defined certain social situations as problems does not mean that they will automatically consider that a governmental or public response is necessary. Before a problem is seen as demanding governmental action it has to be defined not just as a collection of individual problems where individual private solutions are possible, but it has to be defined as a *public* problem where the collective response of public authority is needed to provide a solution and where even private collective effort is regarded as inadequate.

Now if we look at some of the responses of the chairmen in Kensington and Chelsea, we find, for example, that although many would regard housing as a problem, they did not necessarily consider that the solution of this problem demanded an extension of government activity. Some councillors considered that it could best be solved by leaving it to free individuals operating in a free market where there was a total absence of government intervention or private collective effort. They saw the problem, in other words, as essentially a private problem. 'Housing is, I suppose, *the* issue, but I think the mess we are in now is because of the whole history of rent restriction acts as there's no profit in housing anymore. If you took off the rent restrictions by degrees, you would have higher rents, true, but at least there would be property there and people can afford higher rents. All the countries that control rents have a housing problem.' One chairman pointed to the 'racial problem' but again this was a problem which was not seen as involving any government activity, quite the reverse: 'The racial problem is obviously something up in North Kensington, but we should leave this alone and let them find their own feet. I'm anti this Race Relations Act (and so I suspect are most of the people on the council) it will only produce a lot of chippy immigrants.'

In other words, although the chairmen have only a limited awareness of the situation of many in the borough, even where they do recognise the problems of constituents outside their own class then they often see those problems not in public terms, but as private problems the solution of which should lie outside of government. They take this view because they have provided for themselves the basic necessities of the good life and they therefore tend to consider that everybody is, or should be, capable of providing for themselves in the same way without the necessity of any collective response be it public or private. The causes of problems are seen as lying in individual deficiencies rather than in deficiencies of the particular social or economic system; 'self-reliance', 'self-help' (Graham, 1972; and, Haggstrom, 1964) and 'responsibility' are seen as all-important solutions (Thatcher, 1968, esp. pp. 11–12): 'I had a chap round the other day and he said he was living in this and this condition and it really was terrible, but he finished up by saying "What are you going to do about it?" Well, I was brought up in the good old-fashioned way to believe that one should not marry and have children until one is able to provide for them and I felt he was irresponsible, so although I was initially sympathetic, I left feeling that it was his fault.' 'I was brought up in an atmosphere where we talked about the size of family one could afford. I don't see why people have three or four children if they have only a couple of rooms. There's not enough family or parental responsibility, people should do something about their own problems.' 'My philosophy is one which stresses self-help and enterprise, and it expresses the value of work and the importance of this rather than spoonfeeding for all, although one recognises the need for props for the weak. There's more virtue in giving than receiving and it's better still to do things for oneself.'

This view of the chairmen regarding the value of self-reliance and the importance of the private provision of goods and services was a view which was well-known to the other councillors; a North Kensington councillor: '. . . the old people [the senior councillors] start up, and if you say we need pre-school play groups, they say, "Hush, we'll be changing their nappies next". . . . We just couldn't get the Notting Hill Summer Project [a project organised in the summer of 1967 to examine housing provision in North Kensington and to provide play facilities] across. No-one was interested in anything to do with North Kensington, they just pooh-poohed it and said "A lot of do-gooders".' A chairman when looking at the play-space situation made it clear what he saw as the responsibilities of the mothers, as well as his perception of some of the facts of the situation: 'The thing grows. More mothers go out to work instead of looking after the children which is their proper job, and then there's the influx of coloured people who tend to have large families. The situation is that there are more children in the same space with more traffic. . . . I must admit that in the case of Powis Square [a private garden square that was eventually bought by the council to be used as a playground] I would have liked to have seen local people getting up a garden committee without any intervention from us.' This view about the desirability of *private* collective effort was shared by other chairmen: 'The solution we favoured for Powis Square in the past was that the residents should form a committee and get the council to rate it for them. We couldn't get the residents' agreement, however, though practically every square in South Kensington is run by residents.' 'One would like to see more garden committees set up there [in North Kensington]. I know it's easier in a middle-class area than (for want of a better word) a working-class one, where they seem to feel that the recreation of their children is not something they are responsible for.'

Understandably in view of this stress the chairmen often expressed a spirited defence of the rights of private property, and pointed to the desirability of property being held by private persons rather than by any government: 'In general Conservative principles don't agree with the public acquiring property, especially for something like a playground. We believe that property is best administered privately subject to the various acts, . . . the belief in private property and enterprise is a strong one.' 'Conservative principles are the right of the individual; but it's not quite that, it's the right of the individual to run his own life within the framework of the law. A Conservative wants people to run their own lives and groups; Socialists are more inclined to want to run things from the centre. I believe passionately in the private ownership of everything – the Post Office, everything.'

This assertion of the importance of private (over public) rights, and the theme of individualism is associated with their view which suggests that social change occurs 'naturally' without conflict in a society they see as an organic whole: difficult situations adjust themselves by processes of social and economic equilibrium without the necessity of any government interference, which, if it takes place, can be unnecessary and extravagant and prevent more satisfactory developments. A chairman pointed to the way in which the twilight areas in cities develop and improve: 'Our view is that it is quite wrong to deflect money into an area which is quite capable of pulling itself up by its own bootstraps, as if we do then we are loading the housing account with unnecessary expense. Hillgate Village – just behind Notting Hill Gate – was awful just after the war, but now it's looked up fantastically. If there's one decision I'm not happy with it's the decision to go ahead with plans to develop West Chelsea, but it went through in Chelsea days before the merger, and we couldn't stop it because Chelsea was keen on it. The fact is, though, not enough account was taken of the fact that the area was ready to pull itself up and could have been rebuilt and reconditioned privately at no cost to the public purse. This is just what happened at Hillgate Village, the area improved not at our cost but we get an improved rate return.'

Although I have argued that the chairmen tend to see social problems in individual and private terms rather than in public terms, even where they do define a problem as public – as caused by factors outside of the control of individuals and as somehow the product of 'the system' – this still does not mean that they will necessarily consider that *more* government action is the way to alleviate the situation. They may consider that the distributive mechanisms in the economic system are adequate and take the view that the imposition of public authority causes problems; they may see the problems which they define as public as caused by too much government and argue that *less* government action is necessary to provide a solution. Moreover, even where they recognise that public problems are caused by the inadequacies of the economic system, they may still not consider that more public activity is the answer, as they may argue that private collective effort should provide the solution, or they may even consider that a problem is so big as to be insoluble, at least by local activity.

The chairmen tend to see local government as first and foremost a spender of the ratepayers' money, and only secondly (and always with the financial consideration in mind) do they see the council as a provider of services. One situation which they were prepared to define as a public problem was what they saw as the weight of government upon the private citizen, which was symbolised for them in the 'burden of the rates' (Boyson, 1970, esp. pp. 6–7). This was seen as a problem because of their stress on the desirability of private self-sufficiency and their keen awareness of the needs of a certain type of resident who (because he provided for himself the basic amenities of life), not only did not need special government services, but would find the taxation incurred to provide those services for others, impairing his own capacity to provide for himself and narrowing his freedom of choice (Goldman, 1961, p. 10). When the chairmen referred to the problem of the burden of the rates they tended to picture the population of the borough as one composed essentially of old people living on fixed incomes, hit hard by inflation and the rising cost of living, yet still providing for themselves without recourse to any reliance on public services except those of a general kind which maintain the cleanliness and hygiene of the borough: 'We are a borough with a large residential population many of whom are old and retired. The rates go up and up and they can't go and ask for a pay rise. It's totally wrong to ask people like that to subsidise council tenants, many of whom are very well-off.' 'This borough is very highly rated and the individual ratepayer pays more per head than anywhere else in the country. One is conscious of this all the time. There are rich people in the borough but poor as well, and a penny on the rates means a lot of pennies even on the average property. ... I'm careful in spending my own money, and I feel that I should be even more careful in spending that of others. This is my philosophy, and I'm sure that it's that of my colleagues as well.' 'Rates have reached the maximum tolerable for retired people who live in the borough. Rates go up and up and people worry, and you see many old and middle-aged people with a worried look arising out of this millstone round their necks. One is conscious of this all the time, especially when it comes to looking at million pound housing schemes.' 'Value for money is behind the council's policy in everything we've done, and I should think that the percentage increase in the borough rate is probably the lowest in London.' 'We have to remember that every penny spent is contributed by ratepayers and we have to be reasonable in the demands we make on them.'

Although the rate burden was the biggest and most obvious embodiment of the weight of government on the population (a population which was seen as contributing to the cost of government services rather than using those services) – this was not the only problem chairmen saw arising from government activity and intervention. They also stressed their more general objection to 'controls' as making undesirable inroads into the sphere of personal freedom. Note, for example, the council's reluctance to introduce *any* scheme of parking control: 'The council are always reluctant to add to any system of control or to require additional payment from residents, but have concluded that it is an inescapable duty to deal with the existing chaotic conditions caused by irresponsible parking' (*Local Affairs*, September, 1966); and also the explanations given for deciding not to levy a rate on the owners of empty property in the borough, in spite of the fact that the Borough Treasurer's report recommended this as a way of raising some £200,000 per annum: 'Conservatives are predisposed to protect the owners of property and saw this possibility to rate empty property as yet another burden on property owners. It's really Conservative philosophy and part of tradition, though it's hardly logical since other property owners are hardly the beneficiaries of such a decision. There is the argument on practical grounds, but it was primarily why impose a load on property owners: it was seen as yet another impost.' 'There are two ways of looking at it. Firstly, it would entail cost of some sort, whether we took on fresh staff or not, any new work entails cost but if we are to argue on these grounds then one would have to say that there's a definite gain – a return over cost, though it's not as big as is often suggested. But there is another point of view which says it's hard on a person with property who is trying to let it at the highest price to charge rates on that when all through history that has not been so. It seems a bit unfair since while it's empty, no one is having his dustbins emptied and no one is making any use of street lighting.'

The leader of the council pointed to the necessity not only of private effort to solve the housing problem, but also to the necessity of some form of central government initiative as he saw the problem as too big for solutions to be found at the local level: 'When you develop, you can't put the same number back as you took out. That is a simple fact, true of all land-locked boroughs. And when you develop it's bound to cost money. This can either come from the central government or from the private landlord. It can't come from the rates – the increase would be too large. No government, whatever its political complexion, is going to fork out the huge sums needed. So there's bound to be a big part for the private land-lord. Of course, this will cost money, and when you have fewer people in a house, they'll be paying more rent. This is why Kensington is *bound* to become a middle-class community. It's bound to be a well-off community simply because of its situation near the heart of the metropolis. It's much too desirable. If you want a balanced community of all classes, then you can only get it by some sort of subsidy which isn't available. So the lower income people are bound to be excluded' (*Nova*, October 1968).

Not surprisingly in view of the extent to which the chairmen are involved in the day-to-day work and internal activities of the council, they were extremely mindful of the problems of the *council* itself. These problems they invariably saw as embodied in the 'bad press' and 'unjust criticism' which they felt they received and which they considered showed an insufficient regard to the problems and difficulties under which they were labouring and which were beyond their control. Thus in the chairmen's eyes, the housing problem could never be met as there was not enough space in the borough on which to build new housing for those in need, and the problems of 'overspill' meant rebuilding was never able to 'put back the same number as was taken out'. Refuse disposal and street cleansing could not be adequately performed because it was impossible to recruit adequate numbers of staff, and to pay more in wages was not only unfair to the ratepayers but might also incur the wrath of the district auditor. Much of the chairmen's contact with members of the press and public is spent in countering criticisms which are levelled at the council, and they sometimes give the impression that they spend more time in explaining their problems and in looking for a sympathetic audience, than they do in trying, themselves, to be a sympathetic audience to the problems of others – note, for example, their appointment of a public relations officer, and the use of their journal, *Local Affairs*, to explain to the ratepayers the problems which they are facing.

II. THE PROPER SCOPE OF GOVERNMENT

Now we have this information on what the chairmen see as 'problems' and in particular what they see as 'public' problems and the causes of problems, we are better able to appreciate the basis of their views as to the proper role of government, for that conception is based on, and supported by, their perception and categorisation of problems, and their views as to the causes of those problems and the proper way of solving them. The fact that the chairmen take the view that certain problems are caused by individual deficiencies and should be solved by individual effort or else can be solved automatically by forces working outside of government, together with their belief in the public problem of the weight of government and the desirability of maximising the area of private life left uncontrolled by public authority, means that they tend to give government a small role. They take the view that government should restrict itself to the provision of general services used by all ratepayers, but it should also show a concern to safeguard the residential nature of the borough and to develop the shopping areas of the borough, but not in such a way that the latter objective leads to undue 'commercialism': 'We're very sympathetic to the commercial life of the borough; they are very good contributors to the rates, but when we think of the borough we have to remember that it is a residential borough and this is how it should be in the future, and so the more you develop the commercial side the less is left for residential. In practice we try to restrict the commercial life of the borough to shops and then only in certain places and not all over the place.' One councillor of the Royal Borough (not a chairman) published the view that 'local government should confine itself to doing what it is best fitted to do more efficiently than private citizens, firms, and institutions' and he considered: 'It is in local government's best interests to disgorge these new powers [planning and the development of the social services] together with many other excessive activities, and thus regain some of its old qualities. Unburdened by town planning, transport, housing and other entrepreneurial functions, that could be better done privately or contracted out, local authorities would be able to concentrate on public services like amenities (lighting, sewage, open-spaces, anti-pollution), education, public health, police and other *common facilities* which they alone can provide, while *keeping down the rate burden* on their already over-taxed citzens. Locally, as nationally, over-government is misgovernment' (Sherman, 1970, pp. 118, and 132, my emphasis). Since the chairmen saw the proper role of government being mainly restricted to the provision of traditional services (see Williams & Adrian, 1963), and did not see government having any major role in income redistribution through the provision of particular services for sections of the population, it is not surprising that they did not choose to make very full use of the powers available to them under certain permissive acts; a chief officer: 'We don't make much use of permisssive legislation and that's policy. The council are keen on taking a view as to what is desirable and what is essential, and every year it somehow comes about that only the essential is considered.'

III. EXTENDING THE PROPER SCOPE OF GOVERNMENT

Although the chairmen considered that the scope of government should ideally be severely restricted, they nevertheless recognised the necessity of government extending its activity beyond the provision of general services; a chairman recognised the necessity of this with respect to the council's activity in the housing field: 'It would be wrong to say that the Conservative philosophy is unimportant in affecting what we do, but to give you an example, there is the fear that we are building up a lot of property ourselves which is not desirable.' In other words, it is often difficult for the chairmen to fully sustain their views as to the definition of problems and the role of government in their solution, and increasingly they are having to recognise that problems which they have been used to seeing in individual terms are viewed by others as public problems where there is the necessity of some collective response by government if any solution is to be forthcoming. Indeed the activity of many of the interest groups in the area (and particularly those considered by the chairmen as 'unhelpful') is directed towards expanding the role of government into areas of social life that at present lie within the private sphere, outside the scope of government. These groups are successful to the extent that they can impose on the chairmen their definitions of what are 'public' problems and what are the necessary public actions to provide a solution. As Chapters 8 and 9 suggested, however, this is none too easy, and the groups urging an expansion in the role of government have, in terms of tangible results, gained only comparatively minor concessions.

In so far as the chairmen have come to accept a wider view as to what are public problems, then they are still cautious in expanding the role of government to meet those problems since they consider private collective effort is desirable; they point to the need to draw a balance between the needs of the ratepayers and the needs of those who require special government services; and they take the view that the user should pay the full-cost of any special service which they might provide.

. . . . . .

I have already mentioned that many of the councillors considered that the best answer to the problem of the lack of play facilities in North Kensington was for the mothers to look after their children taking them to the open-spaces which existed just outside the borough, but they also recognised the value of private collective effort making use of the garden squares which existed in parts of the borough. In 1971, the council gave a grant to the North Kensington Amenity Trust [previously the North Kensington Playspace group] in order to help it to 'get off the ground' the development of the land under the elevated motorway in North Kensington which was leased to them by the Greater London Council at a peppercorn rent. Many of the councillors considered that a smaller grant was appropriate but the leader expressed the view: 'From now the Trust will have to make its own way in the world. It is on its own to develop its ideas in its own way. I am sure that some of the leading charitable foundations will recognise this as a unique experiment' (*Municipal Review*, March 1971, p. 74). In other words, the council was moving into new areas, but it was doing so with caution, stressing the value of relying on private collective effort and income provided by 'private' sources.

In Chapter 8 the evidence that the chairmen showed a strong preference for those groups that were actually providing some form of service for the public (which if not provided by private collective effort could well have to be provided by themselves as a public authority) is a tangible recognition of their preference for non-governmental collective effort in the solution of certain social problems: 'I'm anti-authoritarian and power and property being centralised in the hands of authorities whether national or local. Where voluntary bodies are willing to do things and can do things and can do them as well as a local authority, the only difference being that the ratepayer has saved money, then I'm all for it.'

Perhaps the most important area where this preference for private, rather than public, collective effort comes to the fore, is in the chairmen's views on the way to solve the housing problem and provide a housing for those who are unable to compete in the private sector. They place considerable emphasis on the role which the housing trusts can play and argue that this is preferable to the council itself assuming an active role in the provision of council housing: 'What do you want to do that for? [the public acquisition of housing accommodation] We don't see any point in acquiring property just on its own. We could acquire property if it was sound and if there was vacant possession or near vacant possession, but there's no point in acquiring property merely in order to manage – it's a pointless exercise. It's politics really, some people just don't like private landlords.' 'Housing trusts and property companies are experts at reconditioning, we are not and we should leave it to them, as if we do it we have to provide higher standards and that only pushes the cost up.' 'We welcome the housing trusts, we think that they complement the work of the council. They are able to do a number of things that we can't do easily. They can deal with cases which it thinks are urgent and which have no priority from the point of view of the council's waiting list. They can in fact deal with families which have aroused public sympathy for various reasons and the council, you see, has to house on the basis of the waiting list because if we didn't then there'd be no point in having a list. A trust doesn't have any list to adhere to, it has informal lists, but it doesn't have to be bound by them. They are not subject to public scrutiny and so they can be more flexible.' 'Conservatives feel that there should be a limit to municipal housing, but the Socialists think there are no limits to this; they would like to see the whole of the borough owned and managed by borough officials. Conservatives would, of course, view this with horror.' 'Socialists would like to see the complete municipalisation of the borough's housing. I personally, as a party member, believe it is a bad thing and destroys the character of a community, as council housing doesn't give the mixed development and the kind of variation which you need in a community.'

Where the chairmen have come to recognise that government has a role to play in the provision of particular services for sections of their population, then they stress the necessity of drawing a 'balance' between the needs of the ratepayers and the needs of those who require special governmental assistance: 'We have to strike a balance between providing for the under-privileged housing and welfare services, and seeing that the ordinary ratepayer is not overburdened and yet has good general services.' 'We are concerned about the rates, but it's a matter of degree and you have to decide whether the interests of the poorer classes should be pushed at the expense of the ordinary ratepayers. Where you put the sword down is critical, but I think that we do a pretty good job.' I suggest that in drawing this balance, or in putting the sword down, the information which I have assembled in this chapter suggests that they will be more mindful of, and sympathetic to, the problems of raising money to provide special services, than they will be to the needs of those who might have recourse to look to public authority for the provision of amenities which they cannot gain in the private sector: 'If you want to keep the rates down you have to be prepared to economise: this is the difference between being in power and being in opposition. The opposition says you're mean and bad, but when you're in power you know that the people who put you there don't want to see the rates go up. At the same time you do have this duty to provide certain services, so you look at everything; does it have to be done? Can it wait till next year? Is it desirable? Is the cost necessary? If you didn't do this then the rates would go up very much more than they have done, but in Kensington and Chelsea we have tried to keep expenditure down in so far as it's under our control.'

In the case of housing, the question of balance is reflected in their refusal to really consider building council houses in parts of the borough that are considered 'expensive'. The point was made clear by a chairman in explaining why the council did not develop the Campden Hill Waterworks site in South Kensington, but instead left the site to private developers: 'The Conservative attitude to it is to let it be developed privately if it is expensive – and it is bound to be – or else for us to invite somebody to develop it for a better class of Kensington resident. It would cost half a million pounds to acquire the site and the space for building is small. It's a matter of simple arithmetic which Labour don't seem to realise. If you divide the site value and the cost of building by the number of flats, even if you had a ten storey block (which would be ridiculous in that area) the real rents would be out of all proportion to what we could charge. Labour would say that the first duty is to the people of the borough and especially to the poor people and they say that we should buy and develop regardless of expense, and if the rents were too high then we should put the difference on the rates. Now we say that's unfair to the ratepayers many of whom are poorer than those on the housing list looking for cheap accommodation. This is the philosophical background to the local political division and it's insoluble. If you did build there, you'd only have thirty or so flats and a debt round our necks for ever, and anyway what is thirty flats when our waiting list is so long?' Another chairman expressed the same sort of view rather more generally: 'I think there is a case for the council staying out of property development in expensive areas as it is not only that you've got very high site costs, as the actual building costs are high in Central London.' In practice, this concern with the cost of development has been translated into a refusal to contemplate public development in South Kensington, as was noted by a chairman from Chelsea: 'The South Kensington people have this thing about there not being council houses in South Kensington, but I can't see why.'

As the chairmen have come to admit that the council can itself assume something of a role in the provision of services for special sections of their population, then they have taken the view which stresses the desirability of the user paying the full-cost of the services whether this be for on-street parking facilities or for council house rents. This idea has almost been elevated into the principle 'the user should pay the full cost', and in the matter of council house rents this position is partly bolstered by the belief that many council house tenants are wealthy when compared to those in the borough not in the position to enjoy the occupancy of what they regard to be the only form of subsidised housing: 'I reckon they [council house rents] are fair, but it's hard in this day and age to make people realise that things have to be paid for somehow, and why can't the user pay?' 'With regard to rents, Conservatives view the question of a rates subsidy as undesirable, but the Socialist view is that up to a point a rate subsidy is a good thing. ... Council tenants are not poor or working class, some are no more working class than my Aunt Fanny, and some are jolly well-off.' A South Kensington councillor: 'I had a daily once who lived in a council flat and she said that the people next door had £80 a week and didn't know what to do with it all. Now these sorts of people can well afford to pay an economic rent.'

Now in expanding their views as to what are to be regarded as public problems (and in recent times this expansion of viewpoint is most noticeable with respect to the problems relating to play facilities), the chairmen have frequently come to see the problems as so big that any solution must lie in the hands of the central government, and even then they doubt if solutions will be possible. These beliefs have served to sustain further the view which considers that the activity of the local authority should be confined to the provision of traditional, general, services because if the larger problems cannot be solved then even to attempt this is worthless, the more so since any attempt must inevitably lead to rate increases which will merely exacerbate the problem experienced by those whose interests have always been uppermost in the minds of the chairmen.

IV. CONCLUDING REMARKS

In this chapter I have given some indication of the chairmen's views as to the proper scope of government, together with the perceptions, beliefs, definitions, and theories of social change, which they use to sustain such a view. This chapter, then, gives an indication of what the chairmen conceive to be the task of their local authority, and these values represent the ethical premises (Simon, 1957) which they take to decisional situations. An understanding of their ideology is fundamental to any appreciation of the policy decisions which they make, but, notwithstanding this, in the situation in which the majority party on the council finds itself, it is of only limited importance in the day-to-day activity of that group, precisely because their activity is largely geared to servicing and *maintaining* established policies and as such they are involved in the taking of routine decisions and these do not necessitate the use of ethical decisional premises. In other words, because they take few policy decisions, their preferences as to the proper scope of government are rarely 'used', even though they are entrenched in the established pattern of commitments. Their ideology really only comes to the fore when the council has to confront some new situation not covered by established policy, and I have already argued that there are factors which tend to restrict the attention of the authoritative councillors to situations with which they are already familiar. However, the fact that major political conflict between the local authority and surrounding interest groups revolves around differences of view as to the proper scope of government, means that councillors are frequently put in the position of having to defend the existing commitments which they seek to maintain, and where they do this then they rely on the arguments which I have set out in this chapter.

Conclusions: The defence of commitment and the control of disturbance

---

If we know what a society's culture is, including its particular system of values and attitudes, we can predict with a fairly high degree of probability whether the bulk of its members will welcome or resist a particular innovation.

> R. Linton, 'Cultural and personality factors affecting economic growth, in B. F. Hoselitz (ed.), *The Progress of Underdeveloped Areas* (Chicago, University of Chicago Press, 1952), pp. 73–88, p. 74.

Nobody can be at the same time a correct bureaucrat and an innovator. Progress is precisely that which the rules and regulations did not foresee; it is necessarily outside the field of bureaucratic activities.

> Ludwig Von Mises, *Bureaucracy* (London, Hodge, 1945), p. 84.

This has been a two-part study, but both parts are intimately related, and each has a bearing on the other. In Part One, I was concerned with the established political science literature which has aimed to explain public policy and the behaviour of governments in representative democracies. In Part Two, I moved from the consideration of established literature to the consideration of one local authority, and I attempted to make sense of public policy in Kensington and Chelsea by noting the factors which I saw as important in accounting for its development. Even though my interest lies in understanding the situation in Kensington and Chelsea, I could not avoid the established literature unless I was prepared to ignore the collective past experience of the discipline, and to assume that the facts of my case could speak for themselves without the aid of any theory.

In this final chapter I do not intend to offer a detailed elaboration and critique of the methods and conclusions embodied in the established literature, for this was the subject of Part One, and I drew together my conclusions in Chapter 5. Now I wish to review the ideas which I used in Part Two to make sense of my case, and to take stock of my empirical findings. I also want to suggest that if students are to account for the development of public policy in other situations then they too may need to pay attention to these ideas, and work from theoretical perspectives other than those which are usually considered in attempts to explain the behaviour of the institutions of representative democracy.

However, before I can satisfactorily do this, it is necessary to recap the major themes I detected in the established literature explaining public policy and the behaviour of government, since the explanatory ideas I developed and used in Part Two arose as a reaction to the deficiencies and omissions which pervaded this literature.

In Chapter 1, I rejected that academic orthodoxy in which local authorities are presented simply as agents administering the policies of the central government. I suggested that local authorities were policy-shaping bodies in their own right. Taking this view meant that in order to explain local policies and the behaviour of local authorities I had to consider factors other than the weight of central control. In Part One, therefore, I outlined political science work which accepted that governments were policy-shaping structures, and I identified the established theories that purported to explain public policy and the behaviour of the institutions of representative government, in the hope that these theories would provide a model which could be used to make sense of my case.

At first, I considered a theory which was developed specifically to make sense of the policy-shaping behaviour of British local authorities, but this was not adequate to the facts of my case, and so I went on to consider other theories which had been developed and used to explain governmental behaviour in Western democracies, in the hope that they would provide more realistic models which might help to interpret my material.

The three bodies of theory which I reviewed have a number of features in common. All emphasised the importance of the impact of the environment in accounting for the pattern of public policies developed by government. Government is seen as a weak organisation operating in a hostile and demanding environment, and it plays but a small, and almost irrelevant, part in the shaping of public policy. It is presented as lacking in autonomy, and is seen as open and responsive to the inputs directed from an all-controlling environment on which it depends for support and survival. However, the theories not only resemble each other in terms of the conclusions as to the respective roles of government and environment in the shaping of public policies, they are similar too in that their conclusions are based on research which has paid but scant attention to the institutions of government. The small and weak part which the institutions of representative government are alleged to play in policy-making is explained by deterministic and mechanistic theories which rest on assumptions that government is weak; that governors are concerned to maintain positions of power; and that security and support are bought at the cost of reduced decisional autonomy by developing public policies favoured by the politically relevant environmental forces. The emphasis in these theories is on the process leading up to policy decisions, the emphasis is on policy-making, on action, on drama, on cases of decision, on change and on disturbance.

The ideas and approaches I developed in Part Two are in almost all respects at variance with the conclusions and methods contained in the established literature. This reflects the fact that I considered there were omissions and deficiencies in these established theories which limited their *general* utility, and, more especially, I considered that the *particular* facts of my case defied explanation and interpretation in terms of these ideas. This means that the theories which I outlined in Part One have not been used in Part Two where I make sense of the situation in Kensington and Chelsea. However, it was necessary to outline the established theories, as coming to terms with the problems which they contained led to the experimentation and the approaches which I eventually adopted in dealing with my empirical data.

As a description Part Two represents a departure from accustomed methods of portraying the policy-shaping behaviour of representative government, and some readers may feel that this departure is unwarranted. I want to deal with such misgivings and to justify my choice of approach and material and to argue that my conclusions about the strength of government and the predominance of policy-maintenance are adequate to the facts of my case.

One probable line of criticism is that it is strange in a study of public policy to find so little consideration given to the detailed policies being pursued by the Borough, to policy issues, and to substantive decisions. Although I touch on these subjects in Chapter 10, it is the case that, given the limitations of time and resources, I did not attempt to undertake a study in which I would *describe* the policy of the Royal Borough. In the introductory chapter I suggested that there were many questions that could legitimately engage the research attention of the student of public policy, and I chose to devote my energy to attempting to account for the pattern of council commitments. I considered that I could only do justice to this subject by analysing systematically the forces which encouraged or inhibited change and innovation, and in the context of Kensington and Chelsea I was drawn to paying particular attention to the manner in which an established and given range of commitments is maintained and defended.

Another criticism might be that I should have approached the task of explanation by introducing case-studies of issues and decisions, showing the council in action. I rejected this approach to the problem, because I do not consider that cases can be used as anything other than illustrations of the validity or otherwise of a particular theoretical position. Not only do cases not speak for themselves, but an emphasis on action and dramatic decisions positively misrepresents the daily reality of those whose task it is to manage the scope of government. Case-studies inevitably emphasise change and disturbance and fail to get to grips with those forces which encourage policy-maintenance and restrict governmental activity to undramatic instances of routine decisions. Questions of this kind will go unnoticed if action, and not structure, is made the subject of research attention.

Although I am not defensive about my failure to describe council policy or include case-studies of the council in action, I am aware of the fact that I have not dealt with the part which the officers of the Royal Borough play in the making and maintenance of council policy, and I would agree that their omission from this study is a major shortcoming, occasioned by a lack of research time, and my difficulty in finding a 'way-in' to study their contribution to the policy process. Many of the officers were interviewed, but it proved impossible to break through the cultural cliche that they were simply servants advising the all-powerful policy-making councillors whose decisions they readily implemented. Of course, ideally, one would have observed instances of interaction between councillors and officers, and would have examined private papers which showed the background to the development of public policies, but neither of these research approaches was possible because of the usual problem of access. In a sense, then, the officers are omitted from this study by default, but notwithstanding this it is reasonable to suggest (as I did in Chapter 9) that the officers are a force which is likely to be disposed to encourage the maintenance of established policy and to discourage change and innovation. In other words, I suggest that if detailed consideration had been given to the official side of the local government machine it would have strengthened my conclusions about the pre-eminence of forces which encourage the maintenance of public policy.

This, then, is my justification and apology for conspicuous omissions from my study, but what is the justification for what is included within the ambit of explanation? Why, in Part Two, did I include what I did in the way that I did?

I have already hinted at an answer to this question, for I have made the point that my approach grew out of my criticism of the established theories both generally, and more specifically, as they made sense of the facts of my case.

First, I considered that it was inadequate to assess the impact of environmental forces on government and public policy by studying the objective environment of government and noting inputs and pressures, while just making assumptions as to the behaviour and response of governmental decision-makers. I took the view that in order to assess the impact and effect of environmental forces on the development of public policy, it was essential to note the psychological environment of those in government, and to appreciate the way in which they imported the surrounding world into their decisional activity. I explored these questions in Section B on the external relations of the council.

Second, however, I considered that this in itself was not enough, because environmental forces are only likely to be decisive in determining the development of public policy where government is weak and operating in a hostile environment. Now although the established literature has posited that governments in the West are in this situation, I argued that these conclusions did not fit the facts of the case in Kensington and Chelsea, where the organisational situation of the governing party was one of strength where it was operating in a comparatively weak environment. This being so, it was not the case that the majority party was lacking in autonomy and independence and was controlled and open to the impact of environmental forces, rather, it was strong and in a secure position, where it could gain cost-free support and resources and so determine the pattern of public policy largely unconcerned by environmental influences.

In this sort of situation any explanation for the development of council policy would need to take into account additional factors besides those relating to external relations, no matter how those relations are considered. The crucial question, therefore, became one of deciding just what was of importance in determining the likely development of public policy. I took the view that since the external influences were of limited importance, then one should, of necessity, look to the influence of factors internal to the council itself. I did this in Section A, when I dealt with the internal regulation of council activity.

In addition, I felt it was important to recognise that developing public policy involves setting the scope of government, and since the governing party of the Royal Borough enjoyed considerable autonomy, it was necessary to identify the councillors' views as to the proper scope of government, since this would probably serve as a bench-mark which could be expected to affect what would be the actual scope of public activity. I outlined councillor ideology in Section C.

When I examined the situation in Kensington and Chelsea; outlined the way council activity was regulated from inside; discussed how external relations were handled; and identified councillor ideology, I concluded that these factors had the effect of maintaining established policy, and of discouraging policy-making activity involving change and innovation. In short, I have explained how an established pattern of public policies is maintained, and have noted how they are defended and how disturbance (either from inside or outside the council) is controlled and shaped so as not to pose a challenge to the continued arrangement of the established commitments.

·   ·   ·   ·   ·

My findings are at variance with the established orthodoxy which I discussed in Part One. Instead of suggesting that government is weak, and open and responsive to environmental influences, I have suggested that government is strong, and is closed and unresponsive, able actively to avoid and resist demands for change or innovation. Instead of suggesting that government is controlled by the environment, I suggested that government is able to control and shape the environment, at least in so far as it impinges on their own activity.[1] Instead of emphasising the importance of factors external to government in order to make sense of governmental behaviour, I have emphasised the importance of factors internal to government. Instead of minimising the role of ideology, I chose to stress its potential importance. Finally, instead of emphasising the process of policy-making, the taking of decisions, action, disturbance and change, I emphasised the structure of policy-maintenance, the restricted scope of decision, the rules which contain and restrain activity, stability and the control of disturbance, and the absence of change and the forces which resist change.

It must be admitted that I have placed deliberate emphasis upon the structure of policy-maintenance to the exclusion of a detailed consideration of the forces which encourage policy-making and change. I have done this because the organisational situation of the governing party in Kensington and Chelsea is one where the forces for maintenance are particularly well-developed, and therefore an understanding of this is of crucial importance if we wish to explain the likely future development of public policy in the Royal Borough. I also chose to pay particular attention to maintenance precisely because the established literature explaining public policy has paid so much attention to the process of policy-making that I felt I could rather underplay this side of the question in the consideration of my case. If the established literature ignores the problem of policy-maintenance, then what bodies of literature provide clues to deal with this?

I have already hinted at this in developing my approach to making sense of the situation in Kensington and Chelsea, and although I do not intend to refer again to the references which I noted then, I do wish to point briefly to general bodies of literature and ideas which I feel need to be taken into account by students who wish to make good sense of the behaviour of representative government.

First, the literature of role theory is of tremendous importance, and I suggest that particular attention should be paid, not so much to the rather clumsy work by policial scientists on conventions and rules of the game, but to the recent contributions by social psychologists and students of organisations (see especially, Gross, Mason, & McEachern, 1958;

1. See Latham, 1952*b*, esp. pp. 386–7. Rice (1963, p. 192) makes the point that 'enterprises have frequently attempted to control their environment, and for a time have succeded in doing so . . . . Such enterprises have been able largely to ignore their environment in considering their internal organisation.'

Kahn, Wolfe, Quinn, Snoek, & Rosenthal, 1964; and, Katz & Kahn, 1966).

Second, my discussion of the external relations of the council, particularly where I considered the councillors' use of information, suggested that theories of selective perception and cognitive dissonance are of importance, and from a different point of view they point to the forces which encourage the stability and rigidity of established views and commitments. In addition, my recognition that certain positions on the council could be expected to be more selective than others owed much to the writings of organisational sociologists. Some students have built theories of organisational change around the patterns of search behaviour displayed by organisations. For example, March and Simon (1958, p. 174) point out that 'where search for new alternatives is suppressed, program continuity is facilitated', and they go on to point out that 'a theory of this kind does not attribute the persistence of behavior to any particular "resistance to change", but simply to the absence of vigorous search for new alternatives under circumstances where the existing program is regarded as satisfactory.' Moreover, even where search does occur, this is unlikely to result in any drastic change of established commitments, since, as Cyert and March (1963, pp. 121-2) point out, 'rules for search are simple-minded' and initially at least there is a tendency to '1) search in the neighbourhood of the problem symptom and 2) search in the neighbourhood of the current alternative.' The effect of this behaviour 'inhibits the movement of the organisation to radically new alternatives'. Ideas of this kind were important in guiding my study, and I suggest that students of government should pay particular attention to patterns of search behaviour and information use, since in this lies an important clue to the likely development of their pattern of policies.

Third, once we recognise that those in government may well enjoy considerable autonomy in shaping public policies, and once we recognise that they are anything but automatons, passively responding to environmental pressures, then it becomes crucially important to recognise that their political ideology is going to be a major factor affecting the way in which they manage the scope of government. This recognition points to the necessity of exploring the literature on political ideology, but in spite of the massiveness of this work, it is of only limited value to the student of political behaviour who wishes to describe and type the ideology of particular political decision-makers, before going on to assess the effect that ideology will have on the likely future development of public policy. Schiff correctly makes the point that 'one variable that has not received sufficient attention in the literature is the role of fundamental administrative outlooks or professional ideologies.' He goes on to suggest that 'despite the difficult incident to a study of the role of administrative ideologies, . . . it can be clearly demonstrated that at least in the attitude of conservationists toward the treatment of land resources, ideology influenced organisational behavior and constrained innovative capability' (Schiff, 1966, pp. 2–3. See also, Mohr, 1969).

Although it may not strike the reader as immediately apparent, I suggest that my description of the structure and organisation of the majority party on the Council of the Royal Borough, shows that it has much in common with the bureaucratic, mechanistic, or monocratic form of social organisation (Gerth & Mills, 1948; Bendix, 1960; Burns & Stalker, 1961; and, Thompson, 1965, 1969). In both my case, and in the ideal type bureaucracy, there is hierarchy, specialisation, careful recruitment, extensive training, and a general plethora of rules affecting and shaping all facets of organisational behaviour. This similarity suggests that students of public policy could also usefully explore this body of literature. In particular they should pay especial attention to the behavioural implications of this organisational form, for there is the strong suggestion that, as in my case, there is rigidity, a lack of flexibility, and a tendency to operate on the basis of precedent which produces not only low innovative capacity, but also a more positive resistance to change. (See the work of Merton, Gouldner, Crozier, Thompson, and Downs. For a contrasting view, see Blau, 1955.)

Interestingly, just as I have chosen to emphasise maintenance and rigidity, so most students of the bureaucratic phenomena have done the same. But Crozier (1964, pp. 195–6) makes the point that this is a 'partial image', for 'crisis is a distinctive and necessary element of the bureaucratic system.' Crozier argues that 'a system of organization whose main characteristic is its rigidity will not adjust easily to change and will tend to resist change as much as possible', but he points out that change will nevertheless occur, although when it does it is likely to be rather unpredictable and unplanned. 'The essential rhythm prevalent in such organisations is, therefore, an alternation of long periods of stability with very short periods of crisis and change' where 'individual initiative prevails'. How far does this view square with the situation in Kensington and Chelsea? I emphasised maintenance, but is this a partial picture? Is there evidence of crisis, and change in the pattern of established commitments?

In my discussion of policy development in Kensington and Chelsea, I pointed to several factors which I felt could have the effect of weakening the forces for policy-maintenance and so encourage the possibility of change and innovation. First, the established recruitment rules were broken with the election of the second leader of the council in 1968, and, given the attributes which the new leader possessed, I considered that he could well be sympathetic to the necessity for change and innovation in the pattern of established council commitments. Additionally, I noted that control of the leader through restraining behaviour rules was likely to be difficult, and as such the leader may have been in a position to take personal initiative in redirecting the activity of the Council. Second, I mentioned that the regular election of new Conservative councillors always posed a certain challenge to established commitments, and I suggested that they were a potentially factional group which could be sympathetic to change and innovation. I noted too that there were an exceptionally large number of new Conservative councillors elected in 1968,[2] because of a considerable number of retirements and because of unusual electoral success in North Kensington. I suggested that this influx posed a particular problem of control for the more senior councillors. Third, I suggested that it was possible that change could be introduced through the activity and initiative of local interest groups, for if an established group took up a demand for change or innovation, or if a new group went about things the proper way, then they might meet with a favourable council response. In 1968, the situation was more favourable for change and innovation than at any time in the recent history of Kensington and Chelsea, as factors encouraging these developments came together at the same time. Inside the Council there was a new leader, and a large number of new councillors, and outside the Council there was an especially significant amount of interest group activity which was geared to urging change and innovation on the council. What was the effect of these forces on the actual development of Council policy?

Casual observation of developments in Kensington and Chelsea since that date does indeed create the impression that there has been substantial change in the pattern of public policies. The new leader created two new committees in 1968 (one of which was specifically concerned to create more effective links with local groups), and in the same year he took a personal initiative in purchasing a private garden square for public use, against the wishes of several of the authoritative councillors. In addition, the Council 'decided to treat a large portion of North Kensington as a proposed Action Area under the terms of the Town Planning Act' (RB of K & C, *Colville Study Area*, 1972), and they sought the active co-operation of local groups. More recently the North Kensington Amenity Trust, and the Kensington and Chelsea Play Association have been established. These groups are specifically concerned with the betterment of conditions in North Kensington; they have received financial help from the Borough Council; and the manner of their organisation involves the cementing of new links between the Council and surrounding organisations.

It may be argued that this short precis of recent developments shows not only change in the pattern of council policies, but also a pattern of relations between the Council and groups which cannot be contained within the framework which I laid out in Chapter 8. I do not take this view. First, the supposed changes in policy do not effect a substantive redistribution of resources. They represent a symbolic response (Edelman, 1964) designed to indicate that something is being done about problems without the necessity of needing to move beyond that indication, as the gesture reduces

2. There were twenty-six new Conservative councillors elected in that year, and this represented well over a third of the strength of the majority party.

dissent and criticism and controls political disturbance (Maniha & Perrow, 1965; and, Selznick, 1952). Second, the new co-operation that is said to exist between the Council and some of the groups from North Kensington in fact represents a technique to control disturbance and channel dissent which is needed where the avoidance of, and resistance to, demanding groups does not lead to those groups either changing the form of their activity or ceasing to exist. In other words, if radical groups survive the period of authoritative siege, then they can expect to be drawn into collaborative relations with the Council, but as junior partners whose activity is channelled towards the pre-ordained goals of the authorities (Bachrach & Baratz, 1970, Appendix E). The tangible benefits of such co-operation to those whose interests are supposedly represented by the groups is usually small, but the symbolic value to the authorities is large, since it creates an impression of flexibility and responsiveness and an illusion not just that problems are being confronted but that they are actually being solved. In a similar way, the authorities' attempts to involve local people in the planning process and the general move towards public participation, are rarely such as to serve the interests of those whose involvement is desired. The authorities need full information on the area they seek to develop, and they need to win local people round to government plans in order to offset the spontaneous but disruptive participation of local protest groups.[3] Both these needs are secured by co-operation and public involvement.

'Decisions are made to guide the course of human action. Two general outcomes of decisions are possible: 1) to select a new course of action different from that being pursued; and 2) to choose the present course of action as the best among available alternatives, thus continuing on-giving activities unchanged' (Dubin, 1959, p. 218). Now the major theme of this study of public policy in the Royal Borough of Kensington and Chelsea has been one which has pointed to the extent to which the decisional activity of the Council is restricted to the making of routine decisions involving the maintenance of established commitments which are themselves defended by a variety of strategies. As Selznick argues, 'it is surely less demanding to preside over an organization that largely runs itself than to be confronted with the question: What shall we *do*? What shall we *be*?' (Selznick, 1957, p. 65). All organisations tend to prefer continuity and stability to change and risk, and over time the process of institutionalisation (Selznick, 1957; Chaffey, 1970; and, Polsby, 1968) tends to mean that organisations are more concerned with internal arrangements and with the defence of established commitments than with confronting and challenging afresh the tasks before them. 'The members of an enterprise that has acquired value can be expected to resist change, including organizational

3. For a comment on the use of this strategy in the U.S.A., see, Cloward & Piven, 1969; Clark & Hopkins, 1969; Van Til & Van Til, 1970; and, Brody, 1970.

change, that appears to them to decrease their opportunities of obtaining personal satisfaction or of defending themselves against insecurity' (Rice, 1963, p. 275). The 'iron law of decadence' – 'that tendency of all organisations to maintain themselves at the expense of needed change and innovation' (Lowi, 1971, p. 5) – means that for organisational members the question becomes not one of considering how the organisation can confront and solve a problematic situation, but one of identifying how the situation affects and threatens the organisation and can be controlled. Of course not all organisations are in this position when they can be self-indulgent and assume an introspective role, but I suspect many are, and certainly the organisational situation of the majority party on the Council of the Royal Borough of Kensington and Chelsea is one where the authoritative councillors can control disturbance and so defend established commitments avoiding the necessity for policy-making, with its inevitable stress on change and innovation.

This has been a study of one local authority. I hope that the way I have described and explained the factors affecting the development of public policy in Kensington and Chelsea convinces students of the desirability of studying policy-maintenance, the defence of commitments, and the control of disturbance (Piven & Cloward, 1972), in other governmental contexts. If this work is undertaken then I am sure we will be better equipped to offer suggestions for the improvement and reform of local government. Traditional assumptions about the functioning of local government need to be questioned, and research needs to be undertaken into the factors which build in stability and inhibit responsiveness and flexibility. Only if research is based upon a keen appreciation of the reality of local politics and political decision-making can reforms be suggested which will make government sensitive and responsive to the needs and demands of all citizens – and no amount of efficiency can make up for that.

Sources and Bibliography

I. PRIMARY SOURCES

The research project reported in this book was started in the early part of 1967 when I first went up to Kensington and Chelsea and met a number of people from the Notting Hill Social Council. Teaching commitments at the University of Sussex meant that I was unable to be permanently resident in the Borough, but initially I was able to attend meetings of the Notting Hill Social Council and the Council of the Royal Borough of Kensington and Chelsea, talk informally to people active in politics in the area, and start reading the local newspapers and the secondary material that was available in the local history collections of the Borough libraries. The written source material I consulted is set out in Section A, below.

During the summer of 1967 I lived in the Borough and I was able to follow more closely a number of 'cases' or 'issues' as they developed. I paid particular attention to the Notting Hill Summer Project and the question of housing in North Kensington, and I also made a special study of the Council's scheme to control car-parking in the southern part of the Borough, noting the political response of the residents affected.[1]

With the close of the vacation I moved back to Brighton and began to assess how far my knowledge of the factors affecting the development of public policy in the area had been advanced by this case approach based on a study of local issues. I concluded that it was impossible to explain the policy of the Council of the Royal Borough by relying on this research method, and I recognised that it would be necessary to interview the councillors and officers of the Royal Borough systematically, in a way which did not concentrate on local issues, but rather used these to identify the structure and rules that were important in their policy activity. In working out my schedule of questions I looked at other surveys,[2] talked with Louis Moss of the Government Social

1. Other issues I followed up during this period included: the Council's plans for underground car parks; their plans to build a new Town Hall; the issue of play facilities and play provision; and the more general question of the development of the Borough.

2. Among the surveys which I consulted were: Lester Milbrath (1963); J. C. Wahlke *et al.* (1962); R. J. Huckshorn (1965); W. L. Francis (1962); Henry Teune (1967); W. H. Riker (1955); L. D. Longley (1967); J. D. Barber (1965); A. M. Scott, &

Survey,[3] and interviewed councillors from other local authorities prior to interviewing in Kensington and Chelsea.

In the summer of 1968 I was ready to interview the 70 aldermen and councillors who made up the Council of the Royal Borough, but in the three months of my vacation I was only able to contact 52 (and interview 47) of the 66 Conservatives on the Council.[4] Interviews ranged from 40 minutes to 4½ hours. I avoided treating these meetings as a chance to fill out a questionnaire, but instead I introduced my questions into the flow of conversation in a way which I hope respected the interests of the councillors in the interview. The basic questions I asked the councillors, as well as a list of the councillors I interviewed, are set out in Section B.

Finally in Section C of this section on the primary sources I used, I give a select list of the meetings I attended and the people I interviewed who were involved in the politics of the area but who were not on the Council.

A. *Written Source Material*

Alexander, Agnes M., *Some Kensington Problems* (Kensington, printed for private circulation, 1904).

Beaver, Alfred, *Memorials of Old Chelsea* (London, Elliot Stock, 1892).

Besant, Sir Walter, *London North of the Thames* (London, Adam and Charles Black, 1911).

Blunt, Reginald, *An Illustrated Handbook to the Parish of Chelsea* (London, Lamley and Co., 1900).

Chesterton, C., *I lived in a Slum* (London, Gollancz, 1936).

Clark, George (ed.), *Community Action in Notting Hill: Summer Project 1967, Report.*

Clarke, M. G., 'Goals and Leadership: The Study of Two Local Conservative Party Associations' (M.A. Dissertation, University of Sussex, 1968).

Faulkner, Thomas, *History and Antiquities of Kensington* (London, T. Egerton, 1820).

An Historical and Topographical Description of Chelsea and its Environs, 2 vols. (Chelsea, Nicols and Son, 1829).

Ferguson, Rachel, *Royal Borough* (London, Jonathon Cape, 1950).

Gaunt, William, *Chelsea* (London, Batsford, 1954).

Gladstone, Florence, and Barker, Ashley, *Notting Hill in Bygone Days*, new edn (London, Anne Bingley, 1969).

James, Godfrey, *London, the Western Reaches* (London, Robert Hale, 1950).

Jephcott, Pearl, *A Troubled Area: Notes on Notting Hill* (London, Faber and Faber, 1964).

Loftie, W. J., *Kensington, Picturesque and Historical* (London, Field and Tuer, 1888).

Mason, David, Ainger, G., and Denny, N., *News From Notting Hill: The Formation of a Group Ministry* (London, Epworth Press, 1967).

Moore, Robin, 'Making the most of motorways', *Help*, 8, Jan./Feb. 1969.

---

3. Joint author of *The Local Government Councillor*.

4. This represented over a 90% response rate, and 70% of the Conservatives were interviewed. In addition four Labour councillors were interviewed.

M. A. Hunt (1965); Committee on the Management of Local Government, vol. 2, *The Local Government Councillor* (1967).

Morton, Jane, 'New hope for Notting Hill?' *New Society*, 21 March 1968, pp. 416–18.

'Notting Hill Survey', *Voice of the Unions*, June 1969

Palmer, F. B., 'The Development of Public Amenities in North Kensington' (Study submitted to the University of London as part of a Diploma of Sociology course, 1969).

Philo, Patricia, 'Notting Hill Today', *Kensington Post*, 24 November, 1 and 8 December 1967.

Richardson, Anthony, *Nick of Notting Hill* (London, George G. Harrap, 1965).

Simon, Oliver, 'Participant Planning' (M.A. Dissertation, University of Sussex, 1968).

'Under elevated roads, wasteland or wonderland?', *Surveyor*, 18 Jan. 1969.

Wearden, Clifford, *The Royal Borough of Kensington and Chelsea, Lancaster Road West Area: Consultants Report on the Proposed Master Plan* (1968).

Wilson, Des (ed.), *Notice to Quit* (A Shelter Report).

Chelsea Post
Chelsea News
Kensington News
Kensington Post
People's News

The Golborne, Information sheet from the Social Rights Committee.

Local Affairs, The Official Journal of the Royal Borough of Kensington, no. 1, Sept. 1961 – no. 7, Sept. 1964.

Local Affairs, The Official Journal of the Royal Borough of Kensington and Chelsea, no. 1, March 1965 – no. 14, Autumn 1971.

The Royal Borough of Kensington and Chelsea, *Abstract of Accounts*, 1965–70.

    Council Minutes, 1964–71, and attention paid to minutes for previous years.

    Estimate for the General Rate, 1964–70.

    Medical Officer of Health, *Annual Report on the Health and Welfare of the Borough*, 1965–70.

    Standing Orders, Committee Terms of Reference, Financial Regulations (1st edn, 1 Feb. 1967, 2nd edn, 1 Jan. 1970.

    Colville Study Area, 1972.

Chelsea Conservative and Unionist Association, *Official Yearbook*, 1963–9.

Chelsea Young Conservatives, *Chelsea Chequer*, 1967–70.

Labour Group on the Council of the Royal Borough of Kensington and Chelsea, *Minutes*, 1964–5.

Newsletter of the Norland and Pembridge Communist Party, *Our View*, 1969–70.

North Kensington Conservative Association, *Journal*, 1961–8.

South Kensington Labour Party, *Labour Report*, 1964–7.

South Kensington Liberal Association, *Newsletter*, 1964–8.

South Kensington Young Conservatives, *Skycon*.

Campden Charities, *Annual Report and Statement of Accounts*, 1948–68.

Chelsea Society, *Annual Report*, 1960–9.

Clydesdale Road Playground, *Annual Report*, 1952–6.

Committee for City Poverty, select documents.

Family Welfare Association, *Annual Report*, 1966–7.

Golborne Neighbourhood Council, *The New Golborne*, 1972–

Housing Action Centre, *Annual Report*, 1972.

Kensington and Chelsea Chamber of Commerce, *Newsletter*, June/July 1965 – October 1969.

Kensington and Chelsea Council Tenants Association, *Executive Committee Minutes*, 1965–9.

  Executive Committee Reports to the Annual General Meeting, 1966–8.

Kensington and Chelsea Inter-Racial Council, *Spectre*, monthly, starting November 1968.

Kensington and Chelsea Play Association, select documents.

Kensington Council of Social Service, *Report*, 1945–65.

Kensington Housing Association, *Annual Report*, 1926–35.

Kensington Housing Trust, *Annual Report*, 1936–68.

Kensington Society, *Annual Report*, 1954–68.

Neighbourhood Service, *Annual Report*, 1968–9.

Norland Conservation Group, *Newsletter*, October 1969.

North Kensington Amenity Trust, select documents.

North Kensington Neighbourhood Law Centre, *Annual Report*, 1972.

North Kensington Playspace Group, *A Scheme of Amenities, Play Facilities, and Open Space for North Kensington*, 1967, and various documents and letters.

Notting Hill Adventure Playground, *Annual Report*, 1965.

Notting Hill Community Workshop, *Community Notebook*, irregular publication starting 1967, and numerous documents and letters.

Notting Hill Housing Service, Initial Housing Survey, Notting Hill Summer Project 1967, *Interim Report* (London, Notting Hill Housing Service, 1969).

Notting Hill Housing Service and Research Group, *Freedom and Choice: A Community Planning Project for Notting Hill* (1969).

  The Rent Acts and the Housing Market in North Kensington: Memorandum of Evidence to the Francis Committee, 1970.

Notting Hill Housing Trust, *Annual Report*, 1964–8.

Notting Hill Housing Trust Tenants Association, *Trust Tenants News*.

Notting Hill Peoples Association, select documents.

Notting Hill Social Council, *Minutes*, monthly, December 1962–March 1969, and select documents.

  Blenheim Project, *Detached Social Work with Young Drifters in London* (2nd annual report, 1966).

  Leisure and Amenities Committee, *Playspace in North Kensington: Report on Local Play Programmes*, 1967–9 (July 1970).

  Summer Play Programme, 1968, *Weekly Worksheets*.

Notting Hill Summer Project, *News and Information*, and numerous documents.

  Report on the Initial Housing Survey and the Public Housing Register (For presentation to the Report Conference on the Notting Hill Summer Project, 14/15 October 1967).

The Housing Register.
Rowe Housing Trust (formerly the Improved Tenements Association), *Report and Accounts*, 1949–68.

B. *Councillor Interviews*

In most cases I commenced councillor interviews by asking councillors when they first served on the council, and how it was that they got involved in council work. At an early stage I asked them to identify the other 'organisations, groups, or clubs' to which they belonged, and I sought to get them to give a general indication of their conception of the role of councillor by asking:

'Suppose you were invited to give a lecture to the civics group of a local school, and you were introduced as a councillor [or alderman] of the Royal Borough, how would you describe the responsibilities of that office, or to put it another way, what would be the sorts of things you would point to which you felt you should do?'

After this general introduction I asked the following questions of most councillors. In addition, however, in the course of the interviews, supplementary and additional questions were asked of specific councillors, though these questions are not laid out in this section.

'When you stand for election do you think that the policies of the local party you support are important in determining the election outcome?'

'Would you regard your seat as marginal? If so, how do you think this affects the way you carry out your civic work and responsibilities?'

'Speaking for yourself, how do you get to know about the needs and attitudes of the people in the borough?'

'In the average month roughly how many people in this area have been in touch with you personally as a member of the council?'

'Could you tell me about council policy with respect to ticket parking and undersquare car parks; the new town hall; rehousing; and play facilities in North Kensington?'

'If a group of constituents, or an organised grouping, has a particular idea which they want to put before the council in one of the sorts of areas we have been discussing, what is the proper or correct way for that idea to be presented to the council?'

'As you know there is a whole range of groups and organisations in this borough as in any other. I'd like to talk to you about them. Do you think they improve local government work? How do you feel about the efforts they make to make their views known to you?'

'Here is a list of groups which I hope is a reasonable cross-section of those in the borough.[5] I wonder if you could advise me as to how helpful you feel

5. Kensington Housing Trust; Notting Hill Community Workshop; Kensington and Chelsea Arts Council; Kensington and Chelsea Inter-Racial Council; Ratepayers Association; Kensington and Chelsea Council Tenants Association; Kensington High Street Association; Neighbourhood Service Unit; Kensington and

they are in making the borough the sort of place you would like to see to live
and work in – not just for their own members but for other people as well?'
'In general terms what do you have in mind, what do you look for, when you
identify a group as "helpful" or "unhelpful"?'

'On the whole are the views of constituents important to you in helping you
to make up your mind on issues before the council?'

'Obviously when you come to decide on issues before you – like the ones
we've been discussing – you assess the information relevant to the problem.
Here are some possible sources of information, I wonder if you could advise
me as to how important they are for you personally in helping you to make
up your mind on an issue?'[6]

'Now I'd like to change the subject and ask you about how policies are
decided here in the council. Obviously not everyone is of equal weight when
it comes to making decisions in the sorts of issues we've been discussing.
Generally speaking who would you say are the members who stand out as
being particularly important in the decision-process? Please don't consider
just your own party members, but include councillors from the other party
as well if you feel they are relevant.'

'You'll remember I asked you a question about the position of councillor [or
alderman], well I'd like to ask you a question about the leader. How would
you describe the responsibilities of that office – what are the sorts of things
which you feel he should and should not do?'

'You'll remember I asked you a question about the position of councillor
[or alderman], well I'd like to ask you a question about some of the other
positions here on the council. What about the committee chairmen, how
would you describe the responsibilities of that office – what are the sorts of
things which you feel they should and should not do?'

'What advice would you give to a new councillor as to how to do his job
properly once he has been elected?'

'What advice, if any, were you given by the other councillors when you were
first elected onto the council?'

In most cases interviews were terminated by my asking:

'Could you tell me what you personally see as the major issues facing the
Royal Borough at the present time?'

and although I would have liked to have asked councillors about their
education, income, employment, and housing situation, I felt that to ask

---

Chelsea Chamber of Commerce; Family Service Unit; Kensington Council of
Social Service; Kensington Architectural Group; Campden Charities; District
Nursing Association; North Kensington Playspace Group; Kensington Society;
Task Force; Notting Hill Social Council; Womens Voluntary Service; North
Kensington Family Study.
6. Borough officers; councillors; local organisations; local press; party officials;
other governments; constituents and residents.

those questions could have made my approaches to other councillors difficult in what I saw as a rather sensitive research situation.

Conservative councillors interviewed

Councillor Mrs J. A. Albert
Councillor John E. Baldwin, M.A. (two meetings)
Councillor Lady Brabazon of Tara
Councillor R. M. Brew
Councillor Mrs Katharine Carver, M.A.
Councillor Mrs Gillian Cassidy
Councillor Miss Elizabeth M. Christmas
Councillor M. A. K. Cocks, B.A.
Councillor Mrs J. Coleridge
Councillor David Collenette, M.C.
Councillor Sir Malby Crofton, Bt, B.A.
Councillor D. A. E. Eaton
Councillor Michael Farrow, M.A.
Alderman F. St G. Fisher, M.A.
Councillor Mrs Muriel Gumbel, J.P., G.L.C.
Councillor The Hon. Archie Hamilton
Councillor Charles Hopkins, B.A., A.R.I.C.S., A.M.T.P.I.
Councillor Miss Barbara Hulme, B.A.
Councillor L. A. Kenny
Councillor Graeme A. Lythe
Alderman F. W. Marshall
Councillor James Mendl (interviewed over the telephone)
Councillor P. H. Methuen

Councillor Gordon Middleton
Councillor C. A. Muller, J.P.
Councillor Miss Shelagh O'Callaghan
Councillor Robert Orme, B.A. (two meetings)
Alderman Mrs Margery Over
Alderman Mrs John Paul
Alderman Lady Petrie
Councillor D. H. Piper
Councillor D. H. C. Pritchard
Councillor Miss Shelagh M. Roberts
Councillor Viscount Sandon, T.D.
Alderman Arthur J. Sims
Councillor J. C. Sorrell
Councillor Arnold H. Stevenson
Councillor John E. Strafford, A.C.A.
Councillor Mrs Brian Sundius-Smith
Councillor S. L. Tanner
Alderman F. Thackway (two meetings)
Councillor Edward Thom
Councillor E. P. Tomlin
Councillor Christopher Walford, M.A.
Councillor Miss Doreen Weatherhead, M.S.R. (R)., S.R.R.
Councillor Michael D. Wigley, B.A.
Councillor John R. H. Yeoman, M.A.

Labour councillors interviewed

Councillor E. A. Briggs
Councillor Bruce Douglas-Mann (councillor till 1968)
Councillor Tom Ives (councillor till 1968)

Councillor Stanley Lawrence (councillor till 1968)
Alderman The Hon. Thomas Ponsonby

C. Meetings and Other Interviews

Council Meetings of the Royal Borough of Kensington and Chelsea, 1967–8.
Meetings of the Notting Hill Social Council, 1967–8.
Public Inquiries with respect to the new Town Hall, and the redevelopment of Lancaster Road (West).

Public Meetings with respect to the parking scheme for the southern parts of the Borough, and various issues affecting North Kensington.

Attendance at numerous meetings associated with the Notting Hill Community Workshop, the Notting Hill Summer Project, and the North Kensington Playspace Group.

Attendance at meetings of the Notting Hill Peoples Association, the Kensington and Chelsea Council Tenants Association, the Management Committee of the Portobello Project, and the Inter-Racial Council.

Interviews with the following officers of the Royal Borough of Kensington and Chelsea:

Mr J. Waring-Sainsbury (Town Clerk of the Royal Borough till 1970)

Mr R. L. Stillwell (Assistant Town Clerk)

Mr L. E. Holmes (Borough Treasurer till 1970, then Town Clerk)

Mr Stack, and Mr Evans (Traffic Management and Parking Control)

Staff at the Electoral Registration Office

In addition, I interviewed spokesmen from the Kensington Housing Trust, the Rowe Housing Trust, and the Notting Hill Housing Trust. I interviewed the three agents of the Conservative and Unionist Associations in the Borough. I had many meetings with people involved in the development of the Council's parking scheme both at County Hall and in the area of the Borough. Finally I met with and spoke to (sometimes on many occasions) members of the Notting Hill Social Council, the North Kensington Family Study, the North Kensington Playspace Group, the Neighbourhood Service Unit, the Notting Hill Adventure Playground, the Notting Hill Peoples Association, the Kensington and Chelsea Council Tenants Association, editors and staff of the local press, the staff of the Local History Collection in the Borough Library (especially Brian Curle), and many, many other people involved with politics in the Borough.

II. SECONDARY SOURCES: LIST OF WORKS CITED IN TEXT

Abrams, M. (1964). 'Party politics after the end of ideology', in E. Allardt, and Y. Littunen (eds.), *Cleavages, Ideologies, and Party Systems* (Helsinki, Academic Bookstore, 1964), pp. 56–63.

and Rose, R. (1960). *Must Labour Lose?* (Harmondsworth, Penguin).

Adeney, M. (1971). *Community Action: Four Examples* (London, Runnymede Trust).

Adrian, C. R. (1960). *State and Local Governments* (New York, McGraw-Hill).

Agger, R. E., Goldrich, D., and Swanson, B. E. (1964). *The Rulers and the Ruled* (New York, Wiley).

Almond, G. A. (1960). 'A functional approach to comparative politics', in G. A. Almond, and J. Coleman, *The Politics of the Developing Area* (Princeton, Princeton University Press), pp. 3–64.

(1965). 'A development approach to political systems', *World Politics*, 17, pp. 183–214.

Alt, J. E. (1971). 'Some social and political correlates of county borough expenditures', *British Journal of Political Science*, 1, pp. 49–62.

American Political Science Association, Committee on Political Parties (1950). 'Toward a more responsible two-party system', *American Political Science Review*, Supplement, 44.

Anson, W. (1922–35). *Law and Custom of the Constitution*, 3 vols. (Oxford, Clarendon Press).

Armbruster, G. H, (1944). 'An analysis of ideologies in the context of discussion', *American Journal of Sociology*, 50, pp. 123–33.

Arnold-Forster, H. O. (1900). *The Citizen Reader* (London, Cassell).

Aron, R. (1957). *The Opium of the Intellectuals* (London, Secker).

Atlee, C. R., and Robson, W. A. (1925). *The Town Councillor* (London, Labour Publishing Co.).

Ayer, A. J. (1967). *Philosophy and Politics*, Eleanor Rathbone Memorial Lecture (Liverpool, Liverpool University Press).

Bachrach, P. (1967). *The Theory of Democratic Elitism* (London, University of London Press).

and Baratz, M. S. (1962). 'Two faces of power' *American Political Science Review*, 56, pp. 947–52.

(1963). 'Decisions and nondecisions: an analytical framework', *American Political Science Review*, 57, pp. 632–42.

(1970). *Power and Poverty* (New York, Oxford University Press).

Backman, C. W., and Secord, P. F. (1966). *Problems in Social Psychology* (New York, McGraw-Hill).

Bagehot, W. (1867). *The English Constitution* (London, Collins, 1963).

Bailey, S. K. (1950). *Congress Makes a Law* (New York, Columbia University Press).

(1959). *The Condition of Our National Political Parties* (New York, Fund for the Republic).

Banfield, E. C. (1961). *Political Influence* (New York, Free Press).

and Wilson, J. Q. (1963). *City Politics* (Cambridge, Mass., Harvard University Press).

Banton, M. (1965). *Roles* (London, Tavistock).

Banwell, H. (1959). 'The new relations between central and local government', *Public Administration*, 37, pp. 201–12.

Barber, J. D. (1965). *The Lawmakers* (New Haven, Yale University Press).

Barker, A., and Rush, M. (1970). *The Member of Parliament and His Information* (London, Allen and Unwin).

Barker, E. (1945). *Essays on Government* (Oxford, Clarendon Press).

Barnard, C. (1940). 'Comments on the job of the executive', *Harvard Business Review*, 18, pp. 295–308.

Barnes, S. H. (1966). 'Ideology and the organisation of conflict: on the relationship between political thought and behaviour', *Journal of Politics*, 28, pp. 513–30.

Barry, B. (1970). *Sociologists, Economists, and Democracy* (London, Collier-Macmillan).

Bassett, R. (1935). *The Essentials of Parliamentary Democracy* (London, Macmillan).

Bauer, R. A. (1968). 'The study of policy formation: an introduction', in R. A. Bauer, and K. J. Gergen (eds.), *The Study of Policy Formation* (New York, Free Press), pp. 1–26.

(1969). 'The obstinate audience: the influence process from the point of view of social communication', in H. C. Lindgren (ed.), *Contemporary Research in Social Psychology: A Book of Readings* (New York, Wiley), pp. 399–412.

Pool, I. de Sola, and Dexter, L. A. (1964). *American Business and Public Policy* (New York, Atherton Press).

Bealey, F., Blondel, J., and McCann, W. P. (1965). *Constituency Politics* (London, Faber).

Beer, S. H. (1956). 'Pressure groups and parties in Britain', *American Political Science Review*, 50, pp. 1–23.

'Group representation in Britain and the United States', *Annals of the American Academy of Political and Social Science*, 319, pp. 130–140.

(1965). *British Politics in the Collectivist Age* (New York, Knopf).

and Ulam, A. B. (eds.), (1962). *Patterns of Government*, 2nd edn (New York, Random House).

Beetham, D. (1970). *Transport and Turbans* (London, Oxford University Press).

Bell, D. (1962). *The End of Ideology*, 2nd edn (New York, Collier).

Bendix R. (1960). *Max Weber: An Intellectual Portrait* (London, Heinemann).

Benewick, R. J., Birch, A. H., Blumler, J. G., and Ewbank, A. (1969). 'The floating voter and the liberal view of representation', (*Political Studies*, 17, pp. 177–95.

Benney, M., Gray, A. P., and Pear, R. H. (1956). *How People Vote* (London, Routledge).

Bentley, A. F. (1908). *The Process of Government*, reprinted and with an introduction by P. H. Odegard (Cambridge, Mass., Belknap Press, 1967).

Berelson, B. R., Lazarsfeld, P. F., and McPhee, W. N. (1954). *Voting* (Chicago, University of Chicago Press).

Biddle, B. J., and Thomas, E. J. (eds.). (1966). *Role Theory* (New York, Wiley).

Birch, A. H. (1959). *Small Town Politics* (London, Oxford, University Press).

(1964). *Representative and Responsible Government* (London, Allen and Unwin).

(1967). *The British System of Government* (London, Allen and Unwin).

Blaisdell, D. C. (1957). *American Democracy Under Pressure* (New York, Ronald).

Blau, P. M. (1955). *The Dynamics of Bureaucracy* (Chicago, University of Chicago Press).

Block, G. (1962). *Party Politics in Local Government*, Local Government Series, 7 (London, Conservative Political Centre).

Blondel, J., *et al* (1969). 'Legislative behaviour: some steps towards a cross-national measurement', *Government and Opposition*, 5, pp. 67–85.

Boaden, N. (1970). 'Central departments and local authorities: the relationship re-examined', *Political Studies*, 18, pp. 175–86.

(1971). *Urban Policy-Making* (London, Cambridge University Press).

and Alford, R. R. (1969). 'Sources of diversity in English local government decisions', *Public Administration*, 47, pp. 203–23.

Bochel, J. M. (1966). 'The recruitment of local councillors: a case study', *Political Studies*, 14, pp. 360–4.

and Denver, D. T. (1971). 'Canvassing, turnout and party support: an experiment', *British Journal of Political Science*, 1, pp. 257–69.

Bonilla, F. (1956). 'When is petition pressure?', *Public Opinion Quarterly*, 20, pp. 39–48.

Bonjean, C. M., Clark, T. N., and Lineberry, R. L. (eds.) (1971). *Community Politics* (New York, Free Press).

Bonnor, J. (1954). 'Public interest in local government', *Public Administration*, 32, pp. 425–8.

Bornfriend, A. J. (1969). 'Political parties and pressure groups', in R. H. Connery, and D. Caraley (eds.), 'Governing the city: challenges and options for New York', *Proceedings of the Academy of Political Science*, 29, pp. 55–67.

Boyle, E. (ed.) (1950). *Tory Democrat: Two Famous Disraeli Speeches* (London, Conservative Political Centre).

Boyson, R. (1970). 'Right Turn', in R. Boyson (ed.), *Right Turn* (London, Churchill Press), pp. 1–13.

Braibanti, R. (1969). 'External inducement of political–administrative development: an institutional strategy', in R. Braibanti (ed.), *Political and Administrative Development* (Durham, N.C., Duke University Press), pp. 3–106.

Brand, J. A. (1965). 'Ministry control and local autonomy in education', *Political Quarterly*, 36, pp. 154–63.

Brehm, J. W., and Cohen, A. R. (1962). *Explorations in Cognitive Dissonance* (New York, Wiley).

Brennan, T., Cooney, E. W., and Pollins, H. (1954). 'Party politics and local government in Western South Wales', *Political Quarterly*, 25, pp. 76–84.

Brier, A. P., and Dowse, R. E. (1966). 'The amateur activists', *New Society*, 29 December, pp. 975–6.

Broady, M. (1968). *Planning for People* (London, Bedford Square Press).

Brody, S. J. (1970). 'Maximum participation of the poor: another holy grail?', *Social Work*, 15:1, pp. 68–75.

Brooke, H. (1953). 'Conservatives and local government', *Political Quarterly*, 24, pp. 181–9.

Brown, R. D. (1955). *The Battle of Crichel Down* (London, Bodley Head).

Bruner, J. S. (1966). 'Social psychology and perceptions', in E. E. Maccoby, T. M. Newcomb, and E. L. Hartley (eds.) *Readings in Social Psychology*, 3rd edn (London, Methuen), pp. 85–93.

Bryce, J., (1923). *Modern Democracies*, 2 vols. (London, Macmillan).

Buchanan, W. (1963). *Legislative Partisanship: The Deviant Case of California* (Berkeley, University of California Press).

Budge, I. (1965). 'Electors' attitudes towards local government', *Political Studies*, 13, pp. 386–92.

Bulpitt, J. G. (1967). *Party Politics in English Local Government* (London, Longmans).

Burdick, E. (1959). 'Political theory and voting studies', in E. Burdick, and A. J. Broadbeck (eds.), *American Voting Behavior* (Glencoe, Ill., Free Press), pp. 136–49.

Burkett, A. J. (1960). 'Conventions and practices in the committee system in selected local authorities in the East Midlands' (M.A. Thesis, University of Nottingham).

Burnett, F. T., and Scott, S. F. (1962). 'Survey of housing conditions in the urban areas of England and Wales; 1960', *Sociological Review (New Series)*, 10, pp. 35–79.

Burns, T. and Stalker, G. M. (1961). *The Management of Innovation* (London, Tavistock).

Butler, D. E., and King, A. (1965). *The British General Election of 1964* (London, Macmillan).

Butler, D. E., and Stokes, D. (1969). *Political Change in Britain* (London, Macmillan).

Canon, L. K. (1964). 'Self-confidence and selective exposure to information', in L. Festinger (ed.), *Conflict, Decision, and Dissonance* (London, Tavistock), pp. 83–95.

Caplow, T. (1964). *Principles of Organization* (New York, Harcourt).

Catlin, G. E. G. (1964). *Political and Sociological Theory and its Applications* (Ann Arbor, University of Michigan Press).

Cecil, Lord Hugh (1912). *Conservatism* (London, Williams and Norgate).

Central Advisory Council for Education (1967). *Children and Their Primary Schools*, 2 vols. (London, H.M.S.O.).

Central Office of Information (1966). *Local Government in Britain*, Reference Pamphlet 1 (London, H.M.S.O.).

Chaffey, D. C. (1970). 'The institutionalization of state legislatures: a comparative study', *Western Political Quarterly*, 23, pp. 180–96.

Chaloner, W. H. (1950). *The Social and Economic Development of Crewe* (Manchester, Manchester University Press).

Chapman, A. (1965). *Local Government and Civil Liberty* (London, Civil Liberty Publication).

Cherry, C. (1966). *On Human Communication*, 2nd edn (Cambridge, Mass., The M.I.T. Press).

Chester, D. N. (1951). *Central and Local Government* (London, Macmillan).

Chomsky, N. (1959). Book Review of B. F. Skinner, *Verbal Behavior* (London, Methuen, 1957), in *Language*, 35, pp. 26–58.

Clapp, C. L. (1963). *The Congressman: His Work as he sees it* (Washington, Brookings Institute).

Clark, K. B., and Hopkins, J. (1969). *A Relevant War Against Poverty* (New York, Harper and Row).

Clark, T. N. (1971). 'Community structure, decision-making, budget expenditures, and urban renewal in 51 American communities', in C. M. Bonjean, T. N. Clark, and R. L. Lineberry (eds.), *Community Politics* (New York, Free Press), pp. 293–313.

Clarke, J. J. (1969). *Outlines of Local Government of the United Kingdom*, 20th edn (London, Pitman).

Clarke, J. W. (1969). 'Environment, process and policy: a reconsideration', *American Political Science Review*, 63, pp. 1172–82.

Cloward, R. A., and Piven, F. P. (1968). 'The professional bureaucracies: benefit systems as influence systems', in R. M. Kramer and H. Specht (eds.), *Readings in Community Organization Practice* (Englewood Cliffs, N.J., Prentice-Hall), pp. 359–72.

Cole, G. D. H. (1921). *The Future of Local Government* (London, Cassell). (1947). *Local and Regional Government* (London, Cassell).

Cole, M. (1956). *Servant of the County* (London, Dobson).

Coleraine, Lord (1970). *For Conservatives Only* (London, Stacey).

Committee on Higher Education (1963). *Appendix One*, Cmnd. 2154–I (London, H.M.S.O.).

Committee on Housing in Greater London (1965). *Report*, Cmnd. 2605 (London, H.M.S.O.).

Committee on Local Authority and Allied Personal Social Services (1968). *Report*, Cmnd. 3703 (London, H.M.S.O.).

Committee on the Management of Local Government (1967):
Vol. 1. *Report*.
Vol. 2. *The Local Government Councillor*.
Vol. 3. *The Local Government Elector*.
Vol. 4. *Local Government Administration Abroad*.
Vol. 5. *Local Government Administration in England and Wales*. (London, H.M.S.O.).

Connelly, D. (1970). 'The councillor and his environment' (B.A. Dissertation, University of Sussex).

Coombes, D. (1966). *The Member of Parliament and the Administration* (London, Allen and Unwin).

Crane, W. (1960). 'A test of effectiveness of interest group pressures on legislators', *Southwestern Social Science Quarterly*, 41, pp. 335–40.

Crick, B. (1964). *The Reform of Parliament* (London, Weidenfeld and Nicolson).

Cross, C. A. (1966). *The Principles of Local Government Law*, 3rd edn (London, Sweet and Maxwell).

Crozier, M. (1964). *The Bureaucratic Phenomena* (London, Tavistock).

Cutright, P. (1963). 'Nonpartisan electoral systems in American cities', *Comparative Studies in Society and History*, 5, pp. 212–26.
(1965). 'Political structure, economic development, and national social security programs', *American Journal of Sociology*, 70, pp. 537–50.

Cyert, R. M., and March, J. G. (1963). *A Behavioral Theory of the Firm* (Englewood Cliffs, N.J., Prentice-Hall).

Dahl, R. A. (1961*a*). 'The problem of participation', in O. P. Williams, and C. Press (eds.), *Democracy in Urban America* (Chicago, Rand McNally), pp. 406–10.
(1961*b*). *Who Governs?* (New Haven, Yale University Press).
(1961*c*). 'The behavioral approach in political Science: epitaph for a monument to a successful protest', *American Political Science Review*, 55, pp. 763–72.
and Lindblom, C. E. (1953). *Politics, Economics and Welfare* (New York, Harper).

Davey, K. J. (1971). 'Local autonomy and independent revenues', *Public Administration*, 49, pp. 45–50.

Davies, B. (1968). *Social Needs and Resources in Local Services* (London, Joseph).

Davis, L. (1964). 'The cost of realism: contemporary restatements of democracy', *Western Political Quarterly*, 17, pp. 37–46.

Davison, W. P. (1959). 'On the effects of communication', *Public Opinion Quarterly*, 23, pp. 343–60.

Dawson, R. E., and Robinson, J. A. (1963). 'Interparty competition, economic variables and welfare policies in the American states', *Journal of Politics*, 25, pp. 265–89.

(1965). 'The politics of welfare', in H. Jacob, and K. Vines (eds.), *Politics in the American States* (New York, Little, Brown), pp. 371–410.

Dearlove, J. N. (1972), 'Public policy in a Royal Borough' (D.Phil. Thesis, University of Sussex).

Dechert, C. R. (1967). 'Availability of information for Congressional operations', in A. de Grazia (ed.), *Congress: The First Branch of Government* (New York, Anchor Books), pp. 154–203.

Dexter, L. A. (1956). 'What do Congressmen hear: the mail', *Public Opinion Quarterly*, 20, pp. 16–27.

(1957). 'The representative and his district', *Human Organisation*, 16, pp. 2–13.

Dicey, A. V. (1959). *Law of the Constitution*, 10th edn (London, Macmillan).

Dolman, F. (1895). *Municipalities at work* (London, Methuen).

Douglas, J. W. B. (1964). *The Home and the School* (London, MacGibbon and Kee).

Ross, J. M., and Simpson, H. R. (1968). *All Our Future* (London, Davies).

Downs, A. (1957). *An Economic Theory of Democracy* (New York, Harper).

Dubin, R. (1959). 'Stability of human organisation', in M. Haire (ed.), *Modern Organization Theory* (New York, Wiley), pp. 218–53.

Duncan, G., and Lukes, S. (1963). 'The new democracy', *Political Studies*, 11, pp. 156–77.

Dye, T. R. (1964). 'Urban political integration: conditions associated with annexation in American cities', *Midwest Journal of Political Science*, 8, pp. 430–46.

(1965). 'Malapportionment and public policy in the States', *Journal of Politics*, 27, pp. 586–601.

(1966). *Politics, Economics, and the Public* (Chicago, Rand McNally).

(1967). 'Governmental structure, urban environment and educational policy', *Midwest Journal of Political Science*, 11, pp. 353–80.

(1968). 'The development of comparative analysis in State politics', Paper presented at the Southern Political Science Association meeting, Gatlinburg, Tennessee, 7–9 November.

Liebman, C. S., Williams, O. P., and Herman, H. (1963). 'Differentiation and cooperation in a metropolitan area', *Midwest Journal of Political Science*, 7, pp. 145–55.

Easton, D. (1953). *The Political System* (New York, Knopf).

(1957). 'An approach to the analysis of political systems', *World Politics*, 9, pp. 383–400.

(1965*a*). *A Systems Analysis of Political Life* (New York, Wiley).

(1965*b*). *A Framework for Political Analysis* (Englewood Cliffs, N. J., Prentice-Hall).

(1969). 'The new revolution in political science', *American Political Science Review*, 63, pp. 1051–61.

Eckstein, H. (1960). *Pressure Group Politics* (London, Allen and Unwin).

(1962). 'The British political system', in S. H. Beer, and A. B. Ulam (eds.),

Patterns of Government, 2nd edn (New York, Random House), pp. 69-269.

(1963). 'Group theory and the comparative study of pressure groups', in H. Eckstein, and D. Apter (eds.), *Comparative Politics* (New York, Free Press), pp. 389–97.

Edelman, M. (1964). *The Symbolic Uses of Politics* (Urbana, Ill., University of Illinois Press).

Ehrmann, H. (1957). *Organized Business in France* (Princeton, Princeton University Press).

(ed) (1958). *Interest Groups in Four Continents* (Pittsburgh, University of Pittsburgh Press).

Eldersveld, S. J. (1958). 'American interest groups: a survey of research and some implications for theory and method', in H. Ehrmann (ed.), *Interest Groups in Four Continents* (Pittsburgh, University of Pittsburgh Press), pp. 173–96.

Emden, C. S. (1956). 'The mandate in the nineteenth century', *Parliamentary Affairs*, 11, pp. 260–72.

Epstein, L. D. (1964). 'Electoral decision and policy mandate: an empirical example', *Public Opinion Quarterly*, 28, pp. 564–72.

Etzioni, A. (1961). *A Comparative Analysis of Complex Organizations* (New York, Free Press).

Eulau, H. (1963). *The Behavioural Persuasion in Politics* (New York, Random House).

and Eyestone, R. (1968). 'Policy-maps of city councils and policy outcomes: a developmental analysis', *American Political Science Review*, 62, pp. 124–43.

and Hinckley, K. (1966). 'Legislative institutions and processes', in J. A. Robinson (ed.), *Political Science Annual*, 1 (New York, Bobbs-Merrill), pp. 85–189.

and March, J. G. (eds.) (1969). *Political Science* (Englewood Cliffs, N. J., Prentice-Hall).

Fabricant, S. (1952). *The Trend of Government Activity in the United States Since 1900* (New York, National Bureau of Economic Research).

Finer, H. (1945). *English Local Government*, 2nd edn (London, Methuen).

(1961). *The Theory and Practice of Modern Government*, 4th edn (London, Methuen).

Finer, S. E. (1956a). 'The individual responsibility of ministers', *Public Administration*, 34, pp. 377–96.

(1956b). 'In defence of pressure groups', *The Listener*, 7 June, pp. 751–2.

(1958). *Annonymous Empire* (London, Pall Mall).

Fletcher, P. (1957). 'The results analysed', in L. J. Sharpe (ed.), *Voting in Cities* (London, Macmillan), pp. 290–328.

Fogarty, M. (1946). *The Reform of Local Government Finance in England and Wales*, Fabian Research Series, 111 (London, Fabian Society).

Francis, W. L. (1962). 'Influence and interaction in a state legislative body', *American Political Science Review*, 56, pp. 953–60.

Frankel, J. (1964). 'Towards a decision-making model in foreign policy', in W. J. Gore, and J. W. Dyson (eds.), *The Making of Decisions: A Reader in Administrative Behavior* (New York, Free Press), pp. 170–9.

Freedman, J. L., and Sears, D. O. (1965). 'Selective exposure', in L. Berkowitz (ed.), *Advances in Experimental Social Psychology*, vol. 2 (New York, Academic Press), pp. 57–97.

Freeman, E. A. (1890). *The Growth of the English Constitution from the Earliest Times*, 3rd edn (London, Macmillan).

Friedrich, C. J. (1953). 'Policy: a Science?', *Public Policy*, 4, pp. 269–81.

(1965). 'Ideology in politics: a theoretical comment', *Slavic Review*, 24, pp. 612–16.

Froman, L. A. (1963). *Congressmen and their Constituencies* (Chicago, Rand McNally).

(1966). 'Some effects of interest group strength in state politics', *American Political Science Review*, 60, pp. 952–62.

(1967). 'An analysis of public policies in cities', *Journal of Politics*, 29, pp. 94–108.

Fry, B. R., and Winters, R. F. (1970). 'The politics of redistribution', *American Political Science Review*, 64, pp. 508–22.

Garceau, O. (1951). 'Research in the political process', *American Political Science Review*, 45, pp. 69–85.

(1958). 'Interest group theory in political research', *The Annals of the American Academy of Political and Social Science*, 319, pp. 104–12.

and Silverman, C. (1954). 'A pressure group and the pressured: a case report', *American Political Science Review*, 48, pp. 672–91.

Geiger, T., and Hansen, R. D. (1968). 'The role of information in decision-making on foreign aid', in R. A. Bauer, and K. J. Gergen (eds.), *The Study of Policy Formation* (New York, Free Press), pp. 329–80.

Gerth, H. H., and Mills, C. W. (1948). *From Max Weber: Essays in Sociology* (London, Routledge).

Gilpatrick, T. V. (1959). 'Price support policy and the Midwest farm vote', *Midwest Journal of Political Science*, 3, pp. 319–35.

Gleeck, L. E. (1940). '86 Congressmen make up their minds', *Public Opinion Quarterly*, 4, pp. 3–24.

Godfrey, J. (1968). 'An approach to interest group success; the case of the Brighton Marina' (M.A. Thesis, University of Sussex).

Goldman, P. (1961). *Some Principles of Conservatism* (London, Conservative Political Centre).

Golembiewski, R. T. (1960). '"The group basis of politics": notes on analysis and development', *American Political Science Review*, 54, pp. 962–71.

Gore, W. J. (1964). *Administrative Decision-Making: A Heuristic Model* (New York, Wiley).

and Dyson, J. W. (eds.) (1964), *The Making of Decisions: A Reader in Administrative Behavior* (New York, Free Press).

Gowan, I. (1963). 'Role and power of political parties in local government', in D. Lofts (ed.), *Local Government Today – and Tomorrow* (London, Municipal Journal), pp. 60–78.

Graham, E. (1972). 'The politics of poverty', in J. L. Roach, and J. K. Roach (eds.), *Poverty* (Harmondsworth, Penguin), pp. 300–14.

Grant, D., and Nixon, H. C. (1963). *State and Local Government in America* (Boston, Allyn and Bacon).

Green, B. S. R. (1968). 'Community decision-making in Georgian city' (Ph.D. Thesis, Bath University of Technology).

Green, L. P. (1959). *Provincial Metropolis* (London, Allen and Unwin).

Griffith, J. A. G. (1963). 'Local democracy: a sorry state?', *New Society*, 14 February, pp. 15–18.

—— (1966). *Central Departments and Local Authorities* (London, Allen and Unwin).

Gross, N., Mason, W. S., and McEachern, A. W. (1958). *Explorations in Role Analysis* (New York, Wiley).

Grundy, J. (1950). 'Non-voting in an urban district', *Manchester School of Economic and Social Studies*, 18, pp. 83–99.

Hadfield, C., and MacColl, J. E. (1948). *British Local Government* (London, Hutchinson).

Hagan, C. B. (1958). 'The group in a political science', in R. Young (ed.), *Approaches to the Study of Politics* (Evanston, Ill., Northwestern University Press), pp. 38–51.

Haggstrom, W. C. (1964). 'The power of the poor', in F. Reissman, J. Cohen, and A. Pearl (eds.), *Mental Health of the Poor* (Glencoe, Ill., Free Press), pp. 205–23.

Hailsham, Viscount (1957). *Toryism and Tomorrow* (London, Conservative Political Centre).

Hale, M. Q. (1960). 'The cosmology of Arthur F. Bentley', *American Political Science Review*, 54, pp. 955–61.

Hampton, W. (1970). *Democracy and Community* (London, Oxford University Press).

Harris, G. M. (1939). *Municipal Self-Government in Britain* (London, King).

Harris, N. (1968). *Beliefs in Society* (London, Watts).

Hart, W. O. (1968). *Introduction to the Law of Local Government and Administration*, 8th edn, (London, Butterworths).

Harvey, J., and Bather, L. (1963). *The British Constitution* (London, Macmillan).

Hasluck, E. L. (1936). *Local Government in England* (London, Cambridge University Press).

Hattery, L. M., and Hofheimer, S. (1954). 'The legislator's source of expert information', *Public Opinion Quarterly*, 18, pp. 300–3.

Hawley, A. H. (1963). 'Community power and urban renewal success', *American Journal of Sociology*, 68, pp. 422–31.

Hawley, C. E., and Dexter, L. A. (1952). 'Recent political science research in American universities', *American Political Science Review*, 46, pp. 470–85.

Hayek, F. (1944). *The Road to Serfdom* (London, Routledge).

Headrick, T. E. (1962). *The Town Clerk in English Local Government* (London, Allen and Unwin).

Hennessy, T. M. (1969). 'Considerations of theory and concept formation in comparative political analysis', Midwest Political Science Association Meeting, Ann Arbor, Michigan, 24–26 April.

—— (1970). 'Problems in concept formation: the ethos "theory" and the comparative study of urban politics', *Midwest Journal of Political Science*, 14, pp. 537–64.

Hepworth, N. P. (1970). *The Finance of Local Government*, rev. edn. (London, Allen and Unwin).

Herring, E. P. (1929). *Group Representation before Congress* (Baltimore, Johns Hopkins).

Heussler, R. (1963). *Yesterday's Rulers: The Making of the British Colonial Service* (London, Oxford University Press).

Higgins, J. (1965). 'Public patronage of the arts', *Planning*, 31:492, November.

Hill, D. (1970). *Participating in Local Affairs* (Harmondsworth, Penguin).

Hofferbert, R. I. (1966a). 'The relation between public policy and some structural and environmental variables in the American states', *American Political Science Review*, 60, pp. 73–82.

 (1966b). 'Ecological development and policy change in the American states', *Midwest Journal of Political Science*, 10, pp. 464–83.

 (1968). 'Socio-economic dimensions of the American states: 1890–1960', *Midwest Journal of Political Science*, 12, pp. 401–18.

Hollander, E. P. (1964). *Leaders, Groups and Influence* (New York, Oxford University Press).

Holman, R. (ed.) (1970. *Socially Deprived Families in Britain* (London, Bedford Square Press).

Homans, G. C. (1951). *The Human Group* (London, Routledge).

Hovland, C. I. (ed.) (1957). *The Order of Presentation in Persuasion* (New Haven, Yale University Press).

Janis, I. L., and Kelley, H. H. (1953). *Communication and Persuasion* (New Haven, Yale University Press).

 and Weiss, W. (1951). 'The influence of source credibility in communication effectiveness', *Public Opinion Quarterly*, 15, pp. 635–50.

Howe, F. C. (1907). *The British City: The Beginnings of Democracy* (London, Fisher-Unwin).

Howell, D., and Raison, T. (eds.) (1961). *Principles in Practice* (London Conservative Political Centre).

Huckshorn, R. J. (1965). 'Decision-making stimuli in the state legislative process', *Western Political Quarterly*, 18, pp. 164–85.

Huitt, R. K. (1957). 'The Morse Committee assignment controversy: A study in Senate norms', *American Political Science Review*, 51, pp. 313–29.

 (1961). 'The outsider in the Senate: an alternative role', *American Political Science Review*, 55, pp. 566–75.

Huntingdon, S. P. (1965). 'Political development and political decay', *World Politics*, 17, pp. 386–430.

Hyman, H. H., and Sheatsley, P.B. (1947). 'Some reasons why communication campaigns fail', *Public Opinion Quarterly*, 11, pp. 413–23.

Inkeles, A. (1964). *What is Sociology?* (Englewood Cliffs, N. J., Prentice-Hall).

Jackson, R. M. (1965). *The Machinery of Local Government*, 2nd edn. (London, Macmillan).

Jacob, H. (1964). 'The consequences of malapportionment: a note of caution', *Social Forces*, 43, pp. 256–61.

and Lipsky, M. (1968). 'Outputs, structure, and power: an assessment of changes in the study of state and local politics', *Journal of Politics*, 30, pp. 510–38.

Janowitz, M., and Delany, W. (1957). 'The bureaucrat and the public: a study of informational perspectives', *Administrative Science Quarterly*, 2, pp. 141–62.

and Marvick, D. (1964). *Competitive Pressure and Democratic Consent* (Chicago, Quadrangle Books).

Jennings, W. I. (1947). *Principles of Local Government Law*, 3rd edn (London, University of London Press).

(1959). *The Law and the Constitution*, 5th edn (London, University of London Press).

Jewell, M. E. (1962). *The State Legislature* (New York, Random House).

Jones, A. (1968). *Local Governors at Work* (London, Conservative Political centre).

Jones, C. O. (1969). 'The policy approach: an essay on teaching American politics', *Midwest Journal of Political Science*, 13, pp. 284–97.

Jones, G. W. (1969). *Borough Politics* (London, Macmillan).

Jones, R. E. (1967). *The Functional Analysis of Politics* (London, Routledge).

Jouvenel, B.de (1965). 'Political science and prevision', *American Political Science Review*, 59, pp. 29–38.

Kahn, R. L., Wolfe, D. M., Quinn, R. P., Snoek, J. D., and Rosenthal, R. A. (1964). *Organizational Stress* (New York, Wiley).

Katz, D., and Kahn, R. L. (1966). *The Social Psychology of Organizations* (New York, Wiley).

Kaufman, H. (1958). 'The next step in case studies', *Public Administration Review*, 19, pp. 52–9.

The Forest Ranger (Baltimore, Johns Hopkins).

Keefe, W. J., and Ogul, M. S. (1964). *The American Legislative Process* (Englewood Cliffs, N. J., Prentice-Hall).

Keith-Lucas, B. (1961). *The Councils, the Press, and the People* (London, Conservative Political Centre).

Kessel, J. H. (1962). 'Governmental structure and political environment: a statistical note about American cities', *American Political Science Review*, 56, pp. 615–20.

Key, V. O. (1943). 'The veterans and the House of Representatives: a study of a pressure group and electoral mortality', *Journal of Politics*, 5, pp. 27–40.

(1949). *Southern Politics in State and Nation* (New York, Knopf).

(1961). *Public Opinion and American Democracy* (New York, Knopf).

(1966). *The Responsible Electorate* (Cambridge, Mass., Belknap Press).

Kingdon, J. W. (1967). 'Politicians' belief about voters', *American Political Science Review*, 61, pp. 137–45.

Kirchheimer, O. (1957). 'The waning of the opposition in parliamentary regimes', *Social Research*, 24, pp. 127–56.

Klapper, J. T. (1960). *The Effects of Mass Communications* (Chicago, Free Press).

Knowles, R. S. B. (1971). *Modern Management in Local Government* (London, Butterworths).

Lane, R. E., and Sears, D. O. (1964). *Public Opinion* (Englewood Cliffs, N. J., Prentice-Hall).

La Palombara, J. (1960). 'The utility and limitations of interest group theory in non-American field situations', *Journal of Politics*, 22, pp. 29–49.

(1964). *Interest Groups in Italian Politics* (Princeton, N. J., Princeton University Press).

Latham, E. (1952*a*). *The Group Basis of Politics* (Ithaca, Cornell University Press).

(1952*b*). 'The group basis of politics: notes for a theory', *American Political Science Review*, 46, pp. 376–97.

Layton, E. (1961). *Building by Local Authorities* (London, Allen and Unwin).

Lerner, D., and Lasswell, H. D. (1951). *The Policy Sciences* (Stanford, Stanford University Press).

Lewis, R. (1968). *Principles to Conserve* (London, Conservative Political Centre).

Lindblom, C. E. (1959). 'The science of "muddling through"', *Public Administration Review*, 19, pp. 79–88.

(1968). *The Policy-Making Process* (Englewood Cliffs, N.J., Prentice-Hall).

Lindsay, A. D. (1935). *The Essentials of Democracy*, 2nd edn (London, Oxford University Press).

Linebery, R. L., and Fowler, E. P. (1967). 'Reformism and public policies in American cities', *American Political Science Review*, 61, pp. 701–16.

Linton, R. (1936). *The Study of Man* (New York, Appleton-Century-Crofts).

(1945). 'Foreword', in A. Kardiner, *The Psychological Frontiers Of Society*, (New York, Columbia University Press).

(1952). 'Cultural and personality factors affecting economic growth', in B. F. Hoselitz (ed.), *The Progress of Underdeveloped Areas* (Chicago, University of Chicago Press), pp. 73–88.

Lipset, S. M. (1963). *Political Man* (London, Mercury Books).

(1964). 'The changing class structure and contemporary European politics', *Daedalus*, 93, pp. 271–303.

Local Government in England and Wales During the Period of Reconstruction (1945), Cmd. 6579 (London, H.M.S.O.).

Local Government Manpower Committee (1950), *First Report*, Cmd. 7870 (London, H.M.S.O.).

(1951), *Second Report*, Cmd. 8421 (London, H.M.S.O.).

Lockard, D. (1959). *New England State Politics* (Princeton, Princeton University Press).

Loewenstein, K. (1965). *Political Power and the Governmental Process*, 2nd edn (Chicago, University of Chicago Press).

Longley, L. D. (1967). 'Interest group interaction in a state legislative system', *Journal of Politics*, 29, pp. 647–58.

Low, S. (1904). *The Governance of England* (London, Unwin).

Lowi, T. J. (1964). 'American business and public policy, case-studies, and political theory', *World Politics*, 16, pp. 677–715.

(1971). *The Politics of Disorder* (New York, Basic Books).

McClosky, H. (1964). 'Consensus and ideology in American Politics', *American Political Science Review*, 58, pp. 361–82.

MacColl, J. E. (1949). 'The party system in English local government', *Public Administration*, 27, pp. 69–75.

McCoy, C. A., and Playford, J. (eds.) (1968). *Apolitical Politics* (New York, Crowell).

McKean, D. D. (1938). *Pressures on the Legislature of New Jersey* (New York, Columbia University Press).

McKenzie, R. T. (1955). *British Political Parties* (London, Heinemann).

MacKenzie, W. J. M. (1951). 'The conventions of local government', *Public Administration*, 29, pp. 345–56.

(1954). 'Representation in plural societies', *Political Studies*, 2, pp. 54–69.

(1957). 'The export of electoral systems', *Political Studies*, 5, pp. 240–57.

(1961). *Theories of Local Government*, Greater London Papers, 2 (London, London School of Economics and Political Science).

MacKintosh, J. P. (1962). *The British Cabinet* (London, Stevens).

Macmillan, H. (1969). *Tides of Fortune* (London, Macmillan).

Macridis, R. C. (1961). 'Interest groups in comparative analysis', *Journal of Politics*, 23, pp. 25–45.

Maddick, H., and Pritchard, E. P. (1958). 'The conventions of local authorities in the West Midlands: Part I. County borough councils', *Public Administration*, 36, pp. 145–55.

(1959). 'The conventions of local authorities in the West Midlands: Part II. District councils', *Public Administration*, 37, pp. 135–43.

Maniha, J., and Perrow, C. (1965). 'The reluctant organisation and the aggressive environment', *Administrative Science Quarterly*, 10, pp. 238–57.

March, J. G., and Simon, H. A. (1958). *Organizations* (New York, Wiley).

Marshall, A. H. (1960). *Financial Administration in Local Government* (London, Allen and Unwin).

(1971). *New Revenues for Local Government*, Fabian Research Series, 295 (London, Fabian Society).

Marvick, D. (1961). 'Political decision-makers in contrasting milieus', in D. Marvick (ed.), *Political Decision-Makers* (New York, Free Press), pp. 13–28.

Massotti, L. H., and Bowen, D. R. (1971). 'Communities and budgets: the sociology of municipal expenditure', in C. M. Bonjean, T. N. Clark, and R. L. Lineberry, *Community Politics* (New York, Free Press). pp. 314–24.

Masters, N. A. (1961). 'Committee assignments in the House of Representatives', *American Political Science Review*, 55, pp. 345–57.

Matthews, D. R. (1959). 'The folkways of the United States Senate: conformity to group norms and legislative effectiveness', *American Political Science Review*, 53, pp. 1064–89.

Meacher, M. (1971). 'Tinkering with twilight homes', *New Society*, 1 July, p. 20,

Meehan, E. J. (1960). *The British Left-Wing and Foreign Policy: A Study of the Influence of Ideology* (New Brunswick, N.J., Rutgers University Press).

Meller, N. (1960). 'Legislative behaviour research', *Western Political Quarterly*, 13, pp. 131–53.

Mellos, K. (1970). 'Quantitative comparison of party ideology', *Canadian Journal of Political Science*, 3, pp. 540–58.

Merton, R. K. (1938). 'Social structure and anomie', *American Sociological Review*, 3, pp. 672–82.

Michels, R. (1911). *Political Parties* (New York, Free Press, 1966).

Milbrath, L. (1960). 'Lobbying as a communication process', *Public Opinion Quarterly*, 24, pp. 33–53.

(1963). *The Washington Lobbyists* (Chicago, Rand McNally).

Mill, J. S. (1861). *Utilitarianism, Liberty, and Representative Government* (London, Everyman's Library, 1964).

Miller, D. C. (1958a). 'Industry and community power structure: a comparative study of an American and an English city', *American Sociological Review*, 23, pp. 9–15.

(1958b). 'Decision-making cliques in community power structures: a comparative study of an American and an English city', *American Journal of Sociology*, 64, pp. 299–310.

Miller, J. G. (1955). 'Toward a general theory for the behavioral sciences', *American Psychologist*, 10, pp. 513–31.

Milne, R. S., and MacKenzie, H. C. (1958). *Marginal Seat* (London, Hansard Society).

Minar, D. W. (1961). 'Ideology and political behaviour', *Midwest Journal of Political Science*, 5, pp. 317–31.

Mises, L. von (1945). *Bureaucracy* (London, Hodge).

Mitchell, W. C. (1967). 'The shape of political theory to come: from political sociology to political economy', *American Behavioral Scientist*, 11:2, pp. 8–37.

Mohr, L. B. (1969). 'Determinants of innovation in organizations', *American Political Science Review*, 63, pp. 111–26.

Monsen, R. J., and Cannon, M. V. (1965). *The Makers of Public Policy* (New York, McGraw-Hill).

Monypenny, P. (1954). 'Political science and the study of groups: notes to guide a research project', *Western Political Quarterly*, 7, pp. 183–201.

Morris-Jones, W. H. (1954). 'In defence of apathy: some doubts on the duty to vote', *Political Studies*, 2, pp. 25–37.

(1969). 'Political recruitment and political development', in C. T. Leys (ed.), *Politics and Change in Developing Countries* (London, Cambridge University Press), pp. 113–34.

(1971). 'Candidate selection: the ordeal of the Indian National Congress, 1966–1967', in M. S. Rajan (ed.), *Studies in Politics: National and International* (Delhi, Vikas), pp. 33–54.

Myrdal, G. (1957). *Economic Theory and Underdeveloped Regions* (London, Duckworths).

Nadel, S. F. (1957). *The Theory of Social Structure* (London, Cohen).

N.A.L.G.O. Survey (1957). 'Interest in local government', *Public Administration*, 35, pp. 305–9.

Nettl, J. P. (1967). *Political Mobilisation* (London, Faber).

Newton, K. (1969). 'City politics in Britain and the United States', *Political Studies*, 17, pp. 208–18.

Oakeshott, M. (1962). *Rationalism in Politics* (London, Methuen).

Odegard, P. H. (1928). *Pressure Politics: The Story of the Anti-Saloon League* (New York, Octagon Books, 1966).

(1958). 'A group basis of politics: a new name for an ancient myth', *Western Political Quarterly*, 11, pp. 689–702.

(1967). 'Preface' to A. F. Bentley, *The Process of Government* (Cambridge, Mass., Belknap Press, 1967).

O'Malley, J. (1970). 'Community action in Notting Hill', in A. Lapping (ed.), *Community Action*, Fabian Tract, 400 (London, Fabian Society), pp. 28–36.

Packman, J. (1968), *Child Care: Needs and Numbers* (London, Allen and Unwin).

Painter, M. (1969). 'Decision-making and change in a local council: the case of "overspill" development in Newmarket' (M.A. Thesis, University of Sussex).

Panter-Brick, K. (1953). 'Local government and democracy – a rejoinder', *Public Administration*, 31, pp. 344–8.

(1954). 'Local self-government as a basis for democracy: a rejoinder', *Public Administration*, 32, pp. 438–40.

Parker, J. (1965). *Local Health and Welfare Services* (London, Allen and Unwin).

Parker, R. S. (1961). '"Group analysis" and scientism in political studies', *Political Studies*, 9, pp. 37–51.

Parsons, T. (1951). *The Social System* (Glencoe, Ill, Free Press).

Patterson, S. C. (1961). 'The role of the deviant in the State legislative system: the Wisconsin assembly', *Western Political Quarterly*, 14, pp. 460–72.

Peterson, P. E. (1969). 'The politics of comprehensive education in British cities: a re-examination of British interest group theory', Paper prepared for delivery at the 65th annual meeting of the American Political Science Association, 2–6 September.

Piven, F. P., and Cloward, R. A. (1972). *Regulating the Poor* (London, Tavistock).

Plamenatz, J. (1958). 'Electoral studies and democratic theory, I. A British view', *Political Studies*, 6, pp. 1–9.

Planning (1947). 'Active democracy – a local election', 261, January.

(1948). 'Local elections, how many vote?', 291, November.

(1955). 'Voting for local councils', 379, May.

Political and Economic Planning (1965). *Sponsorship of Music: The Role of Local Authorities* (London, P.E.P.).

Polsby, N. W. (1968). 'The institutionalization of the US House of Representatives', *American Political Science Review*, 62, pp. 144–68.

Potter, A. (1961). *Organised Groups in British National Politics* (London, Faber).

Presthus, R. (1965). *Behavioral Approaches to Public Administration* (Alabama, University of Alabama Press).

Price, C. M., and Bell, C. G. (1970a). 'Socializing California freshmen assemblymen: the role of individuals and legislative sub-groups', *Western Political Quarterly*, 23, pp. 166–79.

(1970b). 'The rules of the game: political fact or academic fancy', *Journal of Politics*, 32, pp. 839–55.

Prices and Incomes Standstill (1966), Cmnd. 3073 (London, H.M.S.O.).

Raison, T. (1961). 'Principles in practice', in D. Howell, and T. Raison (eds.), *Principles in Practice* (London, Conservative Political Centre), pp. 9–17.

Rakoff, S. H., and Schaefer, G. F. (1970). 'Politics, policy, and political science: theoretical alternatives', *Politics and Society*, 1, pp. 51–77.

Ranney, A. (1962*a*). *The Doctrine of Responsible Party Government* (Urbana, Ill., University of Illinois Press).

(ed.) (1962*b*). *Essays on the Behavioral Study of Politics* (Urbana, Ill., University of Illinois Press).

(1968). 'The study of policy content: a framework for choice', in A. Ranney (ed.), *Political Science and Public Policy* (Chicago, Markham), pp. 3–21.

Redlich, J. (1903). *Local Government in England*, edited and with additions by F. W. Hirst, 2 vols. (London, Macmillan).

Rees, A. (1968). 'Democracy in local government', in B. Lapping, and G. Radice (eds.), *More Power to the People* (London, Longmans), pp. 119–42.

and Smith, T. (1964). *Town Councillors: A Study of Barking* (London, Acton Society Trust).

Rice, A. K. (1963). *The Enterprise and its Environment* (London, Tavistock).

Richards, P. G. (1968). *The New Local Government System* (London, Allen and Unwin).

Riker, W. H. (1955). *The Study of Local Politics* (New York, Random House).

Robinson, J. A. (1962). *Congress and Foreign Policy-Making* (Homewood, Ill., Dorsey).

and Majak, R. R. (1967). 'The theory of decision-making', in J. C. Charlesworth (ed.), *Contemporary Political Analysis* (New York, Free Press), pp. 175–88.

Robson, W. A. (1933). 'The central domination of local government', *Political Quarterly*, 4, pp. 85–104.

(1948). *The Development of Local Government*, 2nd edn (London, Allen and Unwin).

(1966). *Local Government in Crisis* (London, Allen and Unwin).

Rokkan, S., and Valen, H. (1962). 'The Mobilisation of the periphery', in S. Rokkan (ed.), *Approaches to the Study of Political Participation* (Bergen, Chr. Michelson Institute), pp. 111–58.

Rose, R. (1965). *Politics in England* (London, Faber).

and Mossawir, H. (1967). 'Voting and elections: a functional analysis', *Political Studies*, 15, pp. 173–201.

Rothman, S. (1960). 'Systematic political theory: observations on the group approach', *American Political Science Review*, 54, pp. 15–33.

Royal Commission on Local Government in England, Research Studies, 1 (1968). *Local Government in South East England* (London, H.M.S.O.).

Royal Institute of Public Administration (1956). *New Sources of Local Revenue* (London, Allen and Unwin).

Ruck, S. (1963). *London Government and the Welfare Services* (London, Routledge).

Russett, B. (1962). 'International communication and legislative behavior: the Senate and the House of Commons', *Journal of Conflict Resolution*, 6, pp. 291–307.

Ryan, T. (1964). *Day Nursery Provision Under the Health Service: England and Wales, 1948–63* (London, National Society of Childrens Nurseries).

Salisbury, R. H. (1968). 'The analysis of public policy: a search for theories and roles', in A. Ranney (ed.), *Political Science and Public Policy* (Chicago, Markham), pp. 151–75.

Sarbin, T. M. (1954). 'Role theory', in G. Lindzey (ed.), *Handbook of Social Psychology*, vol. 1 (Reading, Mass., Addison-Wesley, 1954), pp. 223–58.

Schattschneider, E. E. (1935). *Politics, Pressures and the Tariff* (Hamden, Conn, Archon Books, 1963).

(1948). 'Pressure groups versus political parties', *Annals of the American Academy of Political and Social Sciences*, 259, pp. 17–23.

(1960). *The Semi-Sovereign People* (New York, Holt).

Schiff, A. L. (1966). 'Innovation and administrative decision-making: the conservation of land resources', *Administrative Science Quarterly*, 11, pp. 1–30.

Schilling, W. R. (1961). 'The H-bomb decision: how to decide without actually choosing', *Political Science Quarterly*, 76, pp. 24–46.

Schnore, L. F., and Alford, R. R. (1963). 'Forms of government and socio-economic characteristics of suburbs', *Administrative Science Quarterly*, 8, pp. 1–17.

Schumpeter, J. A. (1954). *Capitalism, Socialism and Democracy*, 4th edn (London, Allen and Unwin).

Schweitzer, D., and Ginsburg, G. P. (1966). 'Factors of communicator credibility', in C. W. Backman, and P. F. Secord, *Problems in Social Psychology* (New York, McGraw-Hill), pp. 94–101.

Scott, A. M., and Hunt, M. A. (1965). *Congress and Lobbies: Image and Reality* (Chapel Hill, University of North Carolina Press).

Secord, P. F., and Backman, C. W. (1964). *Social Psychology* (New York, McGraw-Hill).

Self, P., and Storing, H. J. (1962). *The State and the Farmer* (London, Allen and Unwin).

Seligman, L. G. (1961). 'Political recruitment and party structure: a case study', *American Political Science Review*, 55, pp. 77–86.

Selznick, P. (1952). *The Organizational Weapon* (New York, McGraw-Hill).

(1957). *Leadership in Administration* (Evanston, Ill., Row-Peterson).

(1966). *T.V.A. and the Grass Roots* (New York, Harper).

Sharkansky, I. (1967a). 'Government expenditures and public services in the American states', *American Political Science Review*, 61, pp. 1066–77.

(1967b). 'Economic and political correlates of state government expenditures: general tendencies and deviant cases', *Midwest Journal of Political Science*, 11, pp. 173–92.

(1968a). 'Economic development, regionalism and state political systems', *Midwest Journal of Political Science*, 12, pp. 41–61.

(1968b). 'Regionalism, economic status and public policies of American states', *Southwestern Social Science Quarterly*, 49, pp. 9–26.

(1968c), *Spending in the American States* (Chicago, Rand McNally).

(1969). *The Politics of Taxing and Spending* (Indianapolis, Bobbs-Merrill).

(1970a). 'Environment, policy, output and impact: problems of theory and method in the analysis of public policy', in I. Sharkansky (ed.), *Policy Analysis in Political Science* (Chicago, Markham), pp. 61–79.

(1970*b*). *Regionalism in American Politics* (Indianapolis, Bobbs-Merrill).

(1970*c*). *Public Administration* (Chicago, Markham).

Sharpe, L. J. (1960). 'The politics of local government in Greater London', *Public Administration*, 38, pp. 157–72.

(1962*a*). 'Elected Representatives in local government', *British Journal of Sociology*, 13, pp. 157–72.

(1962*b*) *A Metropolis Votes*, Greater London Paper, 8 (London, London School of Economics and Political Science).

(1965). *Why Local Democracy?*, Fabian Tract, 361 (London, Fabian Society).

(1966). 'Leadership and representation in local government', *Political Quarterly*, 37, pp. 149–58.

(1967*a*). 'In defence of local politics', in L. J. Sharpe (ed.), *Voting in Cities* (London, Macmillan), pp. 1–14.

(ed.) (1967*b*). *Voting in Cities*, (London, Macmillan).

Shelley, A. N. C. (1939). *The Councillor* (London, Nelson).

Sherbenou, E. L. (1961). 'Class, participation and the council-manager plan', *Public Administration Review*, 21, pp. 131–5.

Sherman, A. (1970). 'The end of local government?', in R. Boyson (ed.), *Right Turn* (London, Churchill Press), pp. 117–37.

Shils, E. (1955). 'The end of ideology?', *Encounter*, November, pp. 52–8.

(1958). 'Ideology and civility: on the politics of the intellectual', *Sewanee Review*, 66, pp. 450–80.

Silverman, C. (1954). 'The legislators' view of the legislative process', *Public Opinion Quarterly*, 18, pp. 180–90.

Simon, H. A. (1957). *Administrative Behavior*, 2nd edn (New York, Free Press).

(1958). 'The role of expectations in an adaptive and behavioristic model', in M. J. Bowman (ed.), *Expectations, Uncertainty, and Business Behavior* (New York, S.S.R.C.), pp. 49–58.

Skilling, H. G., and Griffiths, F. (1971). *Interest Groups in Soviet Politics* (Princeton, Princeton University Press).

Slack, K. M. (1960). *Councils, Committees and Concern for the Old* (Welwyn, Codicote Press).

(1966). *Social Administration and the Citizen* (London, Joseph).

Smallwood, F. (1965). *Greater London: The Politics of Metropolitan Reform* (New York, Bobbs-Merrill).

Smellie, K. B. (1968). *A History of Local Government*, 4th edn (London, Allen and Unwin).

Snyder, R. C., Bruck, H. W., and Sapin, B. (1954). *Decision-Making as an Approach to the Study of International Politics* (Princeton, Princeton University Press).

and Paige, G. D. (1959). 'The U.S. decision to resist aggression in Korea: the application of an analytical scheme', *Administrative Science Quarterly*, 3, pp. 341–78.

Social Science Research Council, Committee on Historiography (1954). *The Social Sciences in Historical Study*, Bulletin, 64 (New York, S.S.R.C.)

Spencer, K. (1970). 'Housing and Socially deprived families', in R. Holman (ed.), *Socially Deprived Families in Britain* (London, Bedford Square Press), pp. 51–108.

Sprout, H., and Sprout, M. (1965). *The Ecological Perspective on Human Affairs* (Princeton, Princeton University Press).

Stanyer, J. (1968). 'Local electoral behaviour', Paper read at the Political Studies Association, annual meeting, University of Sussex, Easter.

Stedman, M. S. (1953). 'A group interpretation of politics', *Public Opinion Quarterly*, 17, pp. 218–29.

Steffens, L. (1904). *The Shame of the Cities* (New York, Hill and Wang, 1957).

Stewart, J. D. (1958). *British Pressure Groups* (Oxford, Clarendon Press).

Stokes, D. E., and Miller, W. E. (1962). 'Party government and the saliency of Congress', *Public Opinion Quarterly*, 26, pp. 531–46.

(1963). 'Constituency influence in Congress', *American Political Science Review*, 57, pp. 45–56.

Storing, H. J. (ed.) (1962). *Essays in the Scientific Study of Politics* (New York, Holt).

Sullivan, J. (1939). *The Reform of the Rating System*, Fabian Research Series, 47 (London, Fabian Society).

Suthers, R. B. (1905). *Mind Your Own Business* (London, Clarion Press).

Sutton, F. X., Harris, S. E., Kaysen, C., and Tobin, J. (1956). *The American Business Creed* (Cambridge, Mass., Harvard University Press).

Teune, H. (1967). 'Legislative attitudes towards interest groups', *Midwest Journal of Political Science*, 11, pp. 489–504.

Thatcher, M. (1968). *What's Wrong With Politics?* (London, Conservative Political Centre).

Thayer, G. (1968). *The Farther Shores of Politics* (London, Allen Lane).

Thompson, V. A. (1965). 'Bureaucracy and innovation', *Administrative Science Quarterly*, 10, pp. 1–20.

(1969), *Bureaucracy and Innovation* (Alabama, University of Alabama Press.).

Tivey, L. (1958). 'The system of democracy in Britain', *Sociological Review (New Series)*, 6, pp. 109–24.

Town Planning Institute (1968). Memoranda submitted to the Committee on Public Participation in Planning, *Journal of the Town Planning Institute*, 54, July/August, pp. 343–4.

Townsend, P. (1962). *The Last Refuge* (London, Routledge).

(1963). 'The timid and the bold', *New Society*, 23 May.

Trist, E. L., Higgin, G. W., Murray, H., and Pollock, A. B. (1963). *Organisational Choice* (London, Tavistock).

Truman, D. B. (1951), *The Governmental Process* (New York, Knopf).

(1955). 'The impact on political science of the revolution in the behavioral sciences', in S. K. Bailey *et al*, *Research Frontiers in Politics and Government* (Washington, Brookings Institute), pp. 202–31.

Utley, T. E. (1949). *Essays in Conservatism* (London, Conservative Political Centre).

Valen, H. (1966). 'The recruitment of parliamentary nominees in Norway', *Scandinavian Political Studies*, 1, pp. 121–66.

Van Dyke, V. (1968). 'Process and policy as focal concepts in political research', in A. Ranney (ed.), *Political Science and Public Policy* (Chicago, Markham), pp. 23–39.

Van Til, J., and Van Til, S. B. (1970). 'Citizen participation in social policy: the end of a cycle?', *Social Problems*, 17:3, pp. 313–23.

Verba, S. (1961). *Small Groups and Political Behavior* (Princeton, Princeton University Press).

Viereck, P. (1950). *Conservatism Revisited: The Revolt Against Revolt* (London, Lehman).

Wade, E. C. S., and Phillips, G. G. (1960). *Constitutional Law*, 6th edn (London, Longmans).

Wahlke, J. C. (1971). 'Policy demands and system support: the role of the represented', *British Journal of Political Science*, 1, pp. 271–90.

Buchanan, W., Eulau, H., and Ferguson, L.C. (1960). 'American state legislators' role orientations towards pressure groups', *Journal of Politics*, 22, pp. 203–27.

Eulau, H., Buchanan, W., and Ferguson, L. C. (1962). *The Legislative System* (New York, Wiley).

Waldo, D. (1962). 'Five perspectives on the cases of the Inter University Case Program', in E. Bock (ed.), *Essays on the Case Method in Public Administration* (Brussels, International Institute of Administrative Sciences), pp. 39–63.

Walker, J. (1966). 'A critique of the elitist theory of democracy', *American Political Science Review*, 60, pp. 285–95.

Warren, J. H. (1950). 'Local self-government: the basis of a democratic state', *Public Administration*, 28, pp. 11–16.

(1952. 'The party system in English local government', in S. D. Bailey (ed.), *The British Party System* (London, Hansard Society), pp. 177–92.

(1962). *The English Local Government System* 6th edn (London, Allen and Unwin).

Weinberg, A., and Weinberg, L. (1964). *The Muckrakers* (New York, Capricorn Books).

Weiner, M. (1962). *The Politics of Scarcity* (Chicago, University of Chicago Press).

A West Midland Study Group (1956). *Local Government and Central Control* (London, Routledge).

White, T. (1968). 'Social services and local government reform', *Case Conference*, 15:5, September.

White, W. S. (1957), *Citadel* (New York, Harper).

Williams, O. P., and Adrian, C. R. (1963). *Four Cities* (Philadelphia, University of Pennsylvania Press).

Herman, H., Liebman, C. S., and Dye, T. R. (1965). *Suburban Differences and Metropolitan Policies* (Philadelphia, University of Pennsylvania Press).

Wilson, H. H. (1961). *Pressure Group: The Case of Commercial Television* (London, Secker and Warburg).

Wilson, J. Q. (1966). 'Problems in the study of urban politics', in E. H. Buehrig (ed.), *Essays in Political Science* (Bloomington, Indiana University Press, 1966), pp. 131–50.

(1968). 'Introduction: City Politics and public policy', in J. Q. Wilson (ed.), *City Politics and Public Policy* (New York, Wiley), pp. 1–14.

and Banfield, E. C. (1964). 'Public regardingness as a value premise in voting behavior', *American Political Science Review*, 58, pp. 876–87.

Wolfinger, R., and Field, J. O. (1966). 'Political ethos and the structure of city government', *American Political Science Review*, 60, pp. 306–26.

Wooton, G. (1963). *The Politics of Influence* (London, Routledge).

Zeigler, H. (1964). *Interest Groups in American Society* (Englewood Cliffs, N.J., Prentice-Hall).

Zisk, B. H., Eulau, H., and Prewitt, K. (1965). 'City councilmen and the group struggle: A typology of role orientations', *Journal of Politics*, 27, pp. 618–46.

Index of Authors

Index of Subjects

activism in political science, 2n
administration, local government as,
see central control of local authorities
agenda as information source for councillors, 179, 198
aircraft noise, 160
aldermen
and beliefs about voters, 42
why no specific study of, 100–1
American state legislatures and rules of the game, 90–1
American states, explanation of policies in, 61, 68
Anslow-Wilson, Ald. E., 114, 119, 121, 150
anthropology and role theory, 92–3
anticipatory socialisation, 149
see also behaviour rules; communication of behavioural expectations
Anti-Saloon League, 47, 50, 53
apathy, 58, 80
apprenticeship
of chairmen, 115–17
of leader, 122–3
of new councillor, 124–5, 127
architect, borough, 18–19
arts, local authority support for, 14
attendance and 'homework', as behaviour rule for new councillor, 125
attributes, *see* expectations for attributes; recruitment rules

authoritative councillors
and behaviour rules, 98
defined, 98
identified, 98
importance of, 97–8
see also chairmen
autonomy of council in Kensington and Chelsea, 80–1, 81–2, 83, 230
avoidance of dissonant information by councillors, 186–90
differences, chairmen/non-chairmen, 196–201
and need to resist, 191
unintentional, 190
see also councillors and information

Baldwin, Cllr J., 114, 120, 122–3
bargains and exchanges, 32, 74
limitations of political science theories centring on, 80
see also support
behavioural expectations
distinguished from behaviour rules, 98–9
and importance of communication, 95, 96
and importance of reinforcement, 96
see also behaviour rules; communication of behavioural expectations; reinforcement of behavioural expectations
for chairmen, 130–2; absence of

M

control of disturbance–*cont.*
  and Chelsea, 86, 230, 236
  from outside the council, 172–4,
    191–5; through co-operation, 235;
    and symbolic response, 234–5
  from within the council, 153; through
    recruitment and behaviour rules,
    86, 140–2; but problem of the new
    councillor, 103, 142 (but success,
    147–8); and the leader, 149–53;
    lack of problem of the chairmen,
    148; of factions, 203
  see also behaviour rules; councillors
    and interest groups; recruitment
    rules; selective use of information
conventions
  in British national government, 9,
    87–8
  in British local government, 88–90
  and Electoral Chain of Command
    Theory, 27
  and similarity to input–output models
    92, and role theory, 92
  see also behaviour rules; recruitment
    rules; role theory; rules of the
    game
co-operation, as control technique, 235
co-optation, 77–9
  defined, 77
  need for, 77–8
co-option, 109, 115, 186
Corbet-Singleton, Cllr J., 114
correlations, problem of use as explanations, 68n
council housing
  chairmen's attitude to, 221, 222, 223;
    in South Kensington, 223–4
  rents in, 19, 36–7, 224–5
councillor ideology, 9, 80, 83, 206–25,
  230
  and reinforcement through informa-
    tion use, 186–7, 190
councillor recruitment and political
  parties, 102–11
  and class, 111–12
  and local government law, 102
  and supply of applicants, 101–2
  see also recruitment rules for Con-
    servative councillors

councillors and information, 9, 175–204
  see also avoidance of dissonant infor-
    mation by councillors; exclusion
    devices; resistance to dissonant
    information by councillors; selec-
    tive use of information
councillors and interest groups, 9, 54,
  57–8, 126–7, 155–74, 186, 213,
  214, 221, 222
  effect of councillor attitudes on
    interest group development, 173–4
  explanation for councillors' differing
    assessments of, 162–8
  see also demanding groups; helpful
    groups; unhelpful groups
councillors and officers, relationship in
  Electoral Chain of Command
  Theory, 27
  see also officers
council meetings, 124, 125, 126, 127,
  133, 143, 147, 156, 157
county boroughs, councillor information use in, 181
Coward, J., 211
Craig-Cooper, Cllr F., 114
critique of political science literature
  explaining public policy, summary
  of, 81–2, 227–8
Crofton, Cllr Sir Malby, 114, 119, 120,
  122, 141, 150–3
credible information sources, 187–8
Crown, 88
customs, *see* conventions

defence of commitment
  as feature of politics in Kensington
    and Chelsea, 230, 236
  and role of leader, 151, 153
  and use of information, 195, 201–2
delegate role, councillor opposition to,
  195
'demanding' groups
  change in, 170, 171, 173
  chairmen's attitudes to, 164–5, 167–8,
    202
  definition of, 164n
  non-chairmen's attitudes to, 164–5,
    202
  see also unhelpful groups

and leader, 139–40
and new councillor, 128, 145;
    response to, 145–6
role consensus, 93, 94, 95
    absence of, for chairmen, 135; and
    leader, 138–40
    and new councillor, 129
role knowledge, 96
    of new councillors, 143
role, searched, 96
    and new councillors, 145
role, sent, 96
    see also communication of behavi-
    oural expectations
role theory, 92–7
    and conventions and rules of the
    game, 92
    importance of literature on, 231–2
    problems of, 93–4; solution to, 96
    see also conventions; rules of the
    game; recruitment rules; behaviour
    rules; communication of behavi-
    oural expectations; reinforcement
    of behavioural expectations
routine decisions
    distinguished from policy decisions,
    4–5
    as feature of politics in Kensington
    and Chelsea, 8, 102, 151, 225, 235
Royal Borough of Kensington and
    Chelsea
    autonomy from central control, 20–1
    distinctive characteristics of, 6–7
    and Doctrine of Responsible Party
    Government, 33–8
    and Electoral Chain of Command
    Theory, 30–1
    location of, 6
    response to central control, 18–20
rules for recruitment and behaviour,
    see behaviour rules; recruitment
    rules
rules of access and interest group
    influence, 51–2, 58
    in Kensington and Chelsea, 155–74
rules of priority, 186, 201
    see also selective use of information
rules of the game, 9, 90–2
    and American legislatures, 90–1

as an explanation for pressure group
    influence, 58
and legislative behaviour, 90–2
problems of, 93–4
and similarity to input–output models
    and simple role theory, 92
    see also behaviour rules; conventions;
    recruitment rules; role theory
rules of thumb, *see* rules of access and
    interest group influence in Ken-
    sington and Chelsea

sanctions and rewards
    absence of; for chairmen, 132–2; and
    leader, 139
    elections as, 26
    enforcing conventions, 88
    enforcing rules of the game, 90–1
    impact on weak organisation, 78–9
    for new councillor, 128, 143
    and position-incumbent, 94
    and role theory, 96
    see also reinforcement of behavioural
    expectations
Sandon, Cllr Viscount, 114
search behaviour
    of councillors, 180–2; *see also* coun-
    cillors and information
    and policy change, 201–2, 232
'searchers', non-chairmen as, 145, 200–1
selection, *see* recruitment rules
Selection Committee of the South
    Kensington Conservative Associa-
    tion, 106–10
selective perception, importance of
    literature on, 232
selective use of information, 175–204,
    213
    differences, chairmen/non-chairmen,
    196–201
    failure of political scientists to recog-
    nise the importance of, 203
    and policy-maintenance, 201–2
    unavoidable, 175; especially for coun-
    cillors, 175–8
    see also avoidance of dissonant infor-
    mation by councillors; differential
    selectivity; resistance to dissonant
    information by councillors

self-confidence, effect on use of information, 197
self-help, councillor attitude to, 160, 215, 216
Senate, 90
senior councillors, 4, 19–20, 152, 163, 168
see also chairmen
separation of powers, 55
Sheffield, councillors and information in, 180–5 *passim*
'silence', as behaviour rule for new councillor, 124–5
Sims, Ald. A., 119, 121
socialisation, *see* behaviour rules; communication of behavioural expectations
Socialist Party of Germany (SPD), 78–9
society, as role definer, 90, 93
irrelevance of, 94, 97
socio-economic variables and public policy, 61–3
sociology and role theory, 92–3
South Kensington councillors, 119, 120, 129–30, 131, 132, 142–3, 143–4, 152
recruitment of, 106–10, 111
Speaker, 88
specialisation
as behaviour rule for new councillor, 125
need for, 177
see also committees
statistical techniques
use in election studies, 30
use in demographic approach, 61; limitations of, 65
status, *see* positions
Stevenson, Cllr A., 114
stimuli–response theories, 74
Stockwell, Cllr Miss E., 114, 116n
street cleansing, 160, 190n, 219
street lighting, 160, 190n, 220
strong organisations in passive environments
and autonomy of, 82
council of Royal Borough as, 80–1, 230
'structural factors and the weak party as an explanation for pressure

group influence, 55–6
substantive policy, distinguished from procedural policy, 2n
Sundius-Smith, Cllr Mrs J., 114
support
cost-free nature of, 80
costs of, 77, 79
government need for, 77
mobilised through elections, 33–4
party need for, 32
supportive information, 187
see also selective use of information
surgeries
chairmen's attitude to, 199
councillor attitude to, 182, 184, 199
as information source, 181
in North Kensington, 182, 200
working-class preference for, 190
symbolic function of elections, 45–6
symbolic policy, 234–5

tacit understandings, *see* conventions
Task Force, 159, 165, 166
Taylor, Cllr Mrs R., 114
teaching, *see* behaviour rules; communication of behavioural expectations
Tennessee Valley Authority (TVA), 77–80
Thackway, Ald. F., 114, 120, 152, 153, 179
theory, need for in empirical studies, 7, 66–7, 71, 226
Theory of Competitive Leadership, 39
Thom, Cllr E., 114, 116n
Tomlin, Cllr E., 114
Tower Hamlets, councillors and information in, 180–5 *passim*
town clerk, and Kensington and Chelsea Chamber of Commerce, 167
Townend, Cllr H., 114
traffic, 18, 160, 190n
training, *see* behaviour rules; communication of behavioural expectations
twilight areas, chairmen's views as to improvement of, 217
two year rule, 113, 118

ultra vires, 15

unhelpful groups, 169–71
  councillor assessments of, 156, 157–9;
    explanation for assessments, 162–8;
    changes in assessments of, 168, 171
  reasons why adopt improper com-
    munication styles, 169–70
  tendency for groups to change, 170,
    171, 173
  tendency for groups to disband, 171,
    173
  see also demanding groups
uniformity, central control and, 13–14
unselective use of information, 189
  see also selective use of information
unwritten rules, 87
  see also behaviour rules; conventions;
    rules of the game; recruitment
    rules
urbanisation, 64–5
urban policy outputs, explanations of,
  61
urgent matters, 133

value theory, 73
verification, problems of in demographic approach, 68
vice-chairmen, 100, 101, 113–16 *passim*,
  133
Villiers, Cllr J., 114

voluntary associations as information
  source for councillors, 181–2
voluntary collective effort, councillors'
  belief in, 160, 166, 215, 216, 221–2
voter, *see* electorate
voting behaviour, politicians' theory of,
  40–2
  in Kensington and Chelsea, 38, 41–2

'waiters', chairmen as, 200–1
Walford, Ald. Mrs J., 114, 117, 118n
ward representative as link to interest
  groups, 161–2
wards, party control of, 34–5
Waring-Sainsbury, Mr, 167
weak organisations in hostile environments, 77–9
  as inadequate characterisation of the
    situation of the council in Ken-
    sington and Chelsea, 79–80
Weatherhead, Cllr Miss D., 106, 114,
  116n
West London Architects, 163
whips, 100, 122
White Papers, 19, 20
Womens Royal Voluntary Service, 159,
  163, 165, 166

Yeoman, Cllr J., 114